LIBRARY
LEWIS-CLARK STATE COLLEGE
LEWISTON, IDAHO
D0044900

Environment, Inc.

STUDIES IN GOVERNMENT
AND PUBLIC POLICY

Environment, Inc.

From Grassroots to Beltway

Christopher J. Bosso

University Press of Kansas

Published by the University Press of Kansas (Lawrence, Kansas 66049), which was organized by the Kansas Board of Regents and is operated and funded by Emporia State University, Fort Hays State University, Kansas State University, Pittsburg State University, the University of Kansas, and Wichita State University

Library of Congress Cataloging-in-Publication Data

Bosso, Christopher J. (Christopher John), 1956–
Environment, Inc. : from grassroots to beltway / Christopher J. Bosso.
p. cm. — (Studies in government and public policy)
Includes bibliographical references (p.).
ISBN 0-7006-1367-6 (cloth : alk. paper) — ISBN 0-7006-1368-4 (pbk. : alk. paper)
1. Environmental sciences—Societies, etc. 2. Environmentalism. 3. Green movement.
I. Title. II. Series.
GE1.B67 2005
333.72—dc22 2004023049

British Library Cataloguing-in-Publication Data is available.

Printed in the United States of America

10 9 8 7 6 5 4 3 2 1

The paper used in this publication meets the minimum requirements of the American National Standard for Permanence of Paper for Printed Library Materials Z39.48-1984.

For my parents, who taught by example

Contents

Figures and Tables

FIGURES

TABLES

Acronyms

AR	American Rivers
CF	Conservation Fund
CHEJ	Center for Health, Environment, and Justice
CI	Conservation International
CWA	Clean Water Action
DoW	Defenders of Wildlife
DU	Ducks Unlimited
EA	Environmental Action
ED	Environmental Defense
EI	Earth Island
EJ	Earthjustice
ELF	Environmental Liberation Front
EPC	Environmental Policy Center
EPI	Environmental Policy Institute
ES	Earth Share
EWG	Environmental Working Group
FoE	Friends of the Earth
IWLA	Izaak Walton League of America
LCV	League of Conservation Voters
NAS	National Audubon Society
NET	National Environmental Trust
NPCA	National Parks Conservation Association
NPT	National Park Trust
NRDC	Natural Resources Defense Council
NWF	National Wildlife Federation
OC	Ocean Conservancy
RAN	Rainforest Action Network
SC	Sierra Club
TNC	The Nature Conservancy
TPL	Trust for Public Land
TWS	The Wilderness Society
WWF	World Wildlife Fund

Preface and Acknowledgments

As often happens, this book's origins can be traced to an unexpected opportunity. In this case, it was an invitation by Burdett Loomis and Allan Cigler, editors of a multiedition volume on interest group politics, to assess the status of the "environmental movement" twenty years after the first Earth Day. A just-published book on federal pesticide policy apparently gave them the idea that I knew something about U.S. environmental groups. I didn't, so I had to do a bit of digging. The chapter I contributed was my first attempt to think about the nation's environmental organizations in any systematic manner.* In the process, I became intrigued by these organizations—where they came from, how they operated, and how they have survived—so what might have been a one-time assignment became more open-ended. Perhaps it was inertia, but I like to think that I grew fascinated by these organizations and what their collective story told us about American politics. This book is, in many ways, the culmination (though hardly an exhaustive one) of years of arm's-length observation, poking around, and musing.

Any work of this kind owes many debts to others. Some of these debts are intellectual: This book would not have been so theoretically informed had it not been for the trails blazed by the political science scholarship on interest groups, including works by Virginia Gray and David Lowery, Jeffrey Berry, William Browne, Frank Baumgartner and Beth Leech, and, of course, the late Jack Walker. Likewise, this book could not have existed were it not for the superb histories, biographies, and studies of environmental politics, which together constitute one of the richest and most well-written literatures imaginable. Some debts are owed for opportunities given: I thank Allan Cigler and Burdett Loomis, and Norman Vig and Mike Kraft, for giving me the chance to write about environmental organizations for two somewhat different audiences—students of

*Christopher J. Bosso, "Adaptation and Change in the Environmental Movement," in *Interest Group Politics,* 3d ed., ed. Allan J. Cigler and Burdett A. Loomis (Washington, D.C.: CQ Press, 1991), 151–76.

interest groups and students of environmental politics, respectively. Other debts are professional: Thanks to Robert Duffy, Lori Brainard, David Hart, Judy Layzer, and Mike Kraft for reading and commenting on all or part of this work, and to Fred Woodward and everyone at the University Press of Kansas for their forbearance and support. Celeste Walker, consummate professional, divined what I wanted as she constructed the index. I also acknowledge the research assistance of several generations of Northeastern University undergraduate and graduate students, including Vanessa Green, Evan Hinckle, Emily Neal, Mark Mesiti, Sabine Schutte, and Sheilagh Scollin, as well as the support and friendship of my Northeastern colleagues. Thanks to all. The final product is better for their help. Any flaws are mine alone, however, which doesn't seem quite fair.

A special note on the data used throughout the book is necessary: I spent a lot of time trying to get my hands on as much data as possible and to corroborate data using at least two published sources; however, the older the data, the less reliable and sparser they got. In many instances, readers should consider the data more illustrative than definitive. Some advocacy organizations have been far more transparent for far longer than others—the Sierra Club, the most democratic national environmental organization of them all, gets special recognition here—but greater demands for transparency now compel all advocacy organizations to make their financial data more readily available. You can also look up their tax forms using guidestar.org and other search engines, and I encourage you to do so.

Finally, thanks of an entirely different kind to Marcia. It only *seems* like I've worked on this project our entire marriage, dear, but now the book's done. Let's play.

1
A Movement Astray?

Earth Day (April 22) 2004 was a busy one for President George W. Bush. That morning, clad in the appropriate outdoor apparel, he appeared before the assembled national press at an estuarine preserve in southern Maine to promote his commitment to wetlands protection and to extol his administration's environmental achievements. "My administration has put in place some of the most important anti-pollution policies in a decade," the president proclaimed, "policies that have reduced harmful emissions, reclaimed brownfields, cut phosphorus releases into our rivers and streams. Since 2001, the condition of America's land, air and water has improved."[1] Later that day, back in his usual business suit, he hosted a White House ceremony honoring winners of the President's Environmental Youth Awards, young people from around the nation recognized by the ten regional offices of the Environmental Protection Agency (EPA).[2] The next day, once again in casual attire, he appeared at a Florida estuarine preserve to promote his wetlands plan and, by extension, his overall environmental record in the run-up to the fall presidential election. "I know there's a lot of politics when it comes to the environment," the president remarked, before taking a few minutes to prune some non-native plants. "But what I like to do is focus on results, and you've got yourself a results-oriented governor when it comes to protecting this environment."[3]

Each of these carefully stage-managed events got the desired local and national media coverage and sent the intended message: President Bush cares about the environment. That he felt compelled to take precious time away from such pressing matters as the conflict in Iraq to make Earth Day–related appearances also said volumes about the centrality of environmental issues in contemporary American politics. As every occupant of the office has understood since the first Earth Day in 1970, no president can afford to appear hostile to environmental protection. Bush, who likes nothing more than to spend time outdoors at his Texas ranch, was not about to be an exception.

For leaders of most of the nation's major environmental organizations, however, Bush's Earth Day appearances must have set their teeth on edge. They knew that months earlier the EPA had proposed to loosen federal protection of wetlands, only to backtrack under White House orders when it became clear that the proposed rule faced major legal hurdles and, more important, political opposition from many in Congress—even Republicans—and from state governments. So great was the uproar that Bush met with representatives of fishing and hunting groups, whose members tend to be politically conservative, to assure them of his intent to maintain the federal commitment to "no net loss of wetlands" begun by his father.[4] These leaders knew, or could argue, that many of the achievements Bush extolled in Maine and Florida were the culmination of years of work in previous administrations or, like the wetlands rule, reflected strategic retreats from original intentions. They also knew that what the administration gave with one hand it might take away with the other. Even as the president talked of protecting a million acres of wetlands, his administration was accused of considering the exclusion of another 20 million acres from protection under the Clean Water Act and of failing to fund a program that encouraged farmers to preserve wetlands on their property.[5]

The tussle over wetlands was just the latest episode in what had become, for environmentalists, an endless struggle with an administration that had pursued a far more ideological tack on environmental and energy issues than many had thought possible, given the president's narrow victory in 2000. It had been a bitter time: seemingly endless legal battles to compel the administration to enforce existing law,[6] rearguard actions in Congress to stave off undesirable statutory and appropriations actions, and efforts to blunt the policy influence of federal officials recruited from the industries they were supposed to regulate. But none of this was publicly apparent on Earth Day as the cameras captured a president at ease in nature, not one who, in the view of many environmental leaders, was more consistently hostile to environmental values than any president in memory. The capacity of the presidency to command the symbolic and rhetorical stage, even if only momentarily, was on full display, and there was little environmentalists could do about it.

Earth Day 2004 typified the frustrations plaguing national environmental organizations. Bush's very ascent to office in 2001 seemed to mock their supposed clout in American politics. Whatever their complaints about the Clinton administration's perceived timidity on environmental issues,[7] most major environmental organizations had rallied behind Vice President Al Gore in 2000 when it became clear that a Green Party challenge headed by longtime consumer activist Ralph Nader might affect the election. For these leaders, Gore's loss to Bush was especially sobering, since broad public support for environmental values had not translated into sufficient votes for their preferred candidate.[8] The 97,000 votes for Nader in Florida put an exclamation point on the message.

Once Bush was in place, only the appointment of former New Jersey governor Christine Todd Whitman to head the EPA deviated from the administration's thoroughgoing conservative agenda on environmental, natural resource, and energy issues.[9] However, Bush soon reversed Whitman (and his own campaign pledge) on the issue of reducing carbon dioxide emissions at coal-fired power plants, making it clear that neither she nor the EPA had much leverage within the administration, particularly compared with the influence wielded by Vice President Richard Cheney.[10] Whitman's eventual departure in June 2003, soon after the White House's public reversal, underscored her marginal status.[11] Her successor, former Utah governor Michael Leavitt, was seen as a team player in an administration known for putting a premium on loyalty.

Environmentalists had encountered similar challenges during the administrations of Ronald Reagan and George H. W. Bush, but most of the time they could rely on Democratic control of Congress as a partisan, ideological, and institutional counterweight. Not anymore: despite considerable efforts to mobilize voters on behalf of more pro-environmental (largely Democratic) candidates, environmentalists were unable to do much to stop the consolidation of Republican power in Congress during the 1990s. With Bush's election, Republicans would control both the executive and the legislative branches of government for the first time since 1953, thereby posing a daunting challenge to many environmentalists, given the wide ideological gulf between them and the conservatives now dominating the party.[12] The House of Representatives in particular reflected the solidification of political power among southern and southwestern conservatives, many of whom had campaigned as stout critics of environmental regulation and, by extension, environmentalists. The Senate, for its part, shifted into firmer Republican control after the 2002 elections, which had been dominated by voter anxiety about national security in the wake of the terrorist attacks of September 11, 2001. Senate Republicans had only a narrow numerical advantage, but it was enough to cause concern, given the chamber's role in approving presidential nominees to the executive branch and, especially, the federal judiciary. The administration had not been shy about nominating conservative jurists before Republicans regained control over the Senate; those efforts became even more assertive thereafter.

As if all this weren't enough to keep environmental leaders awake at night, they and their organizations were caught in the public crosshairs, subject to searing criticism of their way of doing business. One widely disseminated critique came in an April 2001 series, "Environment, Inc.," by *Sacramento Bee* reporter Tom Knudson. The bill of particulars against the major environmental organizations included bureaucratic sclerosis, highly paid executives, constant fund-raising, alleged politicization of scientific data, overuse of lawsuits for policy and organizational ends, and, contrary to the image of a unified movement, friction with local activists. "National environmental organizations, I fear, have grown away from the grass roots to mirror the foxes they had been chasing," wrote Knudson, quoting veteran environmental writer Michael Frome. "They seem to me to have turned tame, corporate and compromising."[13]

Frome's views about the major environmental organizations were common knowledge among longtime observers, if not casual newspaper readers. He had been fired a decade earlier after nearly twenty years as a columnist for *Defenders,* the magazine of Defenders of Wildlife, purportedly because his writings offended middle-of-the-road contributors.[14] To Frome's critique, Knudson offered his own damning summation:

> Put the pieces together and you find a movement estranged from its past, one that has come to resemble the corporate world it often seeks to reform. Although environmental organizations have accomplished many stirring and important victories over the years, today groups prosper while the land does not. Competition for money and members is keen. Litigation is a blood sport. Crisis, real or not, is a commodity. And slogans and sound bites masquerade as scientific fact.[15]

It was a scathing indictment, supported by data and compelling anecdotes. The *Sacramento Bee* is not the *New York Times,* to be sure, but the capacity of the Internet to convey the series beyond Sacramento led to its rapid and widespread dispersal, with predictable results for anyone who follows environmental politics. Newspaper editorials around the country used its assertions to rap environmentalists on their collective knuckles, while grassroots activists worried that the movement had drifted away from its core values. More telling, conservative western Republicans with long-standing ties to extractive industries such as mining and timber latched on to the series and demanded congressional investigations into the fund-raising practices of the national groups. "I have witnessed over the years how environmental groups have changed from actually doing constructive work into self-interest business organizations whose main goals seem to be marketing, self-perpetuating power and growth, and to achieve those ends by any means," proclaimed Representative James Hansen (R-Utah), then chair of the House Committee on Resources.[16] Seasoned veterans of battles with Hansen over western rangelands expressed wonder at his sudden zeal to return environmental advocacy to a more pristine state, but they also worried that environmental organizations had given their political and ideological foes enough ammunition to cause damage.

Nor were the critiques confined to the ideological right. In the December

2001 issue of the *Nation,* left-wing journalist Alexander Cockburn once again lacerated the Sierra Club—and "mainstream" environmental groups in general—for allegedly selling its soul for the sake of affluent donors and well-paid executives.[17] Cockburn's previous targets included the Nature Conservancy, labeled "the heart of darkness" for its willingness to accept corporate donations, and the Wilderness Society for its "cowardice" during one mid-1990s battle over logging on public lands in Idaho.[18] A similar charge was leveled against Greenpeace—long regarded as a no-compromise direct-action group—by Paul Watson, a cofounder who later split with the organization to found the more aggressive Sea Shepherd Conservation Society.[19] Even the apolitical, accommodation-minded Nature Conservancy, an organization long regarded as corporate America's favorite environmental group, drew considerable heat, a Senate committee investigation, and a subsequent Internal Revenue Service (IRS) audit following a May 2003 *Washington Post* series on the fiscal and governance practices of the nation's wealthiest conservation organization.[20]

All this frustration, seeming political impotence, and organizational turbulence might lead an observer of American environmental politics to wonder whether the major environmental organizations had strayed badly from the ideals of the movement that typified American environmentalism in the late 1960s and early 1970s. Had the nation's major environmental organizations lost touch with the American public, lost their capacity to make a difference, or, for that matter, lost their collective soul? A lot of people seemed to think so.

Yet, that same observer might recall identical questions about the health and direction of organized environmental advocacy at other junctures over the decades. Very much the same issues were raised in the early 1980s, in the wake of the Reagan administration's efforts to remake regulatory policy,[21] and in the early 1990s, amidst the recession that followed the first war with Iraq.[22] Indeed, organized environmentalism has been scrutinized and found wanting almost continuously since environmental issues first appeared on the nation's agenda in the late 1960s. The major national environmental organizations in particular *always* seem to have less influence than imagined by their foes or hoped by their friends, and they *always* seem to veer between their desire to push the cause and the more prosaic dictates of organizational survival. Mark Dowie, a trenchant critic of these organizations, makes such an argument:

> American land, air, and water are certainly in better shape than they would have been had the movement never existed, but they would be in far better condition had environmental leaders been bolder; more diverse in class, race, and gender; less compromising in battle; and less gentlemanly in the day-to-day dealings with adversaries. Over the past 30 years environmentalism

> has certainly risen close to the top of the American political agenda, but it has not prevailed as a movement, or as a paradigm.[23]

Not bold enough, not diverse enough, too willing to compromise, too gentlemanly: Dowie's clear disappointment is shared widely, almost unanimously, among environmental writers and pundits. Yet, on reflection, one is struck by another realization: even given its perceived shortcomings, the organized vanguard of national environmental advocacy in the United States *has survived.* Moreover, as even Dowie admits, it has made a difference, although how much of a difference is a matter of debate. Like the hound that did not bark in Arthur Conan Doyle's "The Story of Silver Blaze," the seeming permanence of organizations that work on behalf of environmental values elicits little comment. They are taken for granted as established parts of the contemporary political landscape.

It strikes me as odd that so few commentators consider this fact worthy of examination. But it should be, if for no other reason than the story of how the environmental advocacy community became part of the national political establishment reflects a broader picture of political representation in the United States.[24] For better or for worse, the state of organized environmental advocacy reflects the dominant characteristics of today's political system.

THE ENVIRONMENTAL ADVOCACY COMMUNITY

This book looks at the evolution of organized environmental advocacy in the United States, with particular focus on the period from the early 1970s to the present, as a vehicle for understanding organized advocacy more generally. Studying "organized environmental advocacy" is a pretty tall order, so I limit my attention to the clutch of major organizations that might be called the "national environmental advocacy community." This community is, more or less, the environmental "establishment"—a term I considered but discarded because it so often conjures up caricatures of bespectacled men in gray suits sipping martinis in some smoky private club. Environmentalists don't look like this, of course. But, popular images of tie-dyed T-shirts and Birkenstocks aside, many of them *did* look that way back when the first Earth Day convened, and many still bear some resemblance to that image today—although they're not always men, don't always wear gray, and have probably swapped martinis for a crisp Chardonnay.

Semantics aside, there is no doubt that environmental advocacy at the national level in the United States is dominated by a loosely knit community of

Table 1.1. Snapshot of National Environmental Organizations, 2003

Organization	Members*	Revenue (millions)
Sierra Club	736,000	$83.7†
National Audubon Society	550,000	$78.6
National Parks Conservation Association	375,000	$20.9
Izaak Walton League	45,000	$4.3
The Wilderness Society	225,000	$18.8
National Wildlife Federation	650,000	$102.1
Ducks Unlimited	656,000	$125.1
Defenders of Wildlife	463,000	$21.8
The Nature Conservancy	972,000	$972.4
World Wildlife Fund—U.S.	1,200,000	$93.3
Environmental Defense	350,000	$43.8
Friends of the Earth	35,000	$3.8
Natural Resources Defense Council	450,000	$46.4
League of Conservation Voters	60,000	$7.0†
Earthjustice	70,000	$17.9
Clean Water Action	300,000	$14.5†
Greenpeace USA	250,000	$25.9†
Trust for Public Land	45,000	$126.5
Ocean Conservancy	100,000	$8.9
American Rivers	30,000	$5.5
Sea Shepherd Conservation Society	35,000	$1.0
Center for Health, Environment, and Justice	28,000	$1.0
Earth Island Institute	20,000	$4.9
National Park Trust	33,000	$1.2
Conservation Fund	16,000	$60.1
Rainforest Action Network	35,000	$2.2
Conservation International	70,400	$222.7
Earth Share	–	$7.9
Environmental Working Group	–	$1.8
National Environmental Trust	–	$10.7
Total	7,799,400	$2,135

* Includes "members" or "supporters," where known or possible to estimate.
† Indicates combined revenues of related entities, or for tax-exempt affiliate, FY2003.

established organizations (see table 1.1). Many, though certainly not all, have multimillion-dollar budgets; are led by well-compensated executives; employ scores of professional legal, scientific, and administrative staff; and have the capacity to simultaneously promote multiple goals using multiple techniques at multiple levels (local, state, national, and international) of political action. In this sense, then, we do have an environmental establishment.

Like any establishment, this community of advocacy organizations invites criticism. The complaints have some merit. However, as I will argue, the transformation of environmental advocacy from the relatively inchoate movement of the late 1960s into today's more tightly configured community of professional advocacy organizations was necessary for the long-term success of environmental policy in the United States. In fact, without these organizations, I doubt that environmentalism would have made the successful transition from a largely elite issue to a concern of the mass value system, however lightly held and imperfectly applied.[25] In 1972, Anthony Downs wondered whether nascent public concern about the environment would survive what he termed the "issue-attention" cycle.[26] But it did. No political party, president, or member of Congress can claim credit for this achievement, however. Environmentalists, as persistent advocates for their cause, and the organizations they built deserve the credit.

In making this argument about the centrality of advocacy organizations to the endurance of specific values, this book could have examined the organizational transformation of any social movement into an established advocacy community. It could have been about the organizational evolution of civil rights movements dedicated to racial minorities, women, gays and lesbians, or the physically or mentally disabled, or about those who occupy opposite sides of the debate over abortion.[27] Unlike other, more short-lived movements (e.g., the one seeking a nuclear freeze), none of these movements dissipated. Instead, they spawned an array of advocacy organizations that persisted long enough to become established participants in contemporary political life.[28]

Indeed, this story of the national environmental advocacy community is an apt metaphor for public-interest advocacy in the American political system. These organizational tendencies have always been evident in organizations that lobby on behalf of "private interests." Those who represent corporate or occupational interests are *supposed* to be professionals with long tenures in Washington—the better to establish their bona fides with members of Congress, political appointees, and career civil servants. Public-interest or citizens groups, by contrast, apparently were supposed to stay amateur, small, and poor. For some reason, "Nader's Raiders" and their early 1970s peers were supposed to stay young and ill paid, fueled by little more than zeal and packets of ramen noodles.

But they didn't. This book is about why—and why it shouldn't be any surprise. Whether the critics will ever admit it, the national environmental community is just a larger, broader, and more resilient version of an established public-interest advocacy community in the United States and, to some extent, other mature representative democracies.[29] Rather than an aberration, this community is decidedly normal. That normalcy says volumes about the contours of contemporary American politics, and about American democracy.

Immortals

The organizational roster of environmental advocacy in the United States is dominated by household names: Sierra Club, Audubon Society, National Wildlife Federation, Nature Conservancy, and Greenpeace, to name a few. These organizations are such permanent fixtures in national politics that few bother to ask the most basic questions about them.

For starters, why has this roster remained so remarkably constant over time? Despite mergers and the demise of a few relatively small or narrowly focused organizations, since the early 1970s the organizational topography of the national environmental advocacy community has displayed surprising stability. Two-thirds of the organizations included in this study were created before the mid-1970s, and half of them between 1967 and 1973—to many observers, the formative years of environmental advocacy.[30] The decades since the first Earth Day have seen the transformation of a movement into a mature advocacy community, but there has been no fundamental reshuffling of the organizations that constitute it. Indeed, as Ronald Shaiko notes, more than 80 percent of the environmental organizations listed in Jeffrey Berry's 1972 data set were still in operation in the 1990s. Says Shaiko, "As important as the growth in the public interest sector is the ability of many national organizations to sustain themselves for decades, despite changing policy agendas in Washington and economic difficulties."[31]

Why have so few of these organizations gone out of business? For that matter, how did centenarians like the Sierra Club and the National Audubon Society manage to survive the influx of competitors? And what accounts for the relative paucity of major new organizations created at the national level in the succeeding decades? Is the "marketplace" for environmental advocacy so crowded today that the costs of starting a new national organization are too steep?[32] Do existing organizations cover the range of issues and tactics so thoroughly that no new organizations are needed? Whatever the reason, the organizational stability of the national environmental advocacy community is worthy of analysis.

The few exceptions to this general picture of organizational survival are telling. The demise of Environmental Action (1970–1996), the organizational heir to the first Earth Day, offers clues to these larger questions because its leaders were unable, and in some instances unwilling, to let the organization adapt to changing political and economic conditions.[33] Yet, as I explore more fully in chapter 3, Environmental Action's demise cannot be attributed to a simple case of leadership myopia or ineptitude. Nor did it go out of business because it achieved its stated policy or political goals, so the rent-seeking model implied by rational-choice theories of organizational creation and closure do not apply.[34]

By contrast, most of the other organizations have survived several episodes of fiscal distress, internal disarray, abrupt leadership changes, and reorganization. How were they able to do what Environmental Action could not?

Adaptation is the key: How do these organizations adapt to often sharp changes in external conditions, including economic recession and shifts in partisan control of key governing institutions? Do they compete with one another for supporters, resources, and access to policymakers, or—like the various interests in the agricultural sector, discussed by Browne—do they avoid overt competition and deposit themselves into discrete niches within the broader advocacy population?[35] Or do they do both? Although this book examines the phenomenon of organizational survival as it pertains to the national environmental advocacy community, the questions raised apply to all advocacy communities over time.

Boundaries

To focus on the national environmental advocacy community is to study something far more bounded and substantive than some mystical environmental movement, a term that no longer makes much descriptive or conceptual sense. What has replaced the movement is less well understood and appreciated, but the sooner we move away from an imagery laden with cultural and ideological baggage, the sooner we can fix our gaze on what is, rather than on what some think should be.

In this regard, the national environmental community studied here is composed of professional advocacy organizations that operate on a national and, increasingly, global level, as opposed to a purely local or regional one. However, many of the lessons obtained here apply to long-established regional or state organizations as well. For example, both the Appalachian Mountain Club (1876) and the Massachusetts Audubon Society (1896)—an organization historically autonomous from the National Audubon Society—exhibit the characteristics examined here. I also omit advocacy groups that lack a clearly delineated organizational structure (e.g., Earth First! and the Earth Liberation Front) or local grassroots outfits made up of volunteers. Those dimensions of environmental advocacy are important for other reasons but are beyond the scope of this study.[36]

I do not confine myself to "membership groups," as classically understood. Political scientists have long recognized that "pressure politics" includes nonmembership organizations, public institutions, private foundations, and law firms, among others, even if most scholarship on interest groups continues to focus on the collective action problems central to membership groups.[37] The advocacy community examined here is composed of a broad array of organizations. Some are massive, and others are relatively small, whether measured by budget or membership. A few are organized on the basis of local or state chapters and offer their members a voice in electing leaders and setting advocacy priorities; a larger number can be described as having a mass base without mass participation. Some do not have a dues-paying membership, preferring to rely on foundation support or the patronage of major donors. Still others—perhaps the majority today—treat *any* donor as a "member," thus muddying the concept itself.

Even with these decision rules, some important organizations have been omitted from the environmental advocacy community examined here. For example, I leave out the U.S. Public Interest Research Group and the Union of Concerned Scientists, because each pursues a broad reform agenda of which environmental issues are but one part. They pursue environmental goals but do not portray themselves as environmental organizations to supporters, public officials, or the media. This is an important distinction if we are to understand the evolution of a defined advocacy community over time.

THE ECOLOGY OF THE ENVIRONMENTAL COMMUNITY

This book examines the nation's major environmental organizations as constituent parts of a singular entity, a specific *advocacy community.* As a result, I am less interested in microlevel matters, such as why individuals join organizations or the connections between leaders and members. These questions have been adequately mined in the political science literature on interest groups, and Shaiko in particular thoroughly examines the connections between environmental group leaders and supporters.[38] Instead, I want to understand environmental groups as *organizations*—in this case, nonprofit entities operating within the legal restrictions imposed by the Internal Revenue Code. In this regard, I use the term *organization* rather than *group* to underscore the point that many of them are not the classic membership groups on which theories of representation rest.[39]

Given my focus on the assembly, evolution, and adaptation of a defined advocacy community over time, I incorporate as my theoretical base the population ecology model, as utilized by Gray and Lowery in *The Population Ecology of Interest Representation.*[40] Readers desiring a lengthy discussion on this approach should consult that excellent work. I find the population ecology model useful for understanding the evolution *over time* of a single advocacy *community*—a distinct population—as well as the organizations that make up that community.

My focus on a single national advocacy community over a long period is what distinguishes this study from most scholarship on interest groups. Much of the best large-scale empirical work on groups focuses on the entire population of organized interests at the national level. Walker's magisterial study on the origin and maintenance of interest groups comes to mind, but the list extends to Berry, Schlozman and Tierney, Heinz and associates, and, most recently, the massive undertaking led by Baumgartner.[41] Berry examines the factors that account for the relative longevity of liberal citizens groups since the early 1970s, a category that includes environmental organizations, but his primary purpose is to assess why these groups have been more successful than their conservative counterparts.[42] On the other side of the ledger are many excellent studies of individual organizations, most notably Rothenberg on Common Cause.[43] Gray and Lowery's work examines lobbying patterns in the fifty U.S. states and is more concerned with broader characteristics of advocacy populations in a variety of contexts over time.[44] Finally, Shaiko's study of environmental groups focuses largely on the problematic relationship between leaders and members in the major mass-based organizations.[45]

By contrast, this study follows the gradual assembly of a single advocacy community over time and its adaptation to changes in external political conditions and internal maintenance needs. I want to know how this community came to look the way it does today and to better understand how its development shaped environmental politics and policy. To get at these questions, I treat the national environmental advocacy community as a distinct entity and the organizations within it as distinct "species." Like Gray and Lowery, I rely on biologist E. O. Wilson's definition of species as "populations of closely related and similar organisms," where "similarity is defined in terms of both the internal content or function of organizations and the nature of their external relations."[46] That is, environmental organizations have far more in common with one another than with corporations, labor unions, or political parties, so studying them as a community of similar entities enables us to parse out community-wide dynamics over time. These organizations share an array of characteristics, beginning with a more or less common agenda, so they are part of a "guild" in the language of population ecology. As such, Gray and Lowery argue, the terms of organizational survival are defined within the guild itself:

> Competition for survival as organizations is likely to take place within guilds, not between guilds. Competition for shared resources as members and financial resources will be between one union and another or between one trade association and another, not between a union and a trade association. . . . From this perspective, the primary competitors of an environ-

> mental organization are other environmental organizations, not polluters. Indeed, the presence of more polluters may actually help environmental organizations to survive by convincing their members that lobbying work remains undone.[47]

We can treat organizations as species because, in theory, they too "have beginnings, endings, and a unique history between these two points."[48] The population ecology approach, then, enables us to look at the national environmental advocacy community for what it is: a bounded, contextually derived assemblage of discrete entities whose aggregate shape and internal dynamic make sense only when taken as a whole. It is the unique history of the environmental advocacy community that compels this study.

An important point has to be made about using a conceptual model based on the theory of evolution to study a community of advocacy organizations: *nothing was inevitable*. Although the dynamics observed are explicable organizational responses to internal organizational needs and external political challenges, they are also the products of human agency. Choices were made. Environmental leaders scanned the political landscape around them and moved their organizations in particular directions to ensure organizational survival and, in their minds, effectiveness. Sometimes their choices were, to use the clinical term, less than optimal, but those choices always mattered. They had effects both on the organizations and on environmental policy. But none of this was preordained. Other paths were possible, although not every possible path was equally feasible. Whether the path taken was the best one for the cause in question is a different issue, and one worth considerable debate.

ORIGINS, ADAPTATION, AND IMPACTS

Chapter 2 looks at the origins of the environmental community from the late nineteenth century through the early 1970s. Although the bulk of this study assesses organizational adaptation and change in the decades thereafter, the dimensions of organized environmental advocacy cannot be understood at any moment in time without first tracing the evolution of its constituent organizations back to their respective points of origin. Remarkably little is understood about the patterns of organizational creation and development within a single advocacy community over a long period, or what these patterns reveal about American politics in general. Along the way, I examine the political, societal, and economic contexts that shaped how environmental organizations were created, how they evolved, and how they operated. These contexts, to echo E. E.

Schattschneider, imposed a distinctive bias on the shape and tone of organized advocacy.[49] How organizations emerged reflects these contexts.

Chapter 3 examines the maturation of the national environmental community following the spasm of organizational creation in the late 1960s and early 1970s. In doing so, it pays particular attention to the dimensions of competition among otherwise like-minded organizations and, in particular, the processes by which advocacy organizations move or get moved into distinct policy or tactical niches, where they can operate pretty much on their own. This dynamic of systematic niche seeking is critical to both the survival of individual organizations and the overall dimensions of the present national environmental community.

Chapter 4 looks more closely at how these organizations have managed to survive over the years, seeking lessons from both survivors and the relative few that failed. To do so, it digs into revenues and fund-raising, the elemental details of organizational maintenance that get far less attention than they deserve. National environmental organizations have taken a lot of criticism for their apparently incessant concern over money, and this chapter explores their range of options and why the criticism about their fund-raising practices is accurate but misplaced.

Chapter 5 examines the range of tactics utilized by national environmental advocacy organizations, with a special focus on how advocacy tactics have changed over time in response to shifts in the political opportunity structure. As with the mundane matters of organizational maintenance, not much is known about how organizations adapt their core tactics to, for example, adjust to a major shift in the partisan control of Congress or take advantage of new technologies, particularly the Internet. After all, many of these organizations emerged during an "environmental era" characterized by federal and state judiciaries inclined to expand environmental protection, legislatures that produced major new laws, and the creation of new bureaucratic institutions. None of those conditions held by 2004, so, for the most part, the tactics emphasized by these organizations have had to change accordingly.

Chapter 6 considers lessons that can be extended beyond the particulars of environmental advocacy to other public-interest advocacy communities. Along the way, its asks whether these organizations have mattered. The short answer is that of course they mattered, but in what way and how much are less well understood. As will become evident, I believe that without these organizations, the place of environmental values in American political discourse would be even more marginal than its most disappointed advocates already think it is. The problem is far less the organizations than the political system in which they work.

What do these insights into the national environmental community tell us about organized issue advocacy in the United States? As Baumgartner and Leech argue, "Without a good understanding of the roles of interest groups, our understandings of the functioning of our political system cannot possibly be complete."[50] In this regard, the current state of organized environmental advocacy at the national level is an apt metaphor for American national politics writ large. How we got to this point, and why it matters, are the questions that drive this study.

2
Opportunities and Origins

In February 1936, nationally syndicated political cartoonist and wildlife advocate Jay Norwood ("Ding") Darling convened the first North American Wildlife Conference, drawing to Washington nearly 2,000 state and local conservation officials and activists from around the country. Those in attendance, observed historian Thomas Allen, made up "a real army of conservationists that slogged through a snow storm . . . to launch a crusade to save the nation's wildlife."[1] Darling had long used his cartoons to promote conservation. He had served on the Iowa State Fish and Game Commission and, despite his Republican credentials, had been appointed by President Franklin Roosevelt to head the U.S. Bureau of Biological Survey, forerunner of the Fish and Wildlife Service. It was in his official role that Darling organized the conference.

The gathering was adjudged a success, in no small part because it led to the creation of the National Wildlife Federation, through which the nation's far-flung wildlife advocates now could speak with one voice in national politics. As a federation, Allen observed, it would be "powerful on a national level while drawing strength from numerous organizations still rooted in a myriad of issues and goals on the local or state level."[2] The federation's origins in the halls of national governmental power spoke to its political purpose, and to nobody's surprise, the new organization's first executive director was Ding Darling, who had resigned his government position just before the conference began.

WHY ORIGINS MATTER

Where do advocacy organizations come from? At first glance, this seems like an odd question. They exist because someone like Darling created them to do something. Yet the question isn't as simple (or simplistic) as it appears, and any assessment about advocacy organizations must go back to their origins: Why do they exist at all? How did they emerge, and what do the conditions of their respective origins tell us about the eventual composition of entire contemporary advocacy communities? Moreover, what do the contextual circumstances of their origins tell us about the American political system?

The political science literature on group formation is especially rich.[3] Much of it can be divided into two broad perspectives. The first links group formation to the purposeful actions of rational individuals. That is, the organization is an intentional creation, designed to promote some specific goal. The classic imagery here is of the policy "entrepreneur" who creates an interest group, attracts members to the cause, and through it pursues some political or policy end.[4] A variation on the individual as entrepreneur is a "patron," like Darling, who provides the new organization with critical seed capital and acts as its sponsor until it can walk on its own.[5] Scholars taking this first perspective tend to focus on the range of incentives that entrepreneurs extend to potential and current members in order to mobilize their support, maintain the organization, and wield influence in government.

Scholars working from the second perspective tend to look at group origins in terms of context, the broader societal or structural conditions—the "political opportunity structure"—of the moment.[6] Theirs is a more situational assessment of mobilization. They assume that individuals will always look for the most effective way to organize for political action, but they do not assume that creating an interest group is invariably the preferred option. For example, why don't these individuals create or work through political parties instead? Scholars adopting this perspective tend to focus on the array of access points afforded by the constitutional structure, whether the system favors the formation of parties versus groups,[7] the nature of the administrative state,[8] or the impact of government agendas on group formation.[9] In short, they start with exogenous conditions, not with how individual entrepreneurs overcome the collective action problem. In truth, there is a fair degree of interplay between the perspectives—rational individuals react to the contexts around them, after all—but for present purposes, it is useful to think of them as two distinct explanations of organizational origins.

In either case, interest group scholars (with notable exceptions, such as Walker and Berry) have paid little attention to the creation of organizations within a specific policy area over a long period.[10] This omission seems curious. After all, advocacy organizations are not created in a vacuum. Some undoubtedly emerge as responses to external events or conditions, in line with David Truman's "disturbance" theory of mobilization.[11] Others, however, are created out of perceptions about opportunities to do something, to occupy an otherwise vacant advocacy niche or to take up tactics not being pursued (or being pursued suboptimally) by existing organizations. But, in line with the situational perspective on group formation, the political opportunity structure of the moment may influence the nature of origins in a particular case.

Origins matter. Why and how advocacy organizations are created in the first place shapes what they do, how they do it, and to what effect. I therefore look at the origins of each of these organizations from the perspective that someone decided that it was necessary, that there was a reason to create it in the first place. Any organization is created for a purpose, a response to what sociologist Elizabeth Clemens calls "the complexity of social organization."[12] After all, why else create it? What is it supposed to do? Strip away everything else and you get back to an elemental point: you don't create an organization unless you think that doing so serves a purpose.

In this chapter I examine the assembling of the national environmental advocacy community from the early days of nature conservation through the environmental era of the late 1960s and early 1970s. This historical assessment of organization creation will show that the "movement" as such did not emerge spontaneously out of virgin soil. It was, instead, cultivated by organizations created during earlier spasms of organizational creation dating back to the late nineteenth century. This chapter trails the construction of that advocacy community over time by focusing on the origins of specific organizations in particular eras. In each instance, I also look at the political opportunity structure that affected the particulars of their creation. As will become apparent, the organizational dimensions of the environmental era cannot be understood without a clear picture of what came before. The organizations discussed here are listed in table 2.1. I examine the organizations created in 1972 and later more fully in chapter 3.

PROGRESSIVE PIONEERS

The first conservation organizations were manifest expressions of a growing concern in certain elite social and political circles about the depletion of the nation's natural resources and the despoliation of its landscape as a result of rapid industrialization and development in the late nineteenth century. As would typify nature conservation until the mid-twentieth century, the organizations created were small and regionally based, were elite in composition and tone, and, as historian Samuel Hays argued, reflected Progressive ideals of scientific expertise, professional management, and the practical need to conserve natural resources for the use of later generations.[13]

In some ways, the political opportunity structure of the late nineteenth century could not have been less conducive to the establishment of advocacy

Table 2.1. Origins of Selected Environmental Organizations

	Year Founded	Where	HQ 2004*	Member†	Chapters#	Comments
Sierra Club	1892	CA	CA	yes	yes	Originally San Francisco outdoorsmen seeking to protect Yosemite Park
National Audubon Society	1905	NY	NY	yes	yes	Started with group of Boston women to stop slaughter of birds (1896)
National Parks Conservation Association	1919	DC	DC	yes	no	Organized by National Park Service official to promote park system
Izaak Walton League	1922	IL	DC	yes	yes	Originally Chicago area outdoorsmen; first mass membership conservation group
The Wilderness Society	1935	DC	DC	yes	no	Founded by Interior Dept. official to preserve roadless wilderness
National Wildlife Federation	1936	DC	DC	no	yes	Organized by federal official; DC lobbying arm of wildlife movement
Ducks Unlimited	1937	DC	TN	yes	no	Finances wetlands restoration; works with Fish and Wildlife Service
Defenders of Wildlife	1947	DC	DC	yes	no	Focuses on endangered species in U.S.
Conservation Foundation	*1948*	*NY*	*NY*	*no*	*no*	*Focused on building organizational capacity; merged with WWF in 1985*

Table 2.1. Origins of Selected Environmental Organizations *(Continued)*

	Year Founded	Where	HQ 2004*	Member[†]	Chapters[#]	Comments
The Nature Conservancy	1951	DC	DC	no	no	Land conservancy; purchases "sensitive ecosystems"
World Wildlife Fund—US	1961	DC	DC	no	no	International focus; merged with Conservation Foundation in 1985
Environmental Defense (Fund)	1967	NY	NY	no	no	First environmental law firm; Audubon and Ford Foundation support
Friends of the Earth	1969	CA	DC	yes	no	Spin-off from Sierra Club; merged with Oceanic Society and EPI in 1989
Environmental Action	*1970*	*DC*	*DC*	*yes*	*no*	*Created to organize first Earth Day; closed in 1996*
Natural Resources Defense Council	1970	NY	NY	no	no	"Science and law" organization; founded with Ford Foundation support
League of Conservation Voters	1970	DC	DC	no	no	Political action committee; spin-off from FoE
Earthjustice Legal Defense Fund	1971	CA	CA	no	no	Originally Sierra Club Legal Defense Fund
Clean Water Action	1971	MI	DC	no	no	Loose national coalition of state clean water advocacy organizations

Greenpeace USA	1971	DC	DC	yes	no	Direct-action oriented; merged with Ozone Action in 2000
Environmental Policy Center	*1972*	*DC*	*DC*	*no*	*no*	*Founded by FoE dissidents; merged back with FoE in 1989*
Trust for Public Land	1972	CA	CA	no	no	Land conservancy; acquires land for public use
Ocean Conservancy	1972	DC	DC	no	no	Formerly Center for Marine Conservation
American Rivers	1973	CO	DC	yes	no	Founded by EPC and other groups to protect wild and scenic rivers
Environmental Policy Institute	*1974*	*DC*	*DC*	*no*	*no*	*Founded by EPC; merged with EPC and FoE in 1989*
Sea Shepherd Conservation Society	1977	CA	CA	no	no	Direct-action group founded by Greenpeace dissidents to fight over fishing
Center for Health, Environment, and Justice	1981	DC	DC	no	no	Started by Love Canal activist Lois Gibbs; original focus on toxic wastes
Earth Island Institute	1982	CA	CA	no	no	Spin-off from FoE; focuses on public education and advocacy
National Park Trust	1983	DC	DC	no	no	Spin-off from NPCA; acquires private land in and near national parks
Conservation Fund	1985	DC	DC	no	no	Land conservancy; leverages donations into public-private partnerships

Table 2.1. Origins of Selected Environmental Organizations (*Continued*)

	Year Founded	Where	HQ 2004*	Member†	Chapters#	Comments
Rainforest Action Network	1985	CA	CA	no	no	Earth Island and Earth First! spin-off; Internet-based activism
Conservation International	1987	DC	DC	no	no	Founded by former Nature Conservancy staff; pioneered "debt-for-nature" swaps
Earth Share	1988	DC	DC	no	no	Created by environmental organizations to foster workplace giving
Environmental Working Group	1993	DC	DC	no	no	Research organization; foundation supported
National Environmental Trust	1994	DC	DC	no	no	Established by Pew Trusts to inform citizens about environmental problems

Organizations in italic no longer exist.
* The DC area includes Virginia and Maryland.
† Created as a member-based organization.
# Created with local chapters or state affiliates, versus regional or state offices.

organizations, particularly at the national level. Notwithstanding Theodore Roosevelt's robust presidential leadership and the emergence of a nascent administrative state, the Progressive Era was marked by parties that organized political life down to the ward level, a mass electorate accustomed to voting along partisan lines, congressional dominance, and a post-Reconstruction federalism suffused by strong states' rights sentiments.[14] Any national nonparty organizations that existed (e.g., National Grange, General Federation of Women's Clubs) were, of necessity, federations of state chapters, mimicking the structural realities of both federalism and the national party system.

Even so, the years of the Progressive Era witnessed an explosion of organizational creation at the local and state levels, including civic associations, professional groups, women's clubs, good government groups, and voters' leagues.[15] Many of these organizations embodied the era's faith in scientific management, while others took on a more moralist edge as part of a reformist crusade against what many saw as the corrupting influences of partisanship, the ravages of unchecked industrial development, and the corrosive impact of rampant materialism. These conflicting impulses—management versus morality—recur in environmental debates to this day.

Sierra Club

In 1890, Congress authorized the creation of Yosemite National Park, thereby extending federal jurisdiction over a section of the Sierra Nevada range first set aside in public trust by Abraham Lincoln in 1864. Lincoln's grant gave jurisdiction over Yosemite to the state of California, whose inability to resist local economic interests and curb development in and around the valley generated efforts, led by naturalist John Muir, to shift control of the park to the federal government. The creation of Yosemite National Park in 1890 marked a watershed moment in the nation's history and led directly to the formation of the Sierra Club.[16]

The Sierra Club was founded in San Francisco on May 28, 1892, with 182 charter members and an expressed purpose to promote and protect the new national park. Muir, already a leading national voice for nature preservation, was elected its first president. Its membership consisted of hikers and nature lovers in the San Francisco Bay Area, most of them professors, scientists, businessmen, and other prominent citizens. The club's values embodied California progressivism—it was white, middle class, urban, religious, hostile to partisanship, professional, and reformist. Its official orientation was to encourage development of the cities but to protect Yosemite from local economic interests that were trying to nibble away at the federal protection so recently extended to the park.[17]

From the start, the Sierra Club experienced tension between the pull of activism and the prosaic demands of organizational maintenance, in particular, generating revenues sufficient to support programs and staff. The more militant faction led by Muir pushed for a confrontational stance on preserving the most aesthetically important landscapes in the Sierra Nevada range, while other members stressed a cooperative working relationship with governmental agencies and emphasized the professional management of nature for resource conservation and recreation. The tension between Muir's aesthetic preservation and the utilitarian conservation embodied by Gifford Pinchot, first director of the U.S. Forest Service, marked American conservation for decades.[18]

This philosophical and tactical split became public in the first decade of the new century during the mythic twelve-year battle over the city of San Francisco's proposal to dam the Toulumne River in the Hetch Hetchy Valley, located within Yosemite's boundaries, to serve its pressing need for water. Hetch Hetchy pitted club members who backed the reservoir as key to the Bay Area's economic development against Muir and fellow preservationists who opposed submerging a valley with unsurpassed beauty.[19] Stephen Fox, in assessing Muir's legacy, argues that the dispute went beyond a simple preservationist-utilitarian duality: "Rather, it was occupational, between those who urge the dam *as part of their jobs* and those who *took the time from their jobs to oppose it*."[20] Club leaders, trying to bridge this division, submitted the issue to members in a 1910 referendum. Nearly 80 percent voted to oppose the dam. The club board also set up a legally separate Society for the Preservation of National Parks, with Muir at its helm, to put the campaign against the dam on the national agenda and thereby reduce the local political pressure on members caught in the middle of the dispute.[21]

Congress ultimately responded to the wishes of California's congressional delegation and approved the dam in 1913. Even in defeat, argues historian Michael Cohen, the battle over Hetch Hetchy was "a crucible that transformed the Club, separating—some would say—the pure at heart from those who could be swayed by local interests. But more to the point, these problems opened up a vigorous dialogue, identified the real leaders in the ranks, tested organizational structure, and made the Sierra Club known nationally."[22] It also taught club leaders two important lessons: first, the need to build a broader membership base through the establishment of chapters beyond the Bay Area, and second, the need to elevate local or regional preservation issues to the national agenda to overcome the entrenched political power of local interests.[23] Such lessons would sound familiar to later generations of environmental advocates.

National Audubon Society

On February 10, 1896, Mrs. Augustus Hemenway called together a group of prominent Bostonians to plan a campaign against the continued use of bird plumage in women's fashion, which had led to the virtual extermination of birds such as the white heron throughout the South.[24] That meeting led to others, and the participants decided to call their group the Massachusetts Audubon Society, after famed bird portraitist John James Audubon. They wrote letters about the cause to their members of Congress and, just as important, to friends throughout the country. The myriad local women's clubs already in place proved to be the organizational foundation for the establishment of other state Audubon societies—fifteen within two years—whose members also wrote letters to *their* members of Congress. The aggregate impact of their activism eventually led to passage of the Lacey Act of 1900, outlawing the interstate sale of birds killed in violation of state law.

The National Audubon Society emerged as a national organization in 1901, when representatives of the now thirty-six state societies (which previously had no formal linkage) formed a federation called the National Committee of the Audubon Societies of America.[25] The state chapters retained their individuality, and each sent a representative to a national committee. Formal incorporation as the National Association of Audubon Societies came in 1905 in New York, at the urging of its first de facto officer, William Dutcher. Dutcher, a leading figure in the American Ornithologists' Union (established in 1883), felt that the organization needed more structure, strong central leadership, and financial stability. This decision was aided, indeed impelled, by the wishes of a benefactor who ultimately left the association more than $300,000, provided that it incorporate, expand its focus to all wild animals, and employ paid staff to recruit members and solicit the contributions needed to support the organization. A headquarters was established in New York City, the center of the fashion industry, where the organization could push the battle against the use of plumage in fashions.[26] In what would be a familiar story to any contemporary fund-raising professional, the bequest had the unexpected consequence of making it harder to attract other donations. For example, a 1906 mailing to 4,000 potential members did not produce enough revenue to cover its costs; those contacted apparently figured that the organization already had sufficient resources.[27]

Sierra and Audubon are classic membership groups, created by local elites to work with and, if necessary, put pressure on state and federal officials to counteract the parochial power of business interests in Congress and in the various state legislatures. In the case of the Sierra Club, its original purpose was to defend Yosemite and to expand protection of the Sierra Nevada range. For the Audubon Societies, it was to put a stop to the slaughter of birds. Neither was absolutist in its goals. The Sierra Club, even after Hetch Hetchy, opposed dams only when they would destroy particularly important landscapes, and the Audubon Societies supported the managed hunting of game birds.

More important for our purposes, both organizations began as membership groups with local or state chapters. The Sierra Club established chapters throughout California, and the Audubon Society emerged out of a federation of independent state entities. Those characteristics served both organizations well. Although the Sierra Club and the Audubon Society were not the only conservation organizations created during the Progressive period, nor even the first, their longevity is in stark contrast to other conservation organizations of the day.

A telling counterpoint is the National Conservation Association (NCA), whose story begins with Gifford Pinchot and the American Forestry Association (AFA). The AFA was founded in 1875 as an association of professional botanists and landscape designers. During the 1890s, under Pinchot's leadership, it sharpened its focus on the scientific management of forest resources.[28] Pinchot eventually left the AFA to head the new U.S. Forest Service, where he wielded great influence in the federal government across a wide range of conservation issues while serving under Theodore Roosevelt. Pinchot also used his position to organize and act as official patron for external advocacy organizations. In 1908, he created the Conservation League of America (CLA), largely composed of local waterways associations, to generate external political support for Roosevelt's legislative proposals. A year later, as William Howard Taft's policies began to diverge from those of his predecessor, Pinchot refashioned the CLA into the National Conservation Association to build popular support for conservation and strengthen his own hand in battles with Taft, who had retained Pinchot for fear of alienating Roosevelt.[29] He also saw the NCA as a counterweight to the AFA, from which he had grown estranged because of its reluctance to follow his lead and broaden its agenda beyond forest management.[30] Efforts to make the NCA into a national membership group failed, largely because it was perceived to serve Pinchot's own political agenda. After essentially forcing Taft to fire him as head of the Forest Service in 1910, Pinchot served as the NCA's president, even as he ran for the U.S. Senate and until he was elected governor of Pennsylvania. The organization was dissolved shortly thereafter, having never grown beyond its patron. The AFA, for its part, endures to this day as American Forests, a comparatively small organization that promotes programs (e.g., Arbor Day) to plant trees.

THE INTERWAR PERIOD

The period between the world wars is often overlooked, overshadowed by the formative years of the Progressive Era and, of course, the contemporary environmental age.[31] But the interwar period was essential to the evolution of organized environmental advocacy. First, compared with the Progressive Era, the driving focus at this time was less on the scientific management of nature—or, in the case of preservationists like Muir, appreciation of its aesthetic virtues—than on its *recreational* benefits and opportunities. Nature was not just to be managed and admired, but enjoyed as another consumer good.

Second, the organizations created during the interwar period tended to originate in Washington. This shift in the geography of organizational origin is attributable to the emerging nationalization of public policy, as the federal government took a more active role in conservation and, with the New Deal, economic development.[32] Like the Sierra Club a generation before, many of these organizations would be created *after* government actions—for example, creation of the national parks system in 1916—to maintain and expand on those policy initiatives.

By the late 1920s, with the battle over Hetch Hetchy fading in memory, the Sierra Club was at peace with the Forest Service, supportive of the new National Park Service, and more focused on its mission "to explore, enjoy, and render [nature] accessible" to its members.[33] Club-organized outings constituted a major source of new members and revenues, and club-organized schools trained an entire generation of mountain climbers, skiers, and outdoors experts. Although it did not abandon advocacy, the emphasis on recreation took center stage.

For its part, the National Committee of State Audubon Societies (it changed its name to the National Audubon Society in 1940) had become oriented to serving a membership base largely dedicated to bird-watching and related recreational activities.[34] By the end of the 1920s, the Audubon umbrella covered 125 state and local membership organizations, but decision-making power had become more centralized in the professional staff at the society's headquarters, who tended to favor close working relationships with federal and state government officials.[35] Such elite-level coziness provoked periodic rebellions among more militant volunteer activists in the state affiliates, in one instance leading to the departure of longtime chief executive Gilbert Pearson. For the most part, however, such internal squalls had little long-term impact on the organization.[36]

New organizations were created to foster an ethos of recreation and enjoyment of the outdoors among the widest spectrum of Americans possible. In this regard, two organizational patterns emerged. First, the nationalization of conservation beyond its traditional pockets on the Atlantic seaboard and in California to the Midwest in particular produced several organizations that focused on wildlife management as part of hunting and fishing, not resource development.[37] Second, a set of new national organizations emerged not out of the actions of local citizens but, echoing Pinchot's National Conservation Association, through the sponsorship of federal government officials, in either an official or unofficial capacity, to act as external allies in bureaucratic and legislative politics.

National Parks Conservation Association

The National Parks Conservation Association was established in 1919 as the National Parks Association (NPA) under the guidance of Stephen Mather, former borax mining executive and first director of the National Park Service, and 100 other business leaders, scientists, and scholars.[38] According to the official history, the NPA grew out of Mather's belief in the need for an independent citizens organization to help promote the fledgling park system. However, the story is a bit more complicated than that.

Mather recruited a friend, journalist and editor Robert Sterling Yard, to act as the Park Service's chief publicist, and he paid Yard out of his own pocket to avoid tangling with members of Congress who were unwilling to spend public money for such purposes. In this capacity, Yard was integral to designing the educational programs that quickly boosted the popularity and use of the national parks, but his efforts clashed with the priorities of other Park Service officials and their allies in Congress. When Mather suffered a long period of incapacitation, Yard found himself fighting to maintain his promotional programs, so he decided to look outside the Park Service and build his own network of support.

In June 1918, Yard and several prominent citizens met in an office at the Smithsonian Institution in Washington to form the National Parks Educational Committee. The committee, as historian John Sutter noted, "set itself the task of shaping the system's uses along educational lines, which meant crafting informative publicity to draw Americans to the parks and developing programs to enhance the educational value of the visitor experience."[39] A year later, the committee had grown to more than seventy members—all leading educators, scientists, and businessmen—large enough to require a formal organization: the National Parks Association. Mather (by now back at the helm of the Park Service) could no longer pay Yard's government salary because Congress had outlawed such arrangements, so he made an initial donation that would pay Yard's salary as the NPA's first executive secretary until the organization could generate its own revenues.[40] Yard led the NPA for fifteen years, during which time it worked closely, although not always amicably, with the Park Service to promote the national parks system.

Izaak Walton League

The Izaak Walton League of America (IWLA) stands out as the only grassroots national conservation organization to emerge in the interwar era—and, in some respects, ever. It was organized in response to growing fears among midwestern sportsmen that industrial pollution and loss of wetlands throughout the region threatened its bird and wildlife populations, even those protected by migratory bird treaties or other laws.[41] The organization was incorporated in Chicago in 1922 by a group of more than fifty hunters and anglers, led by advertising executive Will Dilg, "to promote all things piscatorial."[42] They named the organization after seventeenth-century Englishman Izaak Walton, author of *The Compleat Angler.*

The IWLA was a phenomenon of its day. It grew at an astonishing rate, within five years attracting more than 100,000 members spread out among 3,000 local chapters in forty-three states.[43] The league, historian Stephen Fox notes, was "the first conservation group with a mass membership," one organized along the lines of other fraternal organizations (e.g., Kiwanis) of the day.[44] As a result, unlike the Sierra Club or the Audubon Society, the IWLA depended almost entirely on membership dues and revenues from the sale of a new magazine, the *Izaak Walton Monthly* (later *Outdoor America*), the first national conservation magazine aimed at a mass readership.

The IWLA quickly wielded its membership size, breadth, and local connections in national politics, often putting itself squarely in the middle of the most important conservation battles of the era. In 1923, league members, including Secretary of Commerce Herbert Hoover, provided critical support for the creation of a federal wildlife refuge along the Mississippi River, and in 1929, they won passage of a law establishing a system of federal refuges for migratory birds. In each instance, the IWLA succeeded where older, less assertive organizations had failed.[45] In 1934, it pushed to establish a federal Duck Stamp Act as a mechanism to fund federal waterfowl sanctuaries under the Migratory Bird Treaty Act. The inaugural duck stamp was designed by Ding Darling, an active member of the Des Moines, Iowa, chapter of the IWLA and soon-to-be founder of the National Wildlife Federation.

The league's dramatic growth and expansive policy agenda proved traumatic for the organization. It went heavily into debt as Dilg spent whatever was necessary to push the advocacy agenda, and his aggressive leadership style sparked tension with other league leaders. Dilg was pushed out in a virtual coup during the organization's 1926 convention, replaced by a leadership team sworn to greater professional management and a less confrontational stance.[46] Although the league would continue to play a major national role in conservation through the late 1940s, it never again attained the size and influence it wielded in its earliest days.

Wilderness Society

The Wilderness Society traces its origins to an October 1934 roadside discussion in Tennessee among four advocates of wilderness preservation, each concerned about the accelerating pace of a New Deal road-building program designed to make national parks and forests more accessible to automobiles.[47] The American Forestry Association, they agreed, was too focused on resource management, and the National Parks Association had grown too cozy with the Park Service, which seemed to place a premium on providing for the creature comforts of park visitors. What was needed, they agreed, was an organization dedicated solely to preserving what was left of "pure" wilderness, particularly those roadless tracts being managed by the U.S. Forest Service.[48]

The men reconvened in Washington in January 1935 to incorporate the Wilderness Society. They included Robert Sterling Yard, recently separated from the National Parks Association; Benton MacKaye, regional planner with the Tennessee Valley Authority and the "father of the Appalachian Trail"; Aldo Leopold, formerly with the Forest Service and now wildlife ecologist at the University of Wisconsin (his *Sand County Almanac* would make him a household name decades after his death); and Robert Marshall, head forester for the Bureau of Indian Affairs in the Department of the Interior. The society's stated mission was to urge the federal government "to preserve large expanses of road-less and otherwise undeveloped nature in a system of designation wilderness areas."[49]

Marshall, the intellectual father of the Wilderness Society's mission, was the natural choice to head the new organization. However, although Secretary of the Interior Harold Ickes sympathized with its cause (and federal law at the time did not preclude Marshall from taking the post), he did not think it proper for a federal official to head an advocacy group that might oppose policies being pursued by the federal government.[50] The group turned to Yard, who had been forced out of the National Parks Association in large part because of his increasingly strident criticism of the Park Service. Marshall, however, was the chief force behind the society's preservationist orientation.[51]

He was also, as a result of inherited wealth, its primary financial benefactor, enabling the organization to pursue its uncompromising stance on wilderness preservation free of the need to maintain a mass membership (in contrast to the IWLA, for example) and without fear of alienating potential contributors.[52] Marshall even provided for the society in his will, and the Robert Marshall Wilderness Fund played a major role in the society's finances from his untimely death in 1939 to well into the mid-1970s.[53]

In some ways, as wilderness advocate David Brower later wrote, the Wilderness Society "intentionally tied itself closely to the Forest Service, to be its non-governmental supporter and watchdog, even as the National Parks Association had tied itself to the National Park Service."[54] However, relations between the Wilderness Society and the NPA weren't always adversarial, and cooperation between the organizations would grow as the society's preservation ethos began to pervade other old-line conservation organizations.

National Wildlife Federation

The creation of the National Wildlife Federation (NWF) was a direct response to dust bowl–era droughts in the Midwest and fears that no wildlife would be left for future generations. According to historian Thomas Allen, there were some 36,000 local and state conservation groups (including hundreds of Izaak Walton League chapters), bird clubs, and garden clubs in the nation, but no organization aggregated the values of these disparate groups and acted as their collective advocate in the nation's capital. In this regard, as Ding Darling told delegates to the federation's first annual meeting in 1937, the NWF would be an external supporter for wildlife *within* government—in particular, the new U.S. Fish and Wildlife Service—one that could counteract the powerful pull of commercial interests.[55]

Creating the federation was not a foregone conclusion, however. For one thing, existing conservation organizations were wary about a potential competitor. As Darling later observed, "it took a great deal of conferring and reasoning to quiet the fears of several prominent organizations, among them the Izaak Walton League and the representatives of the Audubon Society and the Ornithological Union particularly, that the new Federation would not be a competitor in the membership field."[56] Indeed, the NWF did not recruit its own members as a national organization—and would not do so until the 1960s. Instead, as a *federation* of autonomous state conservation groups, it relied on donations from its affiliates. That funding scheme never worked very well, however; few affiliates had much money during the years of depression and war, so the federation soon looked for independent sources of revenue, particularly publications.

In its earliest years, it survived largely on the patronage of the American Wildlife Institute (later the Wildlife Management Institute), founded in 1935 by Ding Darling—still a federal employee—to establish a wildlife conservation endowment funded by sporting gun companies and other industries with a stake in hunting.[57] Darling in fact used institute funds—and his government staff—to organize the conference that led to the creation of the NWF. This financial patronage from the sporting gun industry would lead to the federation's first major accomplishment, the Pittman-Robertson Act of 1937, requiring the federal government to use funds collected from an excise tax on arms and ammunition to endow state wildlife conservation efforts. Although gun industry support would become a source of much internal debate in the years to come—even Darling eventually felt that the industry had too much influence—with it, the NWF soon became a powerful voice for wildlife conservation among hunters and other recreational users of nature.

Ducks Unlimited

Ducks Unlimited was formed out of the More Game Birds in America Foundation, created in 1930 over concern about the decline in migratory game birds. A 1935 bird census revealed that 75 percent of the ducks shot by hunters in the United States came from breeding grounds in Canada that were under pressure from drought and agricultural development. Preserving those habitats was essential to sustaining North American game bird populations.[58] Ducks Unlimited was incorporated in Washington as a tax-exempt nonprofit organization in January 1937 (although its headquarters remained in New York City until the 1960s) to raise the funds necessary to preserve Canadian breeding grounds and restore wetlands in the southern United States. DU Canada was incorporated later that same year to receive and use the funds raised in the United States.[59] Within two years, the group had nearly 7,000 supporters and had raised nearly $100,000 for wetlands preservation.

By the mid-1940s, conservation was being promoted by an array of national organizations of varying sizes, breadths, and orientations. Whereas the Izaak Walton League had emerged as a mass membership organization and Ducks Unlimited as a vehicle for purchasing and protecting Canadian wetlands, the others were essentially created by federal officials to organize and mobilize external allies—citizens—in their own political battles throughout the federal establishment. Thus, reflecting the near-corporatist dimensions of federal decision-making during the interwar period, the Park Service begat the National Parks Association, the Biological Survey begat the National Wildlife Federation, and the Forest Service begat the Wilderness Society.[60] None maintained a membership base of any significance, and none would have survived long without the patronage of their government benefactors.

THE POSTWAR BRIDGE TO ENVIRONMENTALISM

Conservation organizations were relatively dormant during World War II as their members left to serve in the military and other priorities dominated the national agenda. But a new cohort of leaders, such as the Sierra Club's David Brower, who served in Italy with the Tenth Mountain Division, came back from the war alarmed at how the wilderness in Europe had been exploited over the centuries, not to mention decimated by recent warfare.[61] At home, the demands of national defense had removed any check on industrial output or resource extraction, but with the war's end, air and water pollution, destruction of wildlife habitat, and depletion of natural resources would soon emerge as major public concerns.

New problems, new members, and new leaders characterized conservation in the late 1940s and 1950s. The war's end produced a rush of new outdoors enthusiasts—many of them returning veterans accustomed to being in nature—creating new members for groups such as the Sierra Club. This influx of new members reawakened old tensions between those who favored controlled development of natural areas for recreational opportunities versus preservationists concerned about the accelerated disappearance of undeveloped wilderness.[62] These tensions complicated long-standing working relationships with federal officials, and a growing cohort of preservation-minded advocates expressed increasingly strident opposition to the developmental ethos of the Park Service and Bureau of Land Management.[63] Within the Sierra Club, for example, such concerns would lead to a decision in 1951 to change the wording of its official purpose from "render accessible" to "preserve" nature, moving it closer to the position held by the Wilderness Society.[64] Even the National Parks Association, which had once ousted Robert Sterling Yard over his criticism of the Park Service, now expressed policy goals consistent with those held by the Wilderness Society. Indeed, during the 1950s, the two organizations would share board members and occupy adjacent offices in Washington.[65]

Conservationists also expressed growing alarm over the effects of industrial pollution and the emerging chemical age on wildlife populations and, increasingly, human health. Old-line conservation organizations, influenced by both new members and greater general awareness of environmental degradation, were expressing a more ecological focus. The Audubon Society, for example, initiated one of the first studies of a new chemical pesticide, DDT, in the late 1940s and warned that its unchecked use could endanger bird life.[66] The National Wildlife Federation, despite its conservative reputation and its close ties to business, pushed for a postwar cleanup of environments that had been degraded by war production efforts, with a special focus on rivers polluted by the rubber and steel industries.[67] Even the Wildlife Management Institute, no longer as closely tied to gun industry money, expressed a more preservationist stance.[68]

The postwar era also saw the concomitant nationalization of conservation groups beyond their traditional geographic bases. The Audubon Society, for example, circulated high-quality nature movies to induce local bird clubs to become dues-sharing affiliates. The Sierra Club, following an extensive internal debate, voted to accept new chapters outside California, prompting the resignation of several longtime board members who worried that expansion would dilute the club's emphasis on personal relationships and democratic decision-making.[69]

Their concerns were not unreasonable. With growing memberships (see table 2.2) and a greater national focus came new stresses on organizational maintenance; these, in turn, created a more central role for professional staff and accelerated the centralization of decision-making. The tradition of leadership by the volunteer was fast being eclipsed by the emergence of a new generation of professional managers. In 1953, Brower was picked to serve as the Sierra Club's first executive director, an organizational change that some observers regarded as the most important in the club's history. Brower, already well known within the club for his publishing acumen as well as his mountaineering skills, used his position to develop an array of high-quality picture books to bring the aesthetic beauty of nature to a new, increasingly suburban audience. More important, Brower soon became the club's public face in the advocacy battles to come.[70] Similar professionalization occurred at the National Wildlife Federation, which by the late 1940s began to deploy paid executives to assist volunteer regional directors,[71] and at the Wilderness Society, under the direction of longtime president Howard Zahniser.[72]

The organizations created between the late 1940s and early 1960s would cover a broader spectrum of policy concerns and encompass a broader array of organizational types than before. However, they all differed from interwar organizations in one key respect: none were founded by government officials; they were the offspring of existing organizations. In this sense, the postwar organizations were the first in a series of "niche fillers," each occupying a policy, strategic, or advocacy niche previously unoccupied or, more accurately, unrecognized.

Such differences aside, the political opportunity structure of the postwar era generally mandated that the organizations created during this period follow a by-now established pattern of cautious advocacy, if for no other reason

Table 2.2. Membership Trends of Selected Environmental Organizations, 1950–1971*

Organization	1950–51	1960–61	1965–66	1970–71
Sierra Club	7,000	16,500	31,000	124,000
National Audubon Society	17,000	32,000	40,500	115,000
National Parks Conservation Association	5,400	15,000	31,000	49,000
Izaak Walton League	40,000	51,000	52,000	54,000
The Wilderness Society	5,000	10,000	28,000	62,000
National Wildlife Federation	n/a	n/a	256,000	540,000
Total	74,400	124,500	438,500	944,000

* Figures are two-year averages and are approximations based on conflicting data.

Sources: Annual reports; Stephen Fox, *John Muir and His Legacy: The American Conservation Movement* (Boston: Little, Brown, 1981), 315; Ronald Shaiko, *Voices and Echoes for the Environment* (New York: Columbia University Press, 1999), 40–43; Robert Cameron Mitchell et al., "Twenty Years of Environmental Mobilization: Trends among National Environmental Organizations," in *American Environmentalism: The U.S. Environmental Movement: 1970–1990,* ed. Riley E. Dunlap and Angela G. Mertig (Philadelphia: Taylor and Francis, 1992),13.

than fear of losing tax-exempt status.[73] As reinforced by the 1954 Supreme Court decision in *U.S. v. Harris,* a tax-exempt organization under Section 501(c)(3) of the Internal Revenue Code could foster public education and sponsor research, testify when invited before congressional committees, and even encourage members to write letters to their legislators, but it had to avoid activities that the IRS might classify as overt lobbying or partisan action. Loss of 501(c)(3) status would mean that donations to the organization were no longer tax deductible, a disincentive for the large donors on which most organizations then depended. Some state-level conservation organizations, including the Massachusetts Forestry and Park Association, had already run afoul of the IRS on this matter, so conservation advocates were always on their guard.[74] For example, in the 1950s, the Sierra Club skirted close to the edge of open advocacy in battles over a new wave of dam building in national parks and wilderness areas, but it always stopped just short. The club board, reprising a maneuver taken during the battle over Hetch Hetchy, created independent, non-tax-exempt organizations that could openly lobby through newspaper advertisements or personally in the halls of Congress, but these were always temporary arrangements.[75] So powerful were the constraints imposed by the tax code that, until the 1960s, the conservation community as a whole employed only two registered lobbyists in Washington, each representing entities created by coalitions of conservation groups after the decision in *Harris.*[76]

Conservation organizations were also hemmed in by the lack of access to the courts, since in most cases they could not show standing to sue. In *Frothingham v. Mellon* (1923), the U.S. Supreme Court had ruled that a taxpayer had no standing to challenge the constitutionality of a federal statute because his particular interest was "comparatively minute," and because he failed to show direct injury. The practical impact of *Frothingham* was that citizen access to the courts was limited to negligence, liability, or nuisance suits—all of which required the plaintiff to prove damage.[77] For example, in 1958, a group of Long Island residents sued in federal court to stop the spraying of DDT to eradicate gypsy moths. Despite testimony by medical experts about the accumulating evidence of DDT's danger to human health, the judge ruled that the group had not established persuasive proof of direct harm and thus had no basis to stop the spraying.[78]

Finally, whereas conservationists and federal officials had once enjoyed reasonably close working relationships, by the mid-1950s, they were more often at odds across a wide spectrum of issues, particularly as the Eisenhower administration sided more regularly with its business and agricultural sector allies. Congress, now dominated by a conservative coalition of Republicans and southern Democrats, also sided with local economic interests on issues such as dam construction, pesticide regulation, timber contracts on federal lands, and wildlife conservation. Even the National Parks Association and the National Wildlife Federation, long known for their collaborative orientation, began to express open consternation at the directions taken by the federal government.

In short, the opportunity structure of the postwar era forced advocacy organizations to devise and expand new "outside" strategies rooted in public education and the systematic development of a national constituency to counteract the focused political clout of economic interests. The organizations created after the war also reflected these contexts. They were no longer the tools of government patrons, designed to act as external allies in bureaucratic and legislative politics; they were created by scientists and educators, often with the financial support of private foundations. Their purpose was to raise the public alarm about the degradation of nature, preserve endangered areas, and—most important to the environmental era to come—enhance the organizational capacity of conservation itself.

Conservation Foundation

The Conservation Foundation was founded in 1948 by Fairfield Osborn, president of the New York Zoological Society and author of the influential book

Our Plundered Planet (1948). It was intended to be a nonpartisan, nonpolitical, nonmembership organization to foster research on and public awareness about natural resource depletion and degradation.[79] The foundation's importance lay in its capacity-building contributions to the formative years of the environmental era to come. For example, it sponsored some of earliest significant scientific research on environmental degradation, including much of the research on the impact of pesticides cited in 1962 by Rachel Carson in *Silent Spring*.[80] In the 1950s, it provided critical seed capital for the research institute Resources for the Future (1952) and the International Union for the Conservation of Nature (1957), which in turn formed the World Wildlife Fund for Nature (see below). Later the foundation would support the creation of the Environmental Defense Fund (1967) and the Environmental Law Institute (1969), and it would be a major contributor to the first Earth Day.

Nature Conservancy

The Nature Conservancy was founded by a group of natural scientists, members of the Ecological Society of America, who decided that the best way to preserve scientifically critical parcels of land was to acquire them outright. The Ecological Society had been formed in 1915 as a scientific institution, but from the start its members debated whether it should go beyond research to push for the preservation of important natural areas. In 1917, a dissident group created a Committee for the Preservation of Natural Conditions within the society and for decades used it as a forum to advocate preservation. Leaders of the society dissolved the committee in 1946, following another internal dispute over its advocacy, so the dissidents left to form a new group, the Ecologists Union, which in 1951 changed its name to the Nature Conservancy. The Conservancy was incorporated in Washington, where its handful of staff worked in an office shared with the Wilderness Society. From the start, the Conservancy settled on buying land as its special niche within conservation, and in 1955 it bought its first reserve, sixty acres of river gorge in New York and Connecticut. Its strategy—raising cash to buy land—soon became known within the organization as "bucks and acres."[81]

Defenders of Wildlife

Defenders of Wildlife can trace its origins to the Anti-Steel-Trap League, created in 1925 to oppose the use of steel-jawed leghold traps in hunting. A successor organization, Defenders of Furbearers, was incorporated in the District of Columbia in 1947 and advocated against cruel methods of capturing or killing fur-bearing animals. However, during the 1950s, its agenda became more openly preservationist, dedicated to conserving "the natural abundance and diversity of native wild animals and plants to protect the habitats on which they depend." It changed its name to Defenders of Wildlife in 1959.[82] At first, the organization was more interested in preventing the cruel treatment of individual animals, but in short order, its agenda broadened to include wildlife habitat and endangered species.[83]

World Wildlife Fund

The U.S. chapter of the World Wildlife Fund for Nature (WWF) was incorporated in Washington in 1961 "to preserve the diversity and abundance of life on Earth and the health of ecological systems."[84] The parent organization was conceived as the fund-raising arm of the International Union for Conservation of Nature and Natural Resources (now the World Conservation Union), formed in 1957 by European scientists, naturalists, and business and political leaders, with financial assistance from the Conservation Foundation, to foster conservation throughout the world. The WWF would raise funds through national appeals and, based on scientific advice from the International Union and other sources, provide financial and technical support to appropriate national and local organizations, with a particular focus on preserving endangered species and habitats in less developed nations. The international organization is based in Switzerland. Its first president was Prince Bernhard of the Netherlands; Prince Philip, the Duke of Edinburgh, became president of the British National Appeal, the first national organization created under the WWF umbrella. The U.S. branch was incorporated soon thereafter, with newly retired Dwight D. Eisenhower as its honorary president.[85]

In the main, the new postwar organizations reflected the strategic thinking of their creators: support research and education (Conservation Foundation), buy threatened ecosystems (Nature Conservancy), agitate for animals (Defenders), or act as a fund-raising vehicle for research and conservation (WWF). Compared with interwar organizations, they focused less on advocacy *within* government and more on working *outside* government by supporting research, raising the alarm to the public, and, where necessary, purchasing important land to keep it from being developed or degraded. All could trace their origins to other organizations, a pattern of sponsorship that would become more pronounced in the decade to come.

THE ENVIRONMENTAL ERA

The reformist—even revolutionary—impulses that erupted in the 1960s have been amply analyzed.[86] "Measured in terms of changes in government and legislation," wrote Michael Lacey, "it has been a time of extraordinary ferment, so durable and multifaceted as to make earlier times of great upheaval (the Progressive Era and the New Deal years, for example), seem simpler, if no less important, by comparison."[87]

That ferment had multiple impacts, among them a wave of new advocacy organizations dedicated to noneconomic or "public" interests. Jeffrey Berry notes that two-thirds of the public-interest organizations surveyed in 1972–1973 were formed after 1959, most in the late 1960s.[88] This surge in citizen advocacy, argues Andrew McFarland, grew out of a disproportionate increase in middle-class political participation, a corresponding skepticism about conventional politics, and the displacement of partisan allegiances by the politics of issues, aided by economic prosperity and technical advances in communications, especially television.[89] The rise of public-interest organizations in particular would expand and transform the universe of organized interests studied by pluralist scholars in the 1950s.

The transformation in the political opportunity structure of the era aided the creation of a broader array of new advocacy organizations. The lowering of barriers to access to the federal judiciary,[90] combined with the establishment of the legal concept of "class action,"[91] gave lawyers representing public interests unprecedented opportunities to use lawsuits as advocacy tactics. Equally important, argues Shep Melnick, federal judges increasingly interpreted federal statutes "to guarantee a wide variety of groups the right to participate directly in agency deliberations as well as to bring their complaints to court."[92] Such concerns coalesced in 1971 in the case of *Calvert Cliffs,* in which a federal judge stopped the Atomic Energy Commission from licensing a nuclear power plant until it had considered the plant's "environmental impact" under the National Environmental Policy Act (NEPA) of 1969.[93] *Calvert Cliffs* put teeth into NEPA, and the onus now fell on federal officials to show that they had considered environmental criteria before authorizing new projects.[94]

But the new breed of environmental advocacy organization might not have capitalized on its opportunities were it not for the support of older conservation organizations and, equally important, private foundations. Indeed, the environmental movement survived its tumultuous birth because of organizational patronage rather than mass citizen support. The Ford Foundation played a particularly critical role in bankrolling the entire public-interest law movement that revolutionized American jurisprudence. Ford Foundation grants for public-interest law would total almost $21 million during the late 1960s and early 1970s, with major support going to new organizations such as the Environmental Defense Fund, the Natural Resources Defense Council, and the Sierra Club Legal Defense Fund.[95] The Sierra Club Legal Defense Fund, created in 1971, was formally independent of the club itself and, in the ensuing years, often pursued a more militant course than its parent organization was willing or able to take.[96] It was renamed Earthjustice in 1997 to eliminate any confusion between the two.

For their part, established conservation organizations were challenged by the new issues (e.g., pesticides, pollution, population control, nuclear power) on the public agenda, by a resulting surge in new (and new types of) members, and by competition from new advocacy organizations. Even the most ardent longtime conservationists struggled to adapt to the new environmental ethos and to meet demands for a more aggressive advocacy stance. They expanded their range of issues beyond traditional areas of focus, accompanied in many cases by major alterations in organizational missions and strategies. Some, like the Sierra Club, created legal defense funds and non-tax-exempt affiliates to complement traditional educational activities, adapting to new political opportunities in ways that allowed environmentalists to expand both their legal and legislative efforts. Nearly all of them established formal lobbying operations in the nation's capital. Whereas registered conservation lobbyists had been virtually nonexistent in Washington in the 1950s, by 1970 thirteen environmental organizations employed them, and their ranks expanded thereafter.[97] By 1971, almost seventy environmental organizations had established some type of office in the capital, creating in the process a sense of greater permanency for the movement, a sense of credible "presence" that had previously been absent.[98]

Along the way, established organizations profoundly altered their ways of doing business as organizations. The most dramatic instance came in 1966 when David Brower's newspaper advertising campaign against a proposed dam in the Grand Canyon led the IRS to revoke the Sierra Club's tax-exempt status. Rather than crippling the organization, the controversial and highly public action led to a flood of small contributions and changed the way the club financed itself. Thereafter, the Sierra Club Foundation, a 501(c)(3) organization established in 1960, would continue to get the larger, tax-deductible gifts, while a less constrained Sierra Club would rely on relatively smaller donations from members and other supporters.[99] Brower aggressively recruited new members through newspaper advertising and direct mail, and membership doubled in three years, advancing the transformation of the Sierra Club into a national mass membership organization. It also created internal tensions that led to Brower's ouster and the subsequent creation of new advocacy organizations (see below and chapter 3).

Similar transformations were under way elsewhere. The National Audubon Society broadened its agenda and used direct-mail appeals to expand its national membership base, causing unease among its traditional bird-watching members in the local chapters.[100] The National Wildlife Federation, under Thomas Kimball, for the first time recruited its own national members to complement its base of state affiliates. Although this effort met with some opposition in the affiliates, Kimball recognized that members' dues would be a more dependable source of income than merchandise sales and sporadic larger donations and would generate funds now needed to hire scientists, lawyers, and public-relations experts. A national mass membership base also would help the NWF influence Congress and the executive branch. "Kimball, in effect, called for the creation of a new Federation," Allen notes. "To the existing aggregation of traditional conservation and sportsmen's organizations would be added a new pool of people, each of whom would have his or her own idea of just what 'conservation' was supposed to mean."[101]

A new, more national cohort of dues-paying members required new types of connections to the organization, leading to the creation of the NWF's first general-readership magazine, *National Wildlife*. The Audubon Society, using a foundation grant, reformulated its venerable *Audubon* into a general-interest magazine and an important source for member recruitment and revenue.[102] Even the National Parks Association, concerned that its traditional niche now left it at a competitive disadvantage, expanded its agenda to include forest and wildlife issues, changed its name to the National Parks and Conservation Association, and renamed its magazine *National Parks and Conservation Magazine: The Environmental Journal*.[103]

By decade's end, a direct-mail-generated, magazine-linked national membership had become common for old-line organizations that a few years earlier had relied on contributions from a small, tightly knit base of relatively elite supporters located in local or state chapters. These changes were wrenching, causing internal divisions as members fought over organizational mission and tactics. The Izaak Walton League, in an ironic twist of history, resisted these trends, preferring to stay relatively small and less dependent on a large mass membership base. Yet even the league bent to the changing tenor of the times when, in 1971, it moved its headquarters from Illinois to a suburb of Washington, D.C.—closer to the action.

The generally successful adaptation of the old-line conservation organizations to the challenges and opportunities posed by the emerging environmental era is often overlooked amidst the onrush of new issues, new activists, new laws, and new advocacy organizations. But their ability to adapt was central to the evolution of the national environmental advocacy community as a whole. Moreover, without the early patronage of new outfits by the old, the environmental community might never have attained its eventual scope and elasticity.

Environmental Defense

In 1966, a group of scientists and bird lovers on Long Island joined with lawyer Victor Yannacone and filed suit to halt Suffolk County's spraying of DDT to control mosquitoes. They won a temporary injunction against the spraying, in contrast to the experience of fellow Long Islanders seven years earlier, and sought financial support to carry on the legal fight. The leaders of the National Audubon Society, eager to eliminate DDT use but wary of alienating important board members who worked in the chemical industry, used funds from a major bequest by the recently deceased Rachel Carson to back the lawsuit.[104] Although the judge later ruled that banning DDT use was a political and not a judicial question, the publicity surrounding the suit prompted county officials to suspend spraying. As Thomas Dunlap notes, Yannacone and his allies discovered through this experience a potent "alliance of legal tactics with scientific information in a forum outside the government agencies or Congress."[105] They incorporated the Environmental Defense Fund in 1967 (it dropped "Fund" from its name in 1998), supported financially by the Audubon Society and the Conservation Foundation until they were able to obtain a Ford Foundation grant to establish the organization's own tax-exempt status.

Friends of the Earth

David Brower transformed the Sierra Club into a national political force, but in the process, he provoked a schism over his leadership style and somewhat cavalier attitude about keeping within a budget. Finally, after years of increasingly acrimonious internal conflict, the election of a new board backed by Brower's critics led to his resignation as executive director in May 1969.[106] Brower immediately formed a new advocacy organization, which he named Friends of the Earth (after a John Muir quotation), and took several senior Sierra Club staff members with him.

Brower conceived Friends of the Earth (FoE) as a broad-spectrum national environmental organization that would combine scientific research, major publication campaigns to raise public awareness, and direct lobbying. It would also have an international focus, and FoE affiliates were soon established in Canada and Great Britain. The new organization's style reflected Brower's own, without the need to be concerned about losing tax-exempt status or maintaining local chapters. Instead, FoE would rely on revenues from a direct-mail-generated mass membership, foundation grants to its tax-exempt John Muir Institute (another not-so-subtle jab at the Sierra Club), and income generated by publications.[107]

League of Conservation Voters

The League of Conservation Voters (LCV) was created in Washington in 1970 by the leaders of Friends of the Earth, including David Brower and Marion Edey, who served as executive director until 1986 (and, because of inherited wealth, did not take a salary).[108] Brower had advocated the creation of a league of conservation voters as far back as the late 1950s, but the Sierra Club board had declined to do so for fear of jeopardizing its tax status. As a non-tax-exempt political action committee, LCV could pursue overtly partisan activities, including making campaign donations to candidates.[109]

Environmental Action

Environmental Action (EA) was founded in Washington in 1970 by the student organizers of the original Earth Day (which was aided by a federal grant) as a non-tax-exempt lobby with a particular focus on the human health effects of industrial pollution. EA grew quickly, attracting nearly 10,000 members in its first year, and positioned itself as an aggressive, protest-oriented promoter of environmental and social justice causes. EA also sought to influence elections by disseminating the environmental records of candidates and by making direct contributions through its affiliated Environmental Action Political Action Campaign.[110] During its early years, EA operated as a collective, with all staff sharing in decision-making and earning equal salaries.[111]

Natural Resources Defense Council

The Natural Resources Defense Council (NRDC) was incorporated in New York in 1970 as an environmental law firm modeled on the American Civil Liberties Union and the NAACP Legal Defense Fund. The organization's birth resulted from meetings between a group of Yale Law School students and lawyers involved in fighting a proposed hydropower electric project on the Hudson River, with the Ford Foundation acting as a sponsoring midwife. At first, the NRDC was a classic law firm compared with the Environmental Defense Fund, which employed scientists and lobbyists as well as lawyers, but over the next decade, the two would begin to resemble each other in their "science and law" approaches to advocacy.[112]

Greenpeace

Greenpeace traces its origins to the Don't Make a Wave Committee of Vancouver, British Columbia, formed in 1970 to protest a U.S. nuclear weapons test in Alaska's Aleutian Islands. The group bought an old fishing trawler, renamed it *Greenpeace* to reflect a mix of ecological and anti–nuclear weapons sentiment, and announced plans to stop the test by sailing into the waters near the island. Although the group never made it into the test zone, and the weapon was successfully detonated, the publicity surrounding the protest was a factor in the United States' decision to suspend further tests in the area.

The group's fame spread, and Greenpeace soon grew into a mass membership organization based in Amsterdam, with national affiliates around the world. Its original goals were to end nuclear testing and to preserve marine life, most notably whales. To promote its goals, Greenpeace activists blended the Quakers' tradition of "bearing witness," of putting oneself in the path of an objectionable activity, with the civil rights movement's emphasis on nonviolence. Such "direct-action" protests, which included interposing volunteers between whaling ships and their prey, gained the organization tremendous global recognition.

In some ways, the formation of Greenpeace marked the end of the great spasm of organizational creation that typified the environmental era. More organizations would follow (see chapter 3), but this period is noteworthy for the number of major new organizations created. Environmental Defense and the Natural Resources Defense Council in particular would join older counterparts, notably the Sierra Club, Audubon Society, and National Wildlife Federation, in becoming what Ronald Shaiko calls "full-service" environmental advocacy shops, broad-spectrum advocacy organizations supported by a large base of dues-paying supporters.[113] By contrast, the organizations created thereafter were "niche fillers," relatively narrow, more specialized operations created to fill gaps left by the existing organizations. That phenomenon is covered in the next chapter.

ORIGINS AND OPPORTUNITIES

"The forces leading to the emergence of social movements are not well understood," Jack Walker argues, "but even less is known about the way in which tangible associations arise that purport to represent these movements."[114] The forces leading to the emergence of what became known as the environmental movement originated well before the 1960s. Indeed, from an organizational perspective, the movement did not spring up spontaneously at all, but was birthed into being by mature midwives. Without the Sierra Club, would there have been Friends of the Earth? Without the Audubon Society, would Environmental Defense have survived its early days as a loose group of activists and lawyers? Perhaps some other organizational patron would have taken Audubon's place, but what is clear is that most of the organizations that emerged during the environmental era got critical early help from an older organization. Movements, it seems, don't just happen.

Moreover, the organizations that eventually constituted the movement rarely sprang out of local soil. The Sierra Club, Audubon Society, and, most notably, Izaak Walton League were exceptions, not the rule, and the circumstances of their creation suggest how rare true member-based organizations are. Indeed, the IWLA was the rarest of phenomena—a mass membership organization created and led by a visionary entrepreneur—and its brief heyday speaks volumes about the difficulty of creating, much less sustaining, such groups. The other conservation groups were far smaller and more elite in composition, at least until the onset of mass membership environmentalism in the 1960s.

In contrast to the IWLA and, perhaps, Greenpeace, most of the organizations examined here were created by institutional patrons of one type or another, depending on the political opportunity structure of the moment. Although we know this to be true in the main, based on empirical examinations of group formation,[115] this historically rooted assessment underscores the contextual nature of organizational creation. In this regard, the interwar period stands out as the one moment in American history when government officials apparently felt both the necessity and the ability to create and support external advocacy organizations. Thereafter, the founders and patrons of most environmental advocacy organizations were other organizations, either as a strategic matter, such as Audubon's sponsorship of the Environmental Defense Fund, or because of divisions within older organizations over agendas, tactics, and management issues, such as the Sierra Club and Friends of the Earth. Both dynamics would accelerate in the decades to come.

History also suggests variations in organizational orientation and purpose.

Prior to the 1950s, most organizations tended to focus on places (e.g., national parks, wilderness) or specific wildlife (e.g., birds). Beginning with the creation of the Conservation Foundation, we see the emergence of organizations characterized less by a particular place or animal than by broader tactical or policy orientations. What else is the Nature Conservancy but a tactical organization? This tendency became even more apparent with the unfolding of the environmental era, when virtually every new organization was known for its specific tactics (e.g., lawsuits, campaign contributions, direct action) or ideological orientation.

What accounts for these differences over time? A population ecology perspective suggests that changes in population *density* (the sheer number of organizations that occupy a particular advocacy space) and *diversity* (the different types of organizations within that same guild) are powerful contextual factors. That is, with each era in the development of a national environmental community, new organizations were created to fill previously unoccupied policy niches or to pursue previously unused tactics. With time, assuming a low rate of organizational demise, the advocacy community in question gets more densely populated by a more diverse array of organizations.

At each stage in the evolution of the national environmental community, therefore, any new organization created had to be distinct from existing ones to avoid direct competition over resources, tactics, or areas of policy focus. In this regard, there was little overlap among the old-line conservation organizations for much of the twentieth century, either because of geographic distance (Sierra on the West Coast, Audubon on the East) or because of advocacy focus (e.g., the National Parks Association and national parks). In many respects, these organizations simply weren't bumping into one another all that much. That said, even in the 1930s, Ding Darling had to assure leaders of existing conservation organizations that his new National Wildlife Federation would not recruit individual members in what was perceived to be a limited national pool of potential supporters.

Population diversity and density, Gray and Lowery argue, are shaped by "contextual forces bearing on interest organizations as organizations—the number of potential constituents available to be mobilized by interest organizations, what government is doing or not doing of relevance to those constituencies, and how likely it is to continue doing or not doing it."[116] From this perspective, the growth spurt of new environmental organizations during the 1960s reflected an expansionary context—more potential supporters, more avenues for access, more government policies to promote or defend—that enlarged the organizational carrying capacity of the environmental community beyond what it had been only a decade earlier. The environmental community grew denser and more diverse because it could.

By the 1970s, a greater number and more diverse array of environmental advocacy organizations covered a broader spectrum of issues, ideological orientations, and tactics. The organizations created in the 1960s were different from their predecessors because they occupied different—and different types of—advocacy niches. No new Sierra Club emerged because there already was one. But many new organizations were created, filling open niches and thereby adding to the density and diversity of the environmental advocacy community as it entered the post–environmental era phase.

3
Filling Advocacy Niches

David is David. He always pushes us to be bolder and to be bigger, and to be less practical and more visionary. That's his role. We need to hear from him now and then, but then by the same token, if we ran the Sierra Club according to the David Brower school of organizational management, we wouldn't be around too long.
—Susan Merrow, Sierra Club president, 1990–1991

An organizational archaeologist—if such a profession exists—might be intrigued, if not confounded, by the number of places David Brower's footprints show up. During the 1960s, Brower positioned the Sierra Club in the front and center of the emerging environmental movement. In the process, he cost the club its tax-exempt status, spent beyond its means, infuriated other club leaders, and, in the end, intentionally provoked the fight with the board that led to his ouster. Thereafter, Brower could claim at least indirect responsibility for the creation of four other national environmental advocacy organizations, starting with Friends of the Earth (1969) and ending with the Earth Island Institute (1983). Indeed, Brower's famous dictum, "think globally, act locally," may be best exemplified in the fact that Friends of the Earth International now claims affiliated groups in nearly seventy countries.[1]

Brower's legacy of organizational creation reflects one dimension in the transformation of the somewhat inchoate environmental movement into what today must be considered a mature advocacy community. The contemporary community, as illustrated in later chapters, is characterized by more pervasive norms of professional leadership and attention to organizational maintenance, even within self-labeled "radical" organizations. But it is also differentiated by greater internal organizational density and diversity, population-level conditions that, in turn, generate in constituent organizations a more transparent attention to maintaining secure policy and tactical niches. Such concerns were already apparent by the early 1970s, when the general topography of the contemporary national environmental community was pretty much in place; therefore, any organizations created after this period were going to have to fit into whatever advocacy niches were left unfilled or underexploited. As a result, the types of environmental organizations created were going to differ noticeably from those already established.

This dynamic of "post-movement" organizational creation would proceed on two paths: on one, the formation of new organizations following the departure or ouster of dissidents such as Brower; on the other, the strategic occupation of unoccupied but relatively narrow tactical or policy niches. The two phenomena are not mutually exclusive, to be sure, but for our purposes, they should be treated separately. By *dissident* organizations, I mean those created primarily because a leader or group of leaders left an existing organization over fundamental differences in priorities, tactics, or management style. *Niche seekers,* by contrast, were created primarily because organizational entrepreneurs—whether individuals or leaders of existing organizations—saw opportunities to inhabit unoccupied policy or ideological niches or to pursue tactics that were not being exploited optimally or at all by an existing organization. The distinction here is that these entrepreneurs started new organizations not because of divisive policy or governance differences—although such internal cleavages may well have existed—but to take strategic advantage of new opportunities.

Neither phenomenon is unique to this period, of course. As I mentioned earlier, the Nature Conservancy was formed by dissidents from the Ecological Society, and the Conservation Foundation was created expressly to occupy an open strategic niche, in this case, funding ecological research and supporting organizational capacity building. However, each was created within a much less dense or diverse organizational population, so its creation was less likely to pose competition for existing organizations. By contrast, the spurt of organizational creation during the environmental era produced a population of national environmental organizations that was markedly denser and more internally diverse than before. Put simply, by the 1970s, there were more major environmental organizations of more types catering to a broad range of constituencies, thereby constricting the array of potential policy or tactical niches available to organizational entrepreneurs. As a result, any organization created thereafter faced a greater likelihood of having to compete with existing ones for supporters, resources, and access to policymakers, unless it was consciously designed to occupy an open niche within the broader environmental advocacy community. This explains the reason for treating dissidents and niche seekers as distinct types: organizations created by dissidents might be more likely to compete with former colleagues, at least for a while, given the circumstances of their departure, whereas those created to occupy a strategic niche might avoid direct competition from the start.

Regardless of the specific conditions of their creation, by the 1970s, any new organizations entering the national environmental community were already characterized by greater density and diversity, so any niches that remained were likely to be narrower and more specialized than in previous eras. What is less well understood is the particular logic in the way these remaining niches were filled—the legal, policy-derived, or resource-based "assembly rules" governing which organizations were created at any particular time.[2] For example, the creation of "science and law" organizations such as the Environmental Defense Fund, Natural Resources Defense Council (NRDC), Sierra Club Legal Defense Fund, and their regional counterparts, such as the Boston-based Conservation Law Foundation, must be understood in a context of expanded access to the judiciary and strategic support for public-interest law offered by the Ford Foundation and other patrons. In the same vein, the creation of Washington-oriented organizations such as Friends of the Earth and Environmental Action, with their emphasis on lobbying, elections, and protest-based mobilization, reflected both an expanded federal environmental agenda and the more assertive tactics adopted by new types of citizens groups. One question I examine is what other patterns of organizational creation can be discerned.

Another question is what these dynamics of organizational creation and niche filling add up to over time. That is, what is the bird's-eye view of the environmental advocacy community that emerges by the end of the twentieth century? To provide an initial cut at this question, later in this chapter I lay out a spatial map of the national environmental advocacy community in 2004, displaying constituent organizations in terms of expressed values and advocacy agendas. Subsequent chapters examine competition for resources and differentiated use of tactics as organizations struggle to coexist within what has become a dense and diverse environmental advocacy population. But to get to that point, we need to look at this dynamic of niche filling over time.

DISSIDENTS

David Brower's ouster as executive director of the Sierra Club was attributed to sharp internal differences over his leadership. But the schism went beyond budgets and leadership style into disagreements over agendas, tactics, and the very meaning of membership in a public-interest advocacy organization. These differences went to the heart of the new types of environmental lobbies created during the environmental era and underscored the tensions that reside within advocacy organizations all the time.[3]

Agendas. By the mid-1960s, the faction of Sierra Club leaders led by Brower had come to envision the club as a modern national environmental lobby that pursued an expansive agenda beyond the already broadened postwar focus on wilderness preservation. However, the faction that engineered Brower's eventual ouster feared that the club's agenda was becoming too diffuse and too distant from its historical mission. As historian Michael Cohen argues, this split emerged in a debate over the official club position on inorganic pesticides following the 1962 publication of *Silent Spring* and intensified in debates over the club's position on nuclear power during the fight over the Diablo Canyon power plant.[4] These debates split the organization in ways reminiscent of the Hetch Hetchy controversy five decades earlier. To newer club members in particular, the traditional focus on wilderness seemed antiquated and parochial compared with the holistic perspective embodied by "environmental protection."

Similar tensions over the breadth and shape of policy agendas buffeted other old-line conservation organizations during this time. Although the National Audubon Society and National Wildlife Federation managed to muddle through without experiencing any polarizing leadership battles,[5] the dramatic ousters of Anthony Smith at the National Parks and Conservation Association (see below) and Stuart Brandenborg at the Wilderness Society (see chapter 4) occurred under circumstances eerily identical to Brower's struggle with the Sierra Club board.[6]

Tactics. Brower sought to make the club more tactically aggressive, with much less apparent concern about the impact on finances or organizational maintenance. For example, his ambitious publishing program propelled the club into public awareness and aided membership growth, but it was hugely expensive. By 1967, nearly 40 percent of the club's operating budget was going to the publications program, straining the club's finances.[7] His 1966 national newspaper campaign opposing a Grand Canyon dam was an advocacy success, but it cost the club its tax-exempt status and infuriated board members who valued their long-term working relationships with western members of Congress. Even though the loss of tax-exempt status had unanticipated benefits for the organization (see chapter 2), the question of tactics—and who should approve them—fueled the internal turmoil. Indeed, Brower's unauthorized advertising campaign promoting an "Earth National Park" precipitated his suspension and eventual ouster.

Brower's vision of the Sierra Club as an aggressive, multidimensional advocacy force extended to direct lobbying and election campaigns. He had long advocated that the club maintain a full-time Washington lobbyist, but this idea was rebuffed by board members who were philosophically opposed to the club's becoming a "lobbying outfit," even if they were willing to create the occasional "independent" organization to engage in direct advocacy.[8] As far back as the late 1950s, Brower also had pushed to create a "league of conservation voters," but the board—reflecting the determinedly nonpartisan stance taken by most conservation organizations—refused to go anywhere near such openly political waters.[9] So it was no surprise that an early hallmark of Friends of the Earth was its large and active Washington lobbying office, or that the second organization Brower helped set up was the League of Conservation Voters. For its part, by the mid-1970s, the Sierra Club had established its own Washington lobbying office, its own legal defense fund, and its own political action committee. The difference, it seems, was the process by which it went about initiating these strategies.

Members. Brower came to regard the Sierra Club's traditional governance structure—in particular, the power of its members to elect the board—as unwieldy and an obstacle to the rapid responses needed to carry out the battle on multiple fronts. In his view, the membership was a source of revenue and a base to mobilize for political battle, but an organization's leaders should be free to set the agenda and choose the tactics. Members could always "vote with their feet" if they were unhappy. To many board members, including iconic wilderness photographer Ansel Adams, Brower's actions increasingly threatened to alienate the chapter-based members who were becoming more important, not less, to the club's financial and advocacy future. It was instructive, then, that in the climactic membership vote on a new board, which everyone knew would determine Brower's fate, even a majority of younger members voted with the faction that advocated greater internal democracy.[10]

Yet Brower's attitude about the constraints imposed by an active membership was not unique. None of the environmental advocacy organizations created during or after the wave of the late 1960s and early 1970s made any pretense of giving dues-paying members, assuming they had any, a voice in agendas, tactics, or governance. Only the older conservation organizations—Sierra Club, National Audubon Society, Izaak Walton League, National Wildlife Federation, and, to some extent, Ducks Unlimited—offered members any direct say in how they operated. Not surprisingly, they were also the only environmental organizations built on a base of local chapters or affiliates. For the others, as Ronald Shaiko argues, representation was a mixture of "actual" and "virtual" representation:

> It is actual representation in the sense that active citizens, operating in the noncoercive context of public interest organizations, are free to join as well as to exit the organizations and are also free to act as individual influence

> agents through direct contacts with policy makers. Public interest representation is virtual to the extent that organizational leaders are "acting for" their members as well as for the larger societal interests.[11]

For Brower, as for most other environmental leaders of the period, policy advocacy was not to be constrained by concerns over organizational maintenance or the happiness of members. The stakes were too high.[12]

Leaders versus Managers. At the core of the internal schism over Brower's leadership was a perceptible shift in the types of individuals who were beginning to head major environmental organizations by the late 1960s. If, as Stephen Fox argues, those who once led conservation groups fit the image of the "amateur" advocate, by the 1950s, amateurs were already giving way to full-time professionals like Brower, the club's first executive director.[13] The difference now was the *type* of professional who would typify the new generation of leaders.

By the late 1960s, the Sierra Club, like the Audubon Society, the Wilderness Society, and the National Wildlife Federation, had grown larger (see tables 3.1 and 3.2), more internally complex, and more unwieldy. Tens of thousands of new members, rapidly expanding policy agendas, and the utilization of a wider array of tactics required more full-time staff, more expertise, more money, and, by extension, more professional management. To his critics on the Sierra Club board, Brower's cavalier approach to finances and management had put the organization on the edge of organizational collapse just as it was emerging as a leading national voice on the environment. Although Brower was responsible for getting the club to this point, his intuitive, hands-on style no longer fit the management needs of a large, complex organization.[14] At the Sierra Club, as elsewhere in the environmental community, the visionary leader would have to give way to the professional *manager* if the organization was to survive.

Friends of the Earth

Brower's new organization, Friends of the Earth (FoE), was the antithesis of the Sierra Club and, in many ways, a direct challenge to it and the other old-line conservation organizations that typified environmental advocacy until that time. Whereas the Sierra Club's governance structure radiated out its often fractious membership, FoE—like most environmental organizations created during this period—was a staff-driven organization in which members could do little more than "vote" with their checkbooks.[15] Whereas the Sierra Club was constructed on a base of local chapters, FoE was organized along functional

Table 3.1. Membership Trends of Selected Environmental Organizations, 1950–2003*

Organization	1950–51	1960–61	1965–66	1970–71	1975–76	1980–81	1985–86	1991–92	1996–97	2002–03
Sierra Club	7,000	16,500	31,000	124,000	165,000	246,000	378,000	615,000	569,000	736,000
National Audubon Society	17,000	32,000	40,500	115,000	321,000	400,000	500,000	600,000	550,000	550,000
National Parks Conservation Association	5,400	15,000	31,000	49,000	45,000	27,500	45,000	230,000	375,000	375,000
Izaak Walton League	40,000	51,000	52,000	54,000	50,000	47,930	45,000	51,000	42,500	45,000
The Wilderness Society	5,000	10,000	28,000	62,000	62,500	52,000	145,000	365,000	237,000	225,000
National Wildlife Federation†			256,000	540,000	612,000	818,000	900,000	997,000	650,000	650,000
Ducks Unlimited								469,000	600,000	656,000
Defenders of Wildlife				13,000		50,000	75,000	77,000	215,000	463,000
The Nature Conservancy				22,000		80,000	365,000	545,000	865,000	972,000
World Wildlife Fund—US							450,000	970,000	1,200,000	1,200,000
Environmental Defense				20,000	37,000	46,000	65,000	175,000	300,000	350,000
Friends of the Earth				7,000		25,000	15,000	30,000	20,000	35,000
Environmental Action				7,000	20,000	21,000	15,000	19,000	12,000	defunct
Natural Resources Defense Council				5,000		40,000	65,000	170,000	260,000	450,000
League of Conservation Voters						35,000		25,000	30,000	60,000
Greenpeace USA						250,000	800,000	2,225,000	400,000	250,000
Earthjustice								120,000		70,000
Clean Water Action							400,000	600,000	600,000	600,000
Ocean Conservancy								105,000	110,000	100,000

Trust for Public Land#										45,000
American Rivers								110,000	20,000	30,000
Sea Shepherd Conservation Society								16,000	36,000	35,000
Center for Health, Environment, and Justice								20,000		28,000
Earth Island Institute								32,000	24,000	20,000
National Park Trust										33,000
Rainforest Action Network								32,500	30,000	35,000
Conservation Fund#										16,000
Conservation International								55,000	4,000	70,402
Earth Share#										
Environmental Working Group#										
National Environmental Trust#										
Total	74,400	124,500	438,500	1,018,000	1,312,500	2,138,430	4,263,000	8,653,500	7,149,500	8,099,402

* Figures are two-year averages and are approximations based on conflicting data, nonuniform reporting dates, and elastic definitions of the term member.

† In the mid-1990s, the NWF stopped distinguishing between dues-paying members and other supporters, for example, schoolchildren signed up in Ranger Rick programs, members of affiliated state organizations, and even individuals who purchased merchandise. The figure for 2002–03 is an estimate arrived at by dividing revenues from dues by the lowest possible amount required for designation as a member. Lowry (1993) calculated even lower figures for the NWF for the late 1970s and early 1990s.

Officially a nonmember organization. Figures of support are estimates derived from magazine or newletter circulation data.

Sources: See table 2.2, IRS Form 990; guidestar.org; Tom Knudsen, Environment, Inc., *Sacramento Bee,* April 22, 2001; *Public Interest Profiles* (Washington, D.C.: Foundation for Public Affairs/CQ Press); *Encyclopedia of Associations* (Detroit: Gale Research); Robert C. Lowry, "The Political Economy of Environmental Citizens' Groups" (doctoral dissertation, Harvard University, 1993).

Table 3.2. Operating Budgets, 1970–2002*

Organization	1970	1975	1980	1985	1990	1995	2000	2002
Sierra Club	3.0	6.0	9.5	21.4	40.3	48.3	71.6	86.6
National Audubon Society	3.0		10.0	24.0	35.8	43.1	58.4	70.1
National Parks Conservation Assoc.				1.7	6.0	13.0	16.6	18.5
Izaak Walton League				1.0	1.8	2.3	3.5	4.1
The Wilderness Society		1.8	1.5	6.5	17.7	15.2	17.6	20.6
National Wildlife Federation	13.0	20.0	34.5	46.0	87.2	97.1	96.9	110.8
Ducks Unlimited					67.5		121.0	134.0
Defenders of Wildlife				3.0	4.3	6.6	16.2	29.1
The Nature Conservancy					33.4	48.2	88.5	117.5
*Total TNC budget***					*125.1*	*323.5*	*728.3*	*1,031.8*
World Wildlife Fund—U.S.					64.0	79.0	100.0	102.5
Environmental Defense			2.0	3.4	15.8	24.6	32.2	41.2
Friends of the Earth†	0.4		1.0	1.0	3.0	2.5	4.3	4.3
Natural Resources Defense Council		1.5	3.5	6.8	16.0	26.2	33.7	46.9
League of Conservation Voters			0.5	1.6	1.3	2.5	11.8	6.7
Earthjustice					8.3		17.0	21.1
Greenpeace USA				24.0	63.7	37.8	20.0	22.1
Clean Water Action					5.0	13.0		9.6
Ocean Conservancy					3.7	8.1	11.3	13.6

Trust for Public Land**			78.9	116.8
American Rivers	1.6	2.4	4.9	5.4
Sea Shepherd Conservation Society		0.5	1.1	1.1
Center for Health, Environment, and Justice	0.6		2.0	1.4
Earth Island Institute	1.3		4.4	5.4
National Park Trust			4.5	1.8
Rainforest Action Network	1.2		2.8	2.1
Conservation Fund			45.2	47.3
Conservation International	8.9		34.3	69.0
Earth Share			7.9	8.3
Environmental Working Group			0.2	2.0
National Environmental Trust			17.2	10.5

* In millions of dollars, rounded. Figures are usually for fiscal years. Some are approximations of conflicting data.

** Includes temporary expenditures related to purchasing land for transfer or sale.

† Merged with EPI/EPC in 1989.

Sources: Annual reports; IRS Form 990; Ronald Shaiko, *Voices and Echoes for the Environment* (New York: Columbia University Press, 1999), 40–43; *Public Interest Profiles* (Washington, D.C.: Foundation for Public Affairs/CQ Press); *Encyclopedia of Associations* (Detroit: Gale Research); Robert C. Lowry, "The Political Economy of Environmental Citizen Groups" (doctoral dissertation, Harvard University, 1993), 225–26.

lines. Initially, it had its headquarters in San Francisco, administrative office in New York, a Washington lobbying operation, and a member development and finance division in Albuquerque.[16] (This odd arrangement may have reflected where key FoE leaders happened to live.) Both organizations pursued a broad environmental agenda and, as non-tax-exempt organizations, utilized the broadest possible array of advocacy tactics. Brower, reprising a strategy initiated at the Sierra Club, also created an affiliated foundation to attract tax-deductible donations for tax-exempt activities (e.g., education).

Brower spent heavily to build FoE's national visibility, develop advocacy programs, hire staff, establish affiliates in other countries, and recruit dues-paying members. As a result, FoE quickly went into debt, which, in Brower's view, was the short-term cost of building an effective advocacy organization.[17] Indeed, FoE soon became a central player in national and international environmental advocacy, and in the early 1970s, it led campaigns against construction of the supersonic transport and for restoration of the Florida Everglades.[18]

Defection. FoE grew rapidly in size and stature, but so did the management issues that had dogged Brower at the Sierra Club. Internal disagreements over FoE's awkward organizational structure and Brower's leadership came to a head in 1972, when virtually all the Washington advocacy staff, led by Joseph Browder and Brent Blackwelder, defected to form the Environmental Policy Center (EPC), a broad-spectrum, non-tax-exempt research and lobbying advocacy organization.[19] EPC at first relied heavily on the support of a few wealthy patrons, which, as Robert Cameron Mitchell and colleagues noted, "permitted them to avoid the distractions of having to serve a membership or publish a magazine and instead concentrate on lobbying."[20] Two years later, using seed money obtained from entertainer Arthur Godfrey, EPC created the Environmental Policy Institute (EPI), a tax-exempt research and educational organization that could tap into foundation and government support. In 1977, the affiliated organizations were formally merged, with the EPI wing disseminating information to grassroots groups, the media, and policymakers and the EPC wing acting as a direct lobby. Like FoE, EPI/EPC pursued a broad agenda, including nuclear power and nuclear proliferation, corporate compliance with federal strip-mining regulations, citizen knowledge about chemical plant production and emissions, water pollution, and the use of pesticides in agriculture. Like FoE, it deployed a wide array of tactics, including lobbying, lawsuits, and information campaigns. In fact, on many counts, EPI/EPC looked a lot like FoE.[21]

Departure. By the late 1970s, FoE was finally out of debt and enjoying its largest U.S. membership ever. Perhaps more important, FoE affiliates had been created in thirty-six countries, several of which became major advocacy organizations in their own right.[22] But the issues that had prompted the exodus of the Washington staff in 1972 emerged with new force in the 1980s, as environmental advocacy organizations across the board struggled to respond to the challenges posed by the Reagan administration.[23] Reagan's vigorous deregulatory agenda and cuts in the Environmental Protection Agency (EPA) budget—in particular, grant programs on which many smaller organizations had come to depend—forced environmentalists to escalate their advocacy efforts, build up their own scientific and legal expertise, recruit more members, and spend a lot of money in the process. As a result, many of them experienced serious fiscal crises (explored more fully in chapter 4), forcing significant internal restructuring and a major wave of changes in leadership.[24]

FoE was especially hard hit. On the one hand, Brower's efforts to make it a radical voice in global environmental debates was hemmed in by the media-friendly direct action of Greenpeace, whose global fame, membership rolls, and budget all grew at astonishing rates during the 1980s. On the other hand, FoE's professional staff increasingly found themselves competing for policy space and resources against the larger and better-financed Sierra Club and NRDC and, to a lesser extent, EPI/EPC. As Robert Gottlieb observed, FoE "never really resolved the tension between its organizational emphasis and its activist inclinations," and by the mid-1980s, the organization was in tough fiscal shape.[25] In 1985, FoE's board, following the advice of its professional staff, decided to restructure the organization, focus on advocacy in Washington, and move its headquarters to the nation's capital, actions that Brower and the activist wing opposed. The board prevailed, and Brower resigned.[26] His next organization, the San Francisco–based Earth Island Institute, was designed, in his words, "to instill ecological consciousness into as many spheres of human society as we could enter."[27] To do so, it would rely on Brower's traditional strengths in publication and education.

Reconstitution. The degree to which FoE and EPI/EPC had competed against each other following the split in 1972 was borne out in 1989 when they (along with the smaller Oceanic Society, which focused on coastal pollution) formally merged to pursue an agenda based on global ecological issues. The new organization retained the better-known Friends of the Earth name, even though most of the staff came from EPI.[28] To observers, this was a "remarriage" of organizations with overlapping values and agendas but complementary revenue bases—the foundation-supported EPI and the member-supported FoE.[29] In 2004, the reconstituted, albeit smaller, FoE is led by Brent Blackwelder, who thirty years earlier had led the exodus from Brower's organization.

David Brower died in 2000 at age eighty-eight, but not before one last fling with the Sierra Club. After leaving FoE, he was twice elected to the Sierra Club board and was even given the John Muir Award, the organization's highest honor. Although Brower and the club were somewhat reconciled, his participation often reflected new variations of older tensions. In 1998, a group of dissident members calling themselves "John Muir Sierrans," angry over what they saw as the professional staff's betrayal of the club's preservationist mission, ran a slate including Brower for election to the board. Brower won and served on the board as an in-house critic until his death. That Brower had become the symbol of a grassroots rebellion within the Sierra Club was an irony to anyone who understood his history with it.

Militant Dissidents

Friends of the Earth and EPI/EPC were exceptions among the national environmental advocacy community, in that they were dissident organizations that competed openly—by design or happenstance—with those their founders had left. More typically, dissident leaders left to create smaller, more "militant" outfits that often ended up complementing the work of "mainstream" outfits. For example, David Foreman left the Wilderness Society in the early 1980s over a perceived softening of its traditional militancy on wilderness preservation and cofounded Earth First!, a nonhierarchical "anti-organization" that espoused a radical set of goals (e.g., setting aside much of North America from human habitation) and direct-action tactics (e.g., spiking trees to stop logging). Greenpeace cofounder Paul Watson was eventually tossed out of that organization for violating its pacifist rules and created the far more aggressive (critics call it violent) Sea Shepherd Conservation Society. Neither Foreman nor Watson created an organization that competed directly with his former employer. Indeed, the zeal and tactics of such militants often serve to make the less absolutist views of their former organizations more palatable to government and corporate leaders.[30] In the process, the militants help extend the range of environmental advocacy and, in some ways, redefine the ideological center of environmentalism itself.

A notable example of this dynamic is the Native Forest Council, an Oregon-based organization that coordinates grassroots activism against commercial logging on public lands. The John Muir Sierrans, who backed the candidacies of Brower, Foreman, and Watson to the Sierra Club board, were particularly upset that it had refused to adopt a "zero-cut" stance on logging, calling it impractical. In 1996, the dissidents used the club's referendum process to place the issue before the members, who voted by a two-to-one margin to support the zero-cut stance. Even so, the board continued to move cautiously on the matter, prompting some dissidents to form the Native Forest Council. Like Earth First! and Sea Shepherds, the council occupies a more militant niche in the environmental advocacy community. The militants compete with their former organizations in the sense that they may attract some of their members—although in many cases, members maintain both affiliations[31]—but their goals and tactics typically prove unacceptable (for the moment) to the more middle-class constituency that supports the major environmental organizations. In fact, the leaders of their former organizations may have been perfectly content to see them go. Their departure ends enervating internal turmoil, while the creation of new organizations ultimately extends the aggregate reach of environmental advocacy into a greater number of policy and tactical niches.

NICHE SEEKERS

Whereas dissidents usually leave to form more militant counterparts to established organizations, policy entrepreneurs create organizations to occupy vacant or underpopulated policy niches or to deploy new tactics as a result of changes in the political opportunity structure or the emergence of new technology. As noted, this process did not start in the 1970s, but its pace and dimensions became more pronounced as the diverse elements of the environmental movement sought organizational niches in a maturing advocacy community.

Concern about securing a niche is not confined to new organizations, however. Long-established organizations also struggle to maintain their appropriate places within an evolving advocacy community. Friends of the Earth aside, the organizations created during the environmental era often generated intense, if not always intentional, competition with older conservation organizations over policy niches and resources, forcing the latter to evaluate their missions and ways of doing business. In some respects, the older conservation organizations spent much of the 1970s struggling to balance their traditional missions with the newer environmental ethos—and to simply keep afloat.

The National Parks Association—renamed the National Parks and Conservation Association (NPCA) in 1970—went through a particularly instructive struggle to maintain its niche, and its very relevance. During the first half of the decade, it expanded its agenda beyond the national parks into forestry, wildlife management, regional planning, and even population growth, in part because issues concerning the parks became more complex and more ecologically focused. However, the expanded agenda and name change were also responses to more intense competition with other, usually larger advocacy organizations. For example, in 1973, president Anthony Smith defended the NPCA's growing involvement in international wildlife programs on philosophical grounds—the ecological crisis demanded it—but, more notably, on strategic ones as well:

> The competitive position of the NPCA in the environmental movement in the United States compels us to participate in these activities. The Sierra Club and the National Audubon Society maintain full-time international representatives in New York. The National Wildlife Federation publishes a separate magazine, *International Wildlife,* and maintains an international department. The Friends of the Earth maintains chapters in quite a number of other countries. The NPCA has a special position to maintain in relation to the international movement for international parks.[32]

But the NPCA was small compared with the Sierra Club, Audubon Society, and National Wildlife Federation—not to mention the World Wildlife Fund—and thus lacked the resources to carry on such an expansive mission. It also lacked the edginess and youth of organizations such as Friends of the Earth and Environmental Defense and could not attract the thousands of new members needed to finance new ventures. Worse, the new focus alienated long-time members who cared about the national parks above all else. The NPCA bled members and money through the 1970s, and in 1980, Smith was ousted under conditions reminiscent of Brower's departure from the Sierra Club. The board brought in a new leadership team headed by an experienced professional, Paul Pritchard, which refocused the organization on its traditional mission, embarked on an aggressive marketing campaign built around the protection of the national parks, and returned the NPCA to fiscal health. As if to underscore the parks' centrality to its mission, in 2000 the National Parks and Conservation Association quietly removed the "and" from its name, becoming the National Parks Conservation Association. It was a subtle but telling deletion.

Some organizations have never wavered from their historical missions, with variable results. Ducks Unlimited (DU) has never really gone beyond being an organization of hunters working to protect wetlands in North America. Given its narrow focus and its unique constituency, DU has little direct competition in the overall wildlife niche. For other organizations, staying in an old niche has imposed more serious constraints. The Izaak Walton League, for example, has stuck to its post–Will Dilg ethos of "constructive engagement" with policymakers on pollution issues and to its generally older, politically conservative membership. Yet, in contrast to DU, the IWLA's policy niche (pollution, wildlife, wetlands) is shared with any number of other organizations (see table 3.3), but its ideological niche probably limits it appeal within the broader environmental constituency. The organization has often struggled as a result.

The Nature of Niches

Compared with previous periods, the unfilled policy niches of the environmental era were narrower and more specialized than before. For example, organizations dedicated to specific species and their habitats have long existed (e.g., DU; Trout Unlimited, founded in 1959), but they started to proliferate in the 1970s. Out of the approximately 310 "conservation and environmental" organizations listed in the 2001 edition of the *Encyclopedia of Associations,* about 60 appear to be dedicated to individual species.[33] Two-thirds were created *after* 1973. The North American Wolf Society (1973), National Wild Turkey Federation (1973), Desert Tortoise Council (1975)—not to be confused with the Desert Tortoise Preservation Committee (1974)—North American Loon Fund (1979), Quail Unlimited (1981), and Pheasants Forever (1982) complement broad-spectrum wildlife organizations such as the National Wildlife Federation, Defenders of Wildlife, and World Wildlife Fund. How much they compete for resources with the major wildlife organizations is hard to say, but most are rather small and geographically localized.

Other organizations occupy less narrowly configured but still distinct policy or tactical niches, in most instances reflecting strategic decisions by advocacy entrepreneurs. Some niche organizations were created after the emergence of a new issue on the policy agenda. For example, in the mid-1980s, concerns over the accelerating destruction of tropical rainforests led to the creation of the Rainforest Action Network (1985), the Rainforest Alliance (1986), and, to some extent, Conservation International (1987). American Rivers (1973) and the Ocean Conservancy (1972) reflected perceptions by organizational entrepreneurs that certain policy niches were not fully occupied. Other niche organizations are created in response to changes in government rules, in particular the federal income tax code (e.g., Trust for Public Land), or the advent of new technologies. For example, the Environmental Working Group (1993), whose niche is analyzing mountains of government data, is possible only because of the availability of powerful personal computers.[34]

What follows is a sample of the types of niche organizations created beginning in the early 1970s. It is not an exhaustive list, by any means, but it is fairly representative of the types of environmental advocacy organizations created over the past thirty years. The environmental era produced broad-spectrum advocacy organizations such as Environmental Defense, Natural Resources Defense Council, Friends of the Earth, and Greenpeace, but the full-service "department store" model of advocacy organization has since given way to the "boutique."[35] Some may be rather large specialty shops, but they are niche organizations nevertheless.

Clean Water Action (1971). Clean Water Action—known originally as the Fisherman's Clean Water Action Group—was formed under Ralph Nader's umbrella of public-interest organizations to enlist commercial and recreational fishermen to clean up coastal and inland waters. It soon turned to implementation of the Clean Water Act of 1972. Under founder David Zwick—who continued to run the organization in 2004—Clean Water Action eventually became the coordinator of and clearinghouse for a national coalition of state and local advocacy organizations that focus on clean and affordable drinking water.

Trust for Public Land (1972). The Trust for Public Land was created to exploit a niche left unoccupied by the Nature Conservancy, already the nation's largest land conservancy. Unlike the Nature Conservancy, the Trust for Public Land does not own or manage properties. Rather, it temporarily acquires land through a discounted price or an outright donation, thus providing tax benefits to the seller, and then sells or donates the land to public and nonprofit agencies for use as parks and recreational areas. The trust generally focuses on small parcels, particularly in urban areas and along rivers.[36]

Ocean Conservancy (1972). The Ocean Conservancy's roots lay in the nonprofit Delta Corporation, later renamed the Center for Environmental Education (CEE), which used foundation and government grants to develop educational materials for the classroom. As the official history of the organization tells it, what happened next was classic niche seeking:

> In 1975, after watching a Jacques Cousteau film on whales, [cofounder Bill] Kardash was inspired to find out which organizations opposed whaling. Discovering that few had adopted the whaling issue, Kardash created the Whale Protection Fund (WPF) to save whales and protest commercial whaling by Russia and Japan. The WPF used direct mail (then a new outreach tool) to solicit funds and public support for various petitions and boycotts of Japanese and Russian goods. Direct mail was extremely successful and recruited a large group of active supporters. Consequently, CEE ran ads opposing whaling in major papers, and funded research trips for scientists to discuss ways to address declining whale populations.[37]

During the 1980s, CEE evolved into a member-supported organization that focused on protecting marine life and habitats and fighting coastal pollution.

In 1989, the organization renamed itself the Center for Marine Conservation and, in 2000, became the Ocean Conservancy.

American Rivers (1973). During the 1970 board meeting at which the National Parks Association was renamed the NPCA, a dissenting trustee worried that the organization was moving too far from its core mission. There was plenty of work on the parks yet to do, he argued, as federal actions kept expanding the scope of the park system itself. For example, the Wild and Scenic Rivers Act of 1968 had created a system of national rivers, some to be administered by the National Park Service. "No national organization was soliciting strong public support to ensure that legislation classifying specific rivers, according to the act, passed Congress," historian John Miles recounts, so the trustee argued that the NPCA should do this.[38] He was overruled and, in a telling indicator of the organization's internal dynamics, was not invited to stand for reelection.

But others spotted the opportunity and the need to promote implementation of the 1968 law. In 1973, the leaders of several existing organizations created the American Rivers Conservation Council (renamed American Rivers in 1987) to advocate for the act and prevent the construction of new dams on "wild rivers." The organization's first president was Brent Blackwelder, cofounder of EPC a year earlier. During his earlier stint at Friends of the Earth, Blackwelder had engaged in a fight against river channeling projects sought by the Army Corps of Engineers. Repeating an established pattern, the new organization worked out of space at the EPC's Washington offices until it got on firmer fiscal ground.[39]

Center for Health, Environment, and Justice (1981). The Center for Health, Environment, and Justice was founded as the Citizens Clearinghouse for Hazardous Waste by Lois Gibbs, a self-described former housewife, along with other veterans of the fight over the toxic waste dump in the Love Canal neighborhood of Niagara Falls, New York.[40] The clearinghouse started as a network of grassroots activists who framed toxic waste and other hazards in social justice terms and were willing to openly criticize other environmental organizations (e.g., the National Wildlife Federation) for accepting donations from the same corporations they were fighting. Renamed the Center for Health, Environment, and Justice in 1997, the organization acts as a coordinator of and a resource center for grassroots environmental justice groups organized to fight toxic chemical use and unsafe waste disposal in their neighborhoods.

National Park Trust (1983). The National Park Trust (NPT) was created by the board of the NPCA to address an unexpected by-product of the expansion of the park system during the 1960s and 1970s: the many parcels of private land (or "inholdings") located within park boundaries. The NPT was created to acquire these properties and keep them from being developed, in part because no other land conservancy was focusing on this problem, and in part because the Interior Department under Reagan-appointee James Watt was not interested in adding more land to the park system. The NPT remained part of the NPCA until 1990, when the board, fearing personal liability over acquiring and holding land, made it an independent nonprofit land trust.[41]

Conservation Fund (1985). The Conservation Fund is distinct from both the Nature Conservancy and the Trust for Public Land, in that its focus is on creating public-private partnerships to manage donated land. The fund works with local, state, and federal agencies and nonprofit organizations to acquire property from sellers, with a particular emphasis on urban parks, river corridors, and historic places. The organization also provides financial support, technical assistance, and leadership training to land conservation professionals throughout the nation. In doing so, it occupies a capacity-building niche that was once dominated by the Conservation Foundation, which merged with its offspring and longtime partner, the World Wildlife Fund, the same year that the Conservation Fund was created.[42]

Rainforest Action Network (1985). The Rainforest Action Network (RAN) is but one of several advocacy organizations created during the mid-1980s to address the emerging issue of tropical rainforest depletion. It was founded by Randall Hayes of David Brower's Earth Island Institute (and in whose offices the new organization operated for a while) and Earth First! cofounder Mike Roselle to use Internet-based direct-action tactics (e.g., boycotts) and educational campaigns to generate grassroots pressure on corporations (e.g., Home Depot, Scott Paper) and nations to halt practices that RAN deems harmful to tropical rainforests.

Conservation International (1987). The conceptual basis for the creation of Conservation International can be traced to a 1984 *New York Times* opinion essay by biologist Thomas Lovejoy, then director of the biodiversity program at the World Wildlife Fund. In it, Lovejoy argued that the emerging "debt crisis" facing developing nations offered an opportunity for conservation efforts in those countries. He proposed a "debt-for-nature swap," whereby a country could be relieved of a portion of its debt in return for guarantees that it would protect important ecosystems. Under this scheme, some amount of foreign debt would be purchased by a nongovernmental organization, using tax-deductible donations, and then retired.[43] Conservation International was cofounded by

Peter Seligmann and Spencer Beebe, both formerly of the Latin America program at the Nature Conservancy, in part to use debt-for-nature swaps to conserve threatened ecosystems in developing countries.[44]

Earth Share (1988). Originally established as the Environmental Federation of America, Earth Share is a funding vehicle for around forty tax-exempt (or tax-exempt affiliates of) environmental organizations, including most of those examined in this study. Its purpose and operation mimic the long-established United Way. Earth Share acts as a clearinghouse for workplace contributions, thus providing a convenient means by which individuals can donate to environmental causes. Its board is made up of representatives of the recipient organizations.

Environmental Working Group (1993). The Environmental Working Group (EWG) was created by Ken Cook, former communications director at the World Wildlife Fund, to collect federal government data (often through Freedom of Information Act requests), reorganize them into more user-friendly and Web-accessible formats, and communicate the reformulated information to journalists. For example, its interactive database on recipients of farm subsidies was widely credited with shaping much of the public debate, if not necessarily the outcome, during congressional reauthorization of the farm bill in 2002. The EWG is funded largely by foundation grants.[45]

National Environmental Trust (1994). The National Environmental Trust (NET) was established as the Environmental Information Center under the sponsorship of Josh Reichert, director of environmental programs at the Pew Charitable Trusts. (During the 1990s, Pew became a major—some say pivotal—force in shaping environmental advocacy in the United States; see chapter 4.)[46] NET's stated purpose is to act as a counterweight to industry public-relations efforts by seeking to set the agenda and frame the debate on environmental issues in selected areas, such as global climate change and forest preservation, and to inform citizens about environmental problems and their effects on human health. It also gives grants to other environmental organizations (e.g., Izaak Walton, Defenders, Audubon) for their educational and public awareness programs. NET maintains strong connections to the Pew Trusts but now seeks support from other sources, including individual donations.

Assembly Rules

David Hart, utilizing the population ecology framework to study the formation of agricultural and high-technology advocacy organizations, argues that certain "assembly rules" may govern organizational creation and the partitioning of advocacy niches within a defined population.[47] That is, there may be patterns in the creation of advocacy organizations that result from factors such as the current political opportunity structure and the existence of unoccupied policy or tactical niches. Based on the preceding capsule descriptions, what observations can we make about the creation of niche environmental advocacy organizations starting in the early 1970s?

First, the organizations created during the 1970s tended to occupy vacant or underexploited policy niches. American Rivers was formed because no other organization had dedicated itself to implementing the Wild and Scenic Rivers Act. The history of the Ocean Conservancy reflects a strategy of occupying a niche on marine issues that was not already dominated by another organization, particularly Greenpeace. In the 1980s, by comparison, there were relatively few unoccupied policy niches available to new startups. Even newly emergent issues such as tropical rainforest depletion or global climate change were being covered to some extent by broad-spectrum organizations such as the Sierra Club and NRDC, which continually revise their agendas to include a mix of traditional and new policy concerns. On rainforests, for example, the new organizations created (RAN, Conservation International) were distinguished more by their *tactics* (Internet-based direct action, debt-for-nature swaps) or ideological positioning within the broader environmental advocacy community.

Second, with a few notable exceptions (e.g., the Center for Health, Environment, and Justice), niche organizations are either created by experienced leaders coming out of established organizations or devised by existing organizations for purposes that complement their own. For a number of rational reasons—core mission chief among them—setting up an entirely new niche operation is often preferable to expanding or changing the scope of an established one. Thus, the NPCA begets the National Park Trust, the Nature Conservancy and the World Wildlife Fund beget Conservation International, and the environmental community as a whole begets Earth Share. Sometimes these spin-offs reflect disagreements over priorities within the "parent" organization (apparently part of the story behind the departures of Seligmann and Beebe from the Nature Conservancy to start up Conservation International), while at other times they simply reflect the strategic conclusion that a niche organization fills a need.

In this regard, it is useful to note that the organizations created most recently—Earth Share, Environmental Working Group, and National Environmental Trust—are among environmentalism's most specialized. Although their leaders might contest this observation, all three can be considered "service providers" to the environmental community, rather than advocacy organizations in their own right. Their creation also reflects the maturity of the national environmental advocacy community, which by the early 1990s had become so dense and internally diverse that only the most specialized niche organizations were worth creating.[48]

Competition for finite resources also plays a role in this equation. By 1990, as Michael McCloskey, former executive director of the Sierra Club (1969–1985) observed, competition among existing broad-spectrum organizations was already keen:

> Almost every group faced a logical competitor trying to occupy the same market niche and competing for visibility, leadership, membership, and funds. NRDC competes in this way with the Environmental Defense Fund, the Nature Conservancy with the Trust for Public Lands, the Wilderness Society with the Sierra Club and the National Parks and Conservation Association, Friends of the Earth with Environmental Action, Defenders of Wildlife with the Humane Society of the United States, and the National Wildlife Federation with the National Audubon Society and perhaps increasingly with the World Wildlife Fund.[49]

Competition among existing organizations powerfully defines the niches available to new ones and has independent effects on the pace and shape of new organizational creation. Barring the collapse of an existing major organization, the near-term probability of creating new broad-spectrum organizations like the Sierra Club, or even large but more focused organizations like the Wilderness Society, seems rather low.

MAPPING THE ENVIRONMENTAL ADVOCACY COMMUNITY

What is the topography of the national advocacy community that has been assembled through these processes of organizational creation? Table 3.4 lays out a "spatial map" of the contemporary national environmental advocacy community as it stands in 2004. The vertical axis indicates the relative breadth of an organization's policy agenda, based in part on its public statements about issue priorities (see table 3.3). The horizontal axis portrays an organization's relative place on the ideological spectrum—in this case, the degree to which the organization openly critiques free-market capitalism, mainstream consumer culture, and the policy agenda of the George W. Bush administration.

Jeffrey Berry once observed that "Americans are not only able to find

Table 3.3. Policy Agendas

	Issues															
Organization	1	2	3	4	5	6	7	8	9	10	11	12	13	14	15	16
Natural Resources Defense Council		X	X	X		X	X		X		X			X		X
Sierra Club			X		X	X	X				X			X		X
World Wildlife Fund—US	X	X	X	X	X				X			X	X			
National Wildlife Federation	X	X	X	X		X	X			X						
Environmental Defense	X	X	X	X		X						X			X	
Friends of the Earth	X		X						X					X		
Greenpeace USA			X	X	X		X								X	X
Izaak Walton League		X			X	X	X			X						
National Audubon Society	X	X						X		X		X				
National Parks Cons. Association	X					X						X	X			
The Wilderness Society							X			X		X				
Rainforest Action Network					X		X							X		
National Environmental Trust			X	X		X			X							
Environmental Working Group									X					X		
Earth Island Institute	X			X	X								X			
Defenders of Wildlife	X	X			X											
The Nature Conservancy	X		X					X			X					
Clean Water Action											X		X			

Issues																	
17	18	19	20	21	22	23	24	25	26	27	28	29	30	31	32	33	Total
		X				X		X					X				13
					X		X							X			10
X	X																9
	X				X												8
	X						X										8
X						X			X	X		X					8
		X															7
X																	6
					X												5
			X	X													5
X				X													5
				X													4
																	4
X									X								4
				X													4
X																	3
																	3
		X															3

Table 3.3. Policy Agendas *(Continued)*

	Issues															
Organization	1	2	3	4	5	6	7	8	9	10	11	12	13	14	15	16
Ducks Unlimited		X						X		X						
Trust for Public Land								X							X	
National Park Trust								X		X						
Conservation Fund											X		X			
Ocean Conservancy		X		X												
Conservation International	X							X								
Ctr. for Health, Environment & Justice									X							
American Rivers															X	
League of Conservation Voters																
Sea Shepherd Conservation Society				X												
Earth Share																
Total coverage	10	9	9	9	7	7	7	6	6	6	5	5	5	5	4	4

Legend

1. Biodiversity
2. Wildlife
3. Global warming/climate change
4. Oceans and marine life
5. Forests
6. Clear air
7. Energy
8. Land conservancy
9. Chemicals and toxic waste
10. Wetlands
11. Clean water
12. Arctic National Wildlife Refuge
13. Sustainable resources
14. Trade
15. Rivers
16. Wilderness
17. Agriculture
18. Endangered species
19. Nuclear waste, weapons, etc.
20. National parks

Issues																	
17	18	19	20	21	22	23	24	25	26	27	28	29	30	31	32	33	Total
																	3
								X									3
			X														3
															X		3
																	2
																	2
		X															2
															X		1
											X						1
																	1
																X	1
4	4	4	3	3	3	2	2	2	2	1	1	1	1	1	1	1	

21. Cultural diversity/native populations
22. Population
23. Recycling
24. Sprawl
25. Urban issues
26. Transportation
27. Corporate actions
28. Elections
29. Genetically modified organisms
30. "Green living"
31. Human rights
32. Training
33. Funding environmental groups

Table 3.4. Spatial Map of the National Environmental Advocacy Community

	Ideological Spectrum									
		"Radicals"						*"Accommodationists"*		
Scope of Agenda										
"Keynotes"					SC	NRDC	ED	NWF	WWF	
"Sectoral players"			Greenpeace	FoE [EA]	TWS DoW		NAS NPCA		TNC	IWLA
"Niche players"	ELF	"Militants" Earth First! Sea Shepherds		EI RAN EJ	CWA LCV CHEJ	EWG NET	OC AR ES		CF TPL NPT CI	DU (& other game orgs.)

groups that work in the broad area they are concerned about, but the competition between these lobbies for members creates an incentive for these organizations to develop a policy niche. Is your interest in the environment mostly a concern for endangered species, toxic wastes, national parks, or wilderness? There are groups that specialize in each."[50] Table 3.4 substantiates Berry's point but also shows how this advocacy community can be divided into distinct tiers. The top tier is occupied by those few organizations—NRDC, Sierra Club, Environmental Defense, and World Wildlife Fund—that pursue the broadest policy agendas. NRDC has the most expansive agenda of all, with priorities ranging from urban life and recycling to global warming and nuclear weapons proliferation—and nearly everything in between. The Sierra Club is only slightly narrower, perhaps constrained by the uniquely active role its members play in electing the board and setting priorities. The second tier is occupied by a handful of major organizations (including Audubon and NPCA) that pursue multiple goals within more narrowly focused agendas, and the third tier is occupied by niche organizations.

The criteria used to place organizations along the ideological continuum depicted by the horizontal axis of table 3.4 range from terminology in a mission statement to whether the organization accepts funding from corporations engaged in extractive sectors (e.g., oil, mining) or industrial production (e.g., autos, chemicals). This schema also reflects classifications devised by McCloskey, who sorted environmental organizations into "pragmatic reformers," "radicals," and "accommodationists."[51] Pragmatic reformers, such as NRDC and the Sierra Club, offer varying critiques of market capitalism but tend to focus on achieving change through the political system. The radicals, starting with Friends of the Earth and Greenpeace and heading leftward, express the strongest skepticism about market capitalism and even about the efficacy of working within the political system; they are more likely to support media-oriented protest campaigns and direct-action tactics over lobbying or lawsuits. Finally, accommodationists are willing to embrace market solutions and collaborate with corporations to achieve common goals. This category, using McCloskey's definition, arguably begins with Environmental Defense, which worked with McDonald's to devise "green" packaging, supported tradable pollution credits as part of the 1990 amendments to the Clean Air Act, and advises corporations on technological or market solutions to pollution problems.[52] However, Environmental Defense accepts no corporate funding for these projects and is a frequent critic of the Bush administration. More firmly in this category are "hook and bullet" groups such as the National Wildlife Federation and Ducks Unlimited, generally apolitical land conservancies such as the Nature Conservancy and Conservation International, the World Wildlife

Fund, and the Izaak Walton League. These organizations typically promote "commonsense," market-based approaches; offer muted, if any, criticism of administration policies; and include among their corporate "partners" companies (e.g., General Motors, Chevron Texaco, International Paper) that Friends of the Earth and Greenpeace regard as villains.

Another useful indicator of an organization's relative place on this ideological continuum is its position on international free-trade pacts, such as ratification of the North American Free Trade Agreement (NAFTA) in 1993.[53] That acrimonious battle pitted the Clinton administration and one group of environmental organizations against an organized labor–led coalition that included another set of environmentalists. Strongest support for NAFTA—or, at least, the Clinton administration's position on it—came from "moderates" such as the World Wildlife Fund, the National Wildlife Federation, and Environmental Defense. Strongest opposition came from the left, led by Greenpeace, Friends of the Earth, and the Sierra Club, along with coalitions of environmental justice groups such as the Center for Health, Environment, and Justice.[54]

Finally, the classification scheme incorporates findings by Lowry on the cultural and ideological variations among members of the respective environmental organizations. Although there is some evidence of a growing homogeneity in the membership profiles of the groups studied, the secular liberals likely to join Friends of the Earth as a result of a direct-mail appeal, for example, are different from the hunting and fishing enthusiasts who attend Ducks Unlimited fund-raisers.[55]

When the policy agenda and ideological dimensions are combined, the result is a national environmental advocacy community that is broader, organizationally denser, and more diverse than is commonly understood. That this schema omits dozens of other national niche organizations—American Farmland Trust (1980), Beyond Pesticides (1981), Rainforest Alliance (1984), Surfrider Foundation (1984), and Rails to Trails Conservancy (1986), to name a few—reinforces the point. Amidst this diversity, three modal types of organizations stand out: keystones, sectoral players, and niche players.

Keystones

Gray and Lowery argue that some organizations can be likened to "keystone predators" in nature, in the sense that their size and reach shape entire sectors of a broader advocacy population.[56] These are the relatively few organizations around which all others within an advocacy sector orient themselves in one way or another, consciously or not. One can also use the analogy of the major "anchor tenants" that act as destination points for various wings in any large shopping mall—and without which such a marketplace does not thrive. Whichever analogy is most useful, the centrality of such organizations depends less on gross size or resource capacity—the Nature Conservancy, though wealthy, has a narrow purpose and a muted advocacy stance—than on the degree to which they define and even propel entire sectors within the broader advocacy community.

In this regard, five organizations—Sierra Club, Natural Resources Defense Council, Environmental Defense, National Wildlife Federation, and World Wildlife Fund—arguably are the keystones of their respective sectors. The Sierra Club anchors the "mainstream left" of the national environmental advocacy community and shapes discourse on an array of wilderness and pollution issues for other organizations (e.g., Wilderness Society, Friends of the Earth) on its side of the ideological spectrum. The NRDC and Environmental Defense, the two leading "science and law" organizations, are positioned on opposite sides of what might be considered the ideological center of environmental advocacy and are distinctive enough to offer competing philosophical and tactical arguments on major issues. On climate change, for example, the NRDC is more likely to promote statutory and legal answers, while Environmental Defense proposes market-based or technological solutions.[57] The National Wildlife Federation and World Wildlife Fund are seen as ideologically moderate to slightly conservative, depending on which indicators and values one analyzes. The National Wildlife Federation dominates domestic wildlife, and the World Wildlife Fund defines international wildlife issues, in the sense that the policy stances and actions taken by each has powerful impacts on all other organizations within their respective sectors. Other wildlife organizations (e.g., Defenders, Audubon, Ducks Unlimited) are more likely to react to the actions of these two keystone organizations than the other way around.

Sectoral Players

This category includes organizations that may not dominate an entire sector of the advocacy community but are still large and active enough to coexist, if not necessarily compete, with the keystone organizations. In most instances, an organization of this type pursues a relatively broad policy agenda but has clearly oriented itself with respect to the position occupied by the keystone organization in its particular sector.

For example, by the late 1980s, the National Audubon Society was pursuing a policy agenda that had broadened incrementally beyond its traditional focus on birds and their habitats into such areas as pesticides, air pollution, population control, and international wildlife issues.[58] As a result, however,

Audubon increasingly found itself under pressure to distinguish itself from the Sierra Club on population, the NRDC on pesticides, Environmental Defense on air pollution, the National Wildlife Federation on domestic wildlife, and the World Wildlife Fund on international wildlife, while still maintaining the support of its bird-loving membership base. Grassroots discontent over Audubon's priorities surfaced when it, along with many other environmental organizations, went through a severe fiscal slump in the early 1990s. Older activists in particular accused the leadership of neglecting Audubon's core mission as it sought a jazzier, youth-oriented appeal—trying, as one wit put it, to convert Audubon "into an upper-class Greenpeace."[59] The near rebellion among members compelled the board to change leadership and refocus Audubon's efforts "on a limited set of priorities directly relating birds, other wildlife, and their habitats to the continuance and prosperity of humankind."[60] Audubon continues to pursue a broad policy agenda within the boundaries of its strategic plan, but it does not have the same range of action as the keystone organizations. It has defined its position within its sector as much by what it will *not* do as anything else.

One finds similar strategic or crisis-induced repositioning efforts in the recent histories of almost every organization in this category. Greenpeace, for example, enjoyed remarkable growth during the late 1980s as its parent organization, Greenpeace International, pursued highly publicized protests on issues ranging from ocean dumping of toxic wastes to nuclear weapons tests in the South Pacific. Compared with the sober image cultivated by other organizations, Greenpeace seemed bold, pure, and action oriented, not just another environmental lobby. By 1990, Greenpeace International had become a global "green giant," and its U.S. affiliate alone took in $60 million from an estimated 2.5 million contributors, enabling it to broaden its policy agenda and range of tactics, establish regional offices, and help subsidize the activities of its parent organization.[61] But Greenpeace soon proved susceptible to the challenges that confront any organization that depends on contributions generated through expensive direct-mail campaigns. It was hit hard by the recession of the early 1990s and, to some extent, by its parent organization's stated ambivalence about the Persian Gulf war, leading to staff cuts, leadership turnover, and the closure of regional offices. It never regained its stride, and by the late 1990s, it was in dire fiscal shape.[62] In some respects, Greenpeace had tried to outgrow its traditional niche but had a hard time showing tangible results for contributors' money. Direct-action protests may motivate a subset of the environmental base, but one that is too small to sustain the kind of broad-spectrum organization Greenpeace sought to become, especially when it began to wander into policy and tactical territory dominated by the Sierra Club and the NRDC in particular. A reconstituted Greenpeace continues to pursue a protest-based agenda, but now as a much smaller, more obviously situated sectoral player within the national advocacy community.[63]

Niche Players

The third type of organization encompasses the various policy and tactical niche players discussed throughout this chapter. Most, though certainly not all, are relatively small and are content to act as specialized "boutiques" within the environmental advocacy marketplace. They are spread across the entire ideological spectrum and, more often than not, complement, sometimes openly, the work of their larger counterparts. More than the sectoral actors, these organizations are constrained by their respective policy or tactical niches.

Whereas broad-spectrum organizations such as the National Wildlife Federation or even the Wilderness Society have proved their resiliency over the decades (discussed more fully in chapter 4), the long-term sustainability of niche players is often more problematic. To be sure, some niches seem relatively secure. Earthjustice (formerly the Sierra Club Legal Defense Fund) is the only pure environmental law firm operating on the national level. Ducks Unlimited occupies a policy and ideological niche where it has little competition. The various land conservancies (Trust for Public Land, National Park Trust, Conservation International) are able to maintain identities distinct from one another and from the massive but also narrow Nature Conservancy.

But other organizations reside within more problematic niches. For example, the relatively short history of the Oceanic Society, which merged with the Environmental Policy Institute before EPI's own merger with Friends of the Earth, may foreshadow challenges facing the Ocean Conservancy as it tries to coexist with the NRDC, National Wildlife Federation, and World Wildlife Fund on marine issues. To do so, it must emphasize relatively precise targets—ranging from beach debris to water pollution caused by cruise ships—that the larger, multipolicy organizations usually do not cover. American Rivers safeguards its distinctive role as national coordinator of local and state groups seeking to preserve wild and scenic rivers, and it also collaborates with organizations such as Environmental Defense on specific dam removal or channeling projects. Only especially nimble specialization will enable organizations such as the Environmental Working Group to survive as the smallest of the boutiques in the advocacy mall.

For any advocacy organization, then, long-term survival has as much to do with the relevance and security of the particular niche it occupies as with the vagaries of fund-raising or any purported failures of leadership. For policy and tactical niche organizations in particular, the challenge is to keep from being made redundant.

THE CASE OF ENVIRONMENTAL ACTION

The history of Environmental Action (EA) offers insights into the challenge of surviving in a mature advocacy community, if only because its closure in 1996 was such an anomaly. Other environmental organizations lost their independent identities through mergers (e.g., the Conservation Foundation into the World Wildlife Fund, the Environmental Policy Institute back into Friends of the Earth), but few expired outright. The demise of EA thus merits closer examination.

Founded in 1970 by the student organizers of the original Earth Day, Environmental Action began as a broad-spectrum, non-tax-exempt environmental advocacy organization to the left on the ideological spectrum. Its New Left aura and connection to Earth Day initially enabled EA to attract thousands of members and to expand its focus into a broad array of anti-pollution, energy, and social justice issues. But EA soon found itself at a distinct disadvantage. For one thing, it had a lot of company in its particular neighborhood—FoE and, after the schism there, the EPI, as well as Ralph Nader's Public Interest Research Group, League of Conservation Voters, NRDC, and, on direct-action matters, Greenpeace.[64] By comparison to its neighbors, even FoE, EA was on shakier financial ground from the start. The foundations that supported legal action, scientific research, and capacity building were reluctant to fund grassroots mobilization and social protest, especially after Congress passed the Tax Reform Act of 1969 to force foundations to assume "expenditure responsibility" over their activist recipients. Although the Nixon administration eventually promulgated guidelines that shielded foundations and grantees from IRS penalties, so long as they served the "public good," most so-called liberal foundations shied away from supporting controversial social justice goals.[65] The large individual donors who provided critical support for FoE and EPI were put off by EA's relative lack of professionalism: for many years, it continued to act as a collective, with staff members earning identical salaries and decisions arrived at only after interminable meetings. In the 1980s, when it tried to expand its membership base through direct mail, EA found it so difficult to differentiate itself from competitors like FoE that it suspended the recruitment effort before it lost too much money in the process. Internal disputes over goals and strategies, particularly whether EA should continue to focus on protest or become a more professional advocacy organization, led to the exodus of its more policy-oriented staff.

But the leaders of Environmental Action soldiered on, backed by a small but dedicated cohort of supporters. By the mid-1980s, they had restructured the organization's operations and narrowed its policy agenda to areas such as citizens' right to know about toxic substances in their communities; waste disposal, in particular bottle deposit bills and recycling; and, following a merger with the Energy Conservation Coalition, nuclear power. Even then, however, EA had to differentiate itself from niche organizations such as the Center for Health, Environment, and Justice—which was better known because of its founder, Lois Gibbs—and, at another level, keystone organizations such as the NRDC on recycling and Environmental Defense on right-to-know issues. Its efforts to influence elections by disseminating the environmental records of candidates through its Environmental Action Political Action Campaign always seemed overshadowed by the better-known League of Conservation Voters. Even its most widely publicized product, its "Dirty Dozen" list of members of Congress with the worst voting records on environmental issues, was better known than the organization producing it.

In sum, Environmental Action was too small to compete with the major organizations, too broad to compete with policy or tactical niche organizations, and, in some respects, too purist in its ideals to pursue sources of funding (e.g., advertising in its magazine) that were readily accepted by virtually everyone else. Although widely respected within the environmental community and a steady source of talent for other organizations, EA simply could not sustain itself within its intended niche. By the mid-1990s, it was broke, and it shut its doors in October 1996, leaving behind a diaspora of college campus and foreign EA spin-offs.[66] In a final irony, the "Dirty Dozen" campaign continues, inherited by the League of Conservation Voters.

THE MATURE ADVOCACY COMMUNITY

The national environmental advocacy community in 2004 is characterized by a fairly high degree of organizational density and diversity, marked by a wide array of organizational types, missions, policy and tactical niches, and ideological orientations. A few organizations define entire sectors within the broader advocacy community, while a broad array of smaller or more narrowly configured organizations occupy more defined policy or tactical niches. There is a fair degree of carefully expressed competition over policy leadership and resources, but, as shown in chapter 5, there is also cooperation and coordination when shared goals so dictate.

In these respects, these organizations are constituent elements of a mature advocacy community. The levels of its organizational density and diversity may be unique among public-interest advocacy communities—although the health care advocacy community comes pretty close—but anyone studying advocacy communities oriented around agriculture or defense issues, to offer but two examples, would observe the same characteristics. In agriculture, for example, there are keystone organizations such as the American Farm Bureau Federation, sectoral players such as the National Frozen and Refrigeration Foods Association, and niche organizations ranging from the National Milk Producers Federation to the Missouri Pork Association.[67]

But herein lies a big difference. In an advocacy community such as agriculture, oriented inevitably toward private economic well-being, organizational niches and membership characteristics are rooted in occupations, business sectors, regions, or products. Free-rider problems aside, the organizations that occupy these respective private-sector niches usually can depend on ready-made constituencies of self-interested supporters. Hog producers, after all, ordinarily do not find themselves choosing among a variety of advocacy organizations dedicated to hogs. By contrast, the many organizations that make up the national environmental advocacy community must stake out their respective niches and attract support within a more variegated organizational terrain. Some niches are based on particular animals, issues, or tactics, but the organizations that occupy these niches have to develop and maintain a cohort of supporters, who usually can find at least one other organization to which they can shift their loyalties if they become disenchanted. Unlike the hog producer, an environmentally concerned citizen has several choices.

Private-sector advocacy organizations are not entirely free from such worries, of course, and they have devised all kinds of particularistic benefits (e.g., discounts on goods and services) to reinforce member support, but at the end of the day they can still depend on economic self-interest as a motivating force. For organizations in a public-interest advocacy community, by contrast, self-interest is a more evanescent concept, so the challenge to develop and sustain support is more apparent, and more central to their longevity. Finding a relatively secure policy or tactical niche is only part of the story, but, as the history of Environmental Action suggests, no advocacy organization can survive over the long haul without one.

Finally, the breadth, density, and diversity of the environmental advocacy community give environmentalism itself greater resiliency and impact than are often recognized. Recall the discussion in chapter 1 about the Bush administration's reversal on a proposed wetlands rule. Environmentalists across the ideological spectrum had opposed the rule, but the president's action came only after a coalition of "hook and bullet" organizations, including the National

Wildlife Federation and Ducks Unlimited, expressed their concerns, apparently at the direct urging of outgoing EPA administrator Christine Todd Whitman. Members of these organizations tend to be politically conservative and are an important part of the president's electoral base, so no one was surprised when several of their leaders were invited to meet with the president on the issue. As Jim Martin, a board member of the National Wildlife Federation put it, "I don't think he cares what the environmental community thinks, but he cares what the sportsmen think."[68]

Whether sportsmen are also "environmentalists" probably depends on one's ideological orientation more than anything else, but in the end, the administration's action was counted as a partial gain for the environment and for the environmental community writ large. How else could it be construed? The point here is that contemporary environmentalism is not the marginal value system of a narrow and unrepresentative elite. It is impressively broad, with distinct ideological wings, diverse policy orientations, and clear internal cleavages. As a result, it can be said to represent an immense and diverse national constituency, the breadth of which is critical to the resilience and survival of the organized environmental community itself.

4
Maintaining the Organization

There has been an unfortunate tendency in environmental organizations because the staffs tend to be made up of people who, if they are not alternative lifestylers, they have opted out of the corporate, structured, managed sort of rat race. They don't want people telling them what to do. They want to do their own thing.
—William Turnage, Wilderness Society executive director (1978–1985)

PRESERVING THE WILDERNESS (SOCIETY)

For three decades after its founding, the Wilderness Society, led much of that time by executive director Howard Zahniser, single-mindedly pursued the preservation of millions of acres of roadless federal lands. Passage of the Wilderness Act of 1964 marked a pivotal moment in the achievement of that goal. However, Zahniser died shortly before its enactment. His assistant and successor, Stuart Brandenborg, was determined to maintain the society's core mission, values, and management style, even as other old-line conservation organizations were transforming into multi-issue environmental organizations.[1]

Under Brandenborg—whom critic Mark Dowie called "the last true activist to lead the Wilderness Society"[2]—the society's membership quadrupled, a growth propelled in part by the appeal of the organization's commitment to wilderness preservation, particularly in Alaska. Even so, by the mid-1970s, the society was in serious trouble. Brandenborg had relied heavily on the original Robert Marshall bequest to finance activities, but those dwindling funds were not being augmented by other significant sources of revenue. Moreover, the activists who made up the Wilderness Society's staff were apparently light on management skills and ill-suited for the meticulous and often frustrating process of monitoring the implementation of the Wilderness Act. Tensions between the staff and a worried board intensified as the organization's financial situation worsened. When Brandenborg was fired in January 1976, observes Robert Gottlieb, "the organization seemed least prepared among the traditional groups to reconstitute itself along more professional lines."[3]

Conditions deteriorated even more during the next two years as the society went through two executive directors; saw a 50 percent drop in membership, as supporters drifted away from the fiscally strapped organization; and, as a result, piled up a budget deficit that put the organization near bankruptcy.[4] Finally, in November 1978, the board hired outsider William Turnage, a State Department veteran and former aide to the Sierra Club's Ansel Adams, to "knock heads" and get the organization turned around.[5] In one month, Turnage fired all but one of the society's thirty-seven staff members and began to reshape the traditionally nonhierarchical advocacy group into a more structured, more professional organization. At the same time that Paul Pritchard was reorienting the National Parks Conservation Association (NPCA) back to its traditional emphasis on parks, Turnage accentuated the Wilderness Society's public commitment to nonpark public lands and instituted an array of by-then conventional membership development and management practices. By the time he resigned in 1985, Turnage had tripled the society's membership and doubled its budget. His successors would continue his emphasis on professional advocacy directed at a limited set of goals.

NO GUARANTEES

The organizational struggles of the Wilderness Society after passage of the Wilderness Act remind us that seeking out and keeping a reasonably secure policy niche are not enough. Arguably more important to long-term survival is an advocacy organization's capacity to adapt to changing external conditions, internal needs, and even new opportunities. Despite the emergence of environmentalism as a component of mainstream American culture and politics, and despite the millions of Americans who counted themselves as environmentalists, there was simply no guarantee that organizations created before and during the environmental era would survive to the twenty-first century. As Jeffrey Berry observed about the many advocacy organizations spawned during the late 1960s and early 1970s, "if the gravitation from protest to conventional lobbying was predictable, the endurance and popularity of the citizen organizations were not."[6]

Indeed, the political landscape is littered with the detritus of groups that failed to make that critical transition from protest vehicle to professional advocacy organization. As any activist will point out, it is one thing to enjoy diffuse public support, but it is a far different matter to translate it into sustained backing for policy actions or the resources needed to nourish an advocacy organization over the long haul. Yet these organizations were able to get past those hurdles by continually adapting to changing political, economic, and policy circumstances. Others tried but failed. Like Environmental Action, some succumbed to competition from other organizations in their respective policy, tactical, or ideological niches; others, like the Environmental Policy Institute and the Conservation Foundation, lost their identity in mergers. And, like the Wilderness Society and the NPCA, there were plenty of organizations that careened close to the brink of extinction. Reading their individual histories leaves one a bit amazed that so many of them survived.[7] Their stories underscore the fragility of existence for any advocacy organization. Seeming permanence belies harder reality: nothing is guaranteed.

Taken together, the organizational sagas laid out in previous chapters add up to an advocacy community that has displayed a remarkable resiliency over time. But, as one might surmise, the aggregate evolution of this community into its current state did not follow a seamless path of adaptation and change. It came in spasms, often in piecemeal fashion as individual organizations were forced to adjust to perturbations in their respective niches. For example, the positioning of the Wilderness Society on public lands, the NPCA on national park policy, the Audubon Society on birds and wildlife, or the Ocean Conservancy on marine pollution issues reflect the vagaries of any policy niche over time. Even reasonably secure niches change, and there isn't a single organization that hasn't confronted niche-specific challenges at some time in its history, often more than once.

Even keystone organizations such as the Sierra Club, Environmental Defense, and the National Wildlife Federation endure their share of fiscal challenges, internal strife, and leadership turnover. However, their spasms of organizational duress seem to reflect systemic perturbations rather than niche-specific ones. That is, because of their size and breadth, the keystones are like the proverbial canaries in the coal mine, whose acute sensitivity to methane gas warned miners of impending danger. When keystone organizations struggle, the perturbation seems to cut across policy, tactical, and ideological niches, provoking systemic changes among those organizations that survive. For all environmental organizations, the Reagan administration was one such systemic perturbation.

THE REAGAN REVOLUTION

Any historically informed assessment of the national environmental community must give Ronald Reagan a great deal of the credit—or, depending on one's point of view, the blame—for the transformation in the national environmental organizations. Even though organizational changes had been evident in the previous decade, before Reagan, most of these organizations were still relatively small (see tables 3.1 and 3.2) and, compared with the professionalism of their corporate and labor adversaries, still relatively amateur. After Reagan, environmental organizations typified the professionalism of public-interest advocacy across the board. Although this process was under way before Reagan entered the White House (witness the changes at the Wilderness Society), it was forcibly accelerated for all environmental organizations during his tenure.[8]

In the late 1970s, the national environmental advocacy community as a whole could still afford a bit of organizational immaturity, what with Jimmy Carter in the White House and generally supportive Democrats dominating Congress, especially such critical venues as the Senate Committee on Energy and the Environment.[9] The Environmental Protection Agency (EPA), even with its struggle to implement the clutch of major environmental laws enacted the previous decade, was led by appointees who often came from the environmental community and tended to sympathize with environmentalists on the issues. Moreover, the agency enjoyed solid if not exactly flush budgetary support. The federal courts, for their part, were still inclined to extend rights to citizens claiming environmental harms. In the main, as Robert Gottlieb observed (not necessarily with approval), during the 1970s, the more mainstream environmental advocates went from being outsiders to insiders.[10] They had become part of the policy process.

The Reagan administration changed all that with dramatic speed and severity and, in the process, provoked a fundamental transformation in the national environmental advocacy organization as a species. Environmentalists were suddenly on the outside looking in on an administration that was pledging a smaller federal government, thoroughgoing regulatory reform, and the devolution of decision-making authority to the states, where only older chapter-based organizations such as Audubon and the National Wildlife Federation had any notable local presence. Moreover, Reagan's appointees to the top federal posts that were central to environmental issues—confirmed by a Senate now run by Republicans—typically came from industry and conservative activist circles; they expressed ideological antipathy to federal regulation and, in some instances, a clear cultural dislike for environmentalists.

As J. Clarence Davies concluded, the Reagan administration sought to "reverse the institutionalization process" in environmental policy started in the 1970s.[11] This effort was later judged to have been a failure. Regulatory "reform" frequently became a smokescreen for outright rollbacks or simple short-term relief for business, and the actions of top-level appointees, in particular

Secretary of the Interior James Watt, sparked congressional and public outcry. Watt, EPA administrator Anne Burford, and several subordinates were all forced out in 1983 and replaced by less polarizing appointees. The administration thereafter pursued a more cautious, low-visibility strategy.[12] Even so, the Reagan era produced a smaller and weaker EPA, which in Reagan's first two years was hit by massive budget cuts and the departure of nearly 4,000 experienced employees due to reductions or resignations, seriously eroding its scientific and technical capacity.[13] It also resulted in diminished federal leadership on environmental protection issues and, through a well-crafted appointment strategy, a federal judiciary that began to restrict judicial access and give primacy to property rights over environmental goals.

The irony, in hindsight, is that the Reagan agenda was also the catalyst that forced all constituent parts of the national environmental community to become more self-sufficient, broader, more mass based, and more professional. The following sections consider the ways in which most national environmental organizations transformed themselves during the 1980s.

Greater Self-Sufficiency

Their cultivated public image as outsiders notwithstanding, by the late 1970s, many national environmental organizations were heavily dependent on access to federal government officials, information, and scientific analysis and, in many instances, outright fiscal support through federal grants and contracts. The now-defunct Conservation Foundation, to offer but one example, generated 28 percent of its overall funding from government grants in 1979.[14] With Reagan, that relationship changed quickly. The erosion of expertise in the EPA, the centralization of information and policy clearance in the Office of Management and Budget, and the narrowing of access to Congress after the Republican takeover of the Senate combined to force environmental organizations to develop or expand in-house legal, scientific, and technical expertise. Even politically conservative organizations such as the National Wildlife Federation and Izaak Walton League, which at first tried to develop working relationships with administration officials, were eventually impelled to reposition themselves in the public eye as independent advocates for environmental protection. Given the political orientation of their members, such a visible distancing proved internally challenging.[15]

Their experience with the Reagan administration taught the national environmental organizations an important lesson: never get too close to or too dependent on the administration in office. A decade later, most of these organizations would maintain a degree of public distance from the Clinton administration (even as many of their staffs left to work for it), for fear of being seen as sacrificing independence for access in the eyes of their supporters.[16]

More Members

Membership in national environmental organizations exploded during the 1980s, in many instances outpacing the growth rates of the 1960s (see table 3.1). In 1980, only four organizations claimed 100,000 members or more; by decade's end, fifteen did—and seven claimed over half a million each. More telling, organizations that had long resisted developing a national member base now did so, usually with great success. The World Wildlife Fund, for example, did not start recruiting individual members until 1981; within a few years, its rolls surpassed 400,000 and kept growing. By 1990, aggregate membership in national environmental organizations had quadrupled to more than 8 million. Even though this figure did not account for duplicate, family, or bulk memberships, an impressive number of Americans could be counted as financial and political supporters of the national environmental advocacy community.

Some of this surge in membership was certainly attributable to spontaneous actions by individuals expressing concern about the Reagan agenda and, later, fear of environmental disaster following the explosion at the Chernobyl nuclear power plant and the *Exxon Valdez* oil spill off Alaska. However, most of it was cultivated by environmental organizations as a deliberate strategy to build their national membership ranks. In part, they were compelled to do so. Reagan's effort to "de-fund the Left" by eliminating a range of federal grant programs forced advocacy organizations to diversify their sources of support. This imperative was particularly clear for organizations that had relied on a mix of foundation grants and government contracts for a significant proportion of their revenues, including law and science organizations such as Environmental Defense and the Natural Resources Defense Council (NRDC). Neither had made a real effort to cultivate a membership base before the 1980s, but thereafter, they posted some of the highest membership growth rates among all national environmental organizations.

In the process, individual dues and contributions became more critical to organizational survival and flexibility. Simply put, a mass base financed greater organizational independence. As Carl Pope, executive director of the Sierra Club, argued in the early 1990s, a large base of dues-paying members produces a more consistent revenue stream, enabling the organization "to bring a lawsuit, to fight a political candidate, to respond to a legislative crisis. So, in a rough sense, we will be stronger if we can grow from our current 600,000 members to 750,000 or 800,000. If we were to fall back to 300,000 we would be substantially weakened."[17] The Sierra Club in 2004 claimed nearly 750,000 members. Organizations that were unable (e.g., Environmental Action) or unwilling (e.g., Izaak Walton League) to build a large national membership base would confront a far more constricted capacity to maneuver, making them more vulnerable to fluctuations in other revenue sources. The mergers of the foundation- and grant-dependent Environmental Policy Institute and Conservation Foundation into member-supported organizations (Friends of the Earth and World Wildlife Fund, respectively) reflected the calculation that an organization without a sufficient mass base was on thinner fiscal ice.

Equally important, maintaining a mass membership base connected an organization to a politically potent constituency of middle-class voters, thereby extending the reach of many organizations beyond the corridors of Congress or the EPA. Organizations that once relied almost exclusively on large donors or foundations to pursue "insider" strategies such as lawsuits and lobbying now developed complementary "outsider" strategies based on public communications and member mobilization (see chapter 5), a strategy intertwined with the usual appeals for member financial support. More members, spread out over more of the nation, meant greater national visibility and a stronger political presence in the minds of members of Congress and even the administration in power. As Audubon chronicler Frank Graham put it, a large membership "gives the Society high visibility and much political leverage from coast to coast. . . . Numbers imply power in a democracy."[18]

Mass membership environmentalism produced its own share of controversies, among them charges of crisis-driven fund-raising, reliance on expensive direct mail, an incessant focus on middle-class lifestyle concerns rather than the health and environmental justice issues affecting less affluent sectors of society, and perceptions that members were little more than passive donors.[19] Whatever the merits of these charges, the shift to mass membership environmentalism clearly connected the national environmental advocacy community as a whole to a national constituency that it previously lacked. Even organizations without local chapters or that gave members little direct voice in governance or policy directions now had to worry about showing results to a larger, broader audience of donors.[20] In the process—and despite images to the contrary—they became a lot less elitist than the conservation organizations of old. How well these organizations represent this mass constituency is always a matter for discussion, but without its development during the 1980s, the national environmental community would be a lot smaller and weaker and, as a result, more politically marginal than critics claim it is.

Accelerated Professionalism

Greater organizational capacity and the need to maintain a mass membership base require more professional staff in more areas of expertise. As table 4.1 shows, the number of full-time staff employed by many major environmental organizations nearly doubled during the 1980s, and many of them were assigned to tasks essential to organizational maintenance—administration, finance, fund-raising, and development.[21]

In the process, the centrality of professional staff to the operations, tactics, and policy directions of environmental organizations only deepened, usually to the dismay of the activists in the ranks. Indeed, the intraorganizational clashes that erupted during the period typically echoed the tensions between the "professionals" and the "amateurs" in the Sierra Club during the battle over Hetch Hetchy.[22] "There really are two separate Sierra Clubs," explained Michael Fischer, executive director from 1987 to 1992. "One is the national club that's focused on Washington, D.C., and the United Nations and the World Development Bank . . . [while the other] is the chapters and the groups, the grassroots, the volunteer-driven."[23] In the case of Environmental Action, that conflict generated paralyzing organizational disarray that figured in its demise. For others (e.g., Wilderness Society, Friends of the Earth), it generated schisms that provoked leadership battles, staff turnover, and the exodus of the activists. But the result was always the same: the professionals won. The imperatives of organizational maintenance and the need to establish a permanent advocacy presence in national politics typically outweighed ideological purity—as it would for mature advocacy organizations across the board.

Triumph of the Manager

Environmental organizations were already trying to balance visionary leadership with greater professional management before the 1980s—recall the issues surrounding the ousters of Brower at the Sierra Club, Brandenborg at the Wilderness Society, and Smith at the NPCA—but the shocks of the Reagan challenge accentuated this shift. In 1984 and 1985 alone, new presidents or executive directors were installed at the Sierra Club, National Audubon Society, Wilderness Society, Friends of the Earth, Environmental Defense, Environmental Action, Greenpeace USA, World Wildlife Fund, and League of Conservation Voters, in several instances following major organizational shakeups.[24] The Sierra Club, in fact, changed executive directors twice during the mid-1980s after having had only two (Brower and Michael McCloskey) during the previous thirty years. Even hard-charging William Turnage was succeeded at the helm of the Wilderness Society by a more "analytic, rational manager," George Frampton.[25]

Table 4.1. Staff of Selected Environmental Organizations, 1970–2000*

Organization	1970	1975	1980	1987	1990	1995	2000
Sierra Club (includes SC Fund)	60	90	145	269	250	294	290
National Audubon Society	275	212		260	315	270	550
National Parks Conservation Assoc.					43	50	89
Izaak Walton League				28	23	24	38
The Wilderness Society				105	135	123	118
National Wildlife Federation			464	540	800	474	692
Ducks Unlimited					275		622
Defenders of Wildlife				37	34	60	121
The Nature Conservancy			77	550	1,150	1,804	2,773
World Wildlife Fund—US				54	244	302	392
Environmental Defense			41	75	110	166	230
Friends of the Earth/EPI/EPC	12		70	40	45	22	32
Natural Resources Defense Council		45	77	150	128	168	195
League of Conservation Voters			5	9	67	22	25
Greenpeace USA				120	250	300	90
Clean Water Action				60	90	50	90
Earthjustice			10				113
Trust for Public Land						200	310
Ocean Conservancy					38	59	63
American Rivers				23	38	25	53
Center for Health, Environment and Justice				12			12
Earth Island Institute					18	38	85
Rainforest Action Network				8	10	23	38
Conservation Fund						41	75
Conservation International					57	88	534
Total				2,340	4,120	4,603	7,630

* Full-time staff, where a distinction is possible.

Sources: IRS Form 990, line 90b (1998–2002) ; annual reports; *Public Interest Profiles* (Washington, D.C.: CQ Press); *Encyclopedia of Associations* (Detroit: Gale Research).

This new cohort was better known for its management expertise, not its environmental activism. The centrality of the managerial ethos is perhaps best personified in Rodger Schlickeisen, selected to lead Defenders of Wildlife in 1991. Defenders had failed to capitalize on the membership surge of the 1980s, and Schlickeisen was its fifth president in a little over a decade—a high turnover rate, even by the turbulent standards of the period. His appointment was noteworthy on two counts: First, his background was in economics and budgeting, not in natural science or the law. Second, his career had not included a succession of positions within the ranks of environmental advocacy. Rather, he had started out at the Office of Management and Budget during the Carter administration, spent time on Capitol Hill as chief of staff to Senator Max Baucus (D-Montana), and, most telling, got experience in the fund-raising world as chief executive officer of Craver, Matthews, Smith & Co., a direct-mail and telemarketing firm that counted among its clients Greenpeace, the Sierra Club, NRDC, and Defenders.[26] Within five years, using direct mail, Schlickeisen doubled Defenders' member base—and its revenue—even as membership leveled off at other environmental organizations. In the process, he also shook up the organization and, as noted in chapter 1, allegedly fired longtime *Defenders* magazine columnist Michael Frome for not being a team player. Schlickeisen was still at the helm in 2004, his longevity underscoring the degree to which the imperatives of organizational maintenance shape leadership needs at national environmental organizations.

Accelerated Niche Positioning

Though only a handful of national advocacy organizations made a serious effort to develop and maintain a national membership base before the 1980s, by 1990, almost all were fishing in the mass membership waters, many with nets in the same ponds.[27] But cultivating a major membership base through direct mail and communications campaigns in a competitive environmental advocacy market required greater attention to the "product" being sold—in particular, the need to differentiate it from the products offered by other organizations in the same sector. This imperative, in turn, required heightened organizational attention to policy, ideological, and tactical niches. Strategic planning and market analysis soon became common practice, producing more purposeful and open niche positioning. Environmental Defense, for example, oriented itself more openly toward market-based solutions after Fred Krupp came on as president in 1984; this allowed it to better distinguish itself from a longtime rival, the more market-skeptical NRDC. In other instances (e.g., NPCA, Wilderness Society, Audubon

Society), the process resulted in a refocusing on historical missions or, like the Conservation Foundation, a merger with a kindred organization.

Greater Cooperation

Finally, Reagan's agenda impelled environmentalists to work with one another. Surprisingly, prior to the 1980s, the national environmental organizations rarely collaborated. In many respects, the national environmental advocacy community was like a very small town where relations among the inhabitants were marked by intense, if usually submerged, competition, often suffused with personal animosities. "Though increasingly professionalized in their composition and their outlook," says Gottlieb, "the groups still had failed to construct a coherent, movement-wide, institutional framework commensurate with their role in establishing a policy nexus in Washington."[28]

But creating such a framework for cooperation was not going to happen on its own. It had to be brokered by a concerned third party. In 1981, the heads of the Henry P. Kendall Foundation brought together the leaders of nine major environmental organizations to discuss the incoming administration and, in the foundation's view, the need for environmentalists to coordinate their agendas, public messages, and advocacy actions. This initial meeting turned into quarterly gatherings of the chief executives of ten national organizations: Friends of the Earth, Environmental Policy Institute, Sierra Club, Wilderness Society, NRDC, National Audubon Society, Environmental Defense, NPCA, National Wildlife Federation, and Izaak Walton League.

Formation of this so-called Group of Ten generated considerable controversy within the broader environmental community. To grassroots activists outside the nation's capital, it appeared exclusionary, open to only a handful of professional advocacy organizations with a strong Washington orientation. To others, its ideological breadth meant that any actions or pronouncements would amount to little more than a lowest common denominator of agreement. Even with their common concerns about the Reagan administration, the ideological gap between Friends of the Earth and, say, the Izaak Walton League was (and is) significant. This concern crystallized in 1985 when the Group of Ten produced a common declaration of priorities for American environmentalism. *An Environmental Agenda for the Future* was hailed by backers as the first expression of common values by the national environmental advocacy community, but it was derided by critics as a watered-down compromise that failed to address fundamental issues of corporate power and social injustice.[29]

The sense of crisis leading to the formation of the Group of Ten subsided as the Reagan administration retreated from its original agenda, but it left behind an acknowledged need to maintain some kind of framework of discussion and collaboration among environmental organizations. Today, a larger and less exclusive "Green Group" comprises the original Group of Ten plus American Rivers, Earthjustice, Defenders of Wildlife, League of Conservation Voters, National Environmental Trust, Nature Conservancy, Ocean Conservancy, and World Wildlife Fund. Other national organizations that include environmental advocacy in their agendas, such as the Children's Defense Fund, Public Interest Research Group, Union of Concerned Scientists, Native American Rights Fund, and Planned Parenthood, also participate. In all, nearly thirty organizations take part.

The Green Group is not a formal association like the Chamber of Commerce or the Business Roundtable, notes the Sierra Club's Carl Pope. It has more of an informal "convening function," enabling leaders to meet three times a year to discuss issues "unique to the roles of executive directors managing national environmental organizations"; it is "an informal way of coordinating activities such as meeting with a key cabinet officer or member of Congress."[30] Without the Reagan challenge or the impetus of the Kendall Foundation, one wonders whether environmentalists would have overcome their own intramural competition to create such a group on their own.

More than any other single factor, then, the tectonic shocks generated by Reagan's term in office transformed the national environmental groups into more professional and more mass-based advocacy organizations. Environmental commentators and activists on the ideological left, in particular, often argue that the size and professionalism of the national organizations do little to challenge orthodox economic or political values, prevent the election of environmentally suspect candidates, or even protect the environment.[31] I address these issues in the last chapter. Less debatable is the fact that most of the organizations that survived the Reagan years were far better prepared individually and collectively to meet the next set of external shocks—in particular, the Republican takeover of Congress after the 1994 elections—than they might have been otherwise.

CARRYING CAPACITY

Professional policy advocacy requires money, and professional advocacy at the national level requires a lot of it. Resources are always limited, but advocacy organizations, unlike most biological species, do not face a fixed resource base. They can devise new sources of support or reposition their organizations to take advantage of resource availability.[32] In short, to some extent, they can go where the money is. How advocacy organizations generate resources or adapt themselves to exploit available resources is a critical element in their evolution as organizations and the roles they play in the broader political system.

Unlike farm groups, business firms, labor unions, or trade associations, environmental organizations depend almost entirely on voluntary donations for their financial lifeblood. They, like all citizens groups, confront the "free-rider" problem: one cannot be forced to contribute, nor does failure to do so forfeit one's right to benefit from any environmental gains obtained.[33] Moreover, every potential donor is fair game. An individual's membership in the Wilderness Society does not preclude the Sierra Club from seeking that person's support. As a result, these organizations exist in a competitive market for environmental advocacy support, conditioned by the aggregate decisions of millions of relatively small donors and a few thousand larger ones. How these individuals will "vote" with their dollars is always on the minds of an organization's fund-raising specialists, since any major shift in mass attitude on a particular issue or in the public image of a particular organization can spell fiscal trouble. Ask Greenpeace.

These organizations share a common concern about the overall carrying capacity for environmental advocacy; that is, whether there are sufficient resources to sustain existing organizations—forget about new ones. Table 4.2 shows annual revenues for each of the organizations in this study for fiscal years 1994 to 2002, organized by the categories listed in chapter 3. I also provide revenues for fiscal year 1991 for a subset of organizations to provide an additional reference point. Revenue figures include all sources (e.g., individual donations, income from investments), so they offer a good overall picture of an organization's fiscal health.

The time span is constricted. owing to the availability of complete data, but there are some telling indicators. Between 1994 and 2000, aggregate revenues for the organizations included here more than doubled. Revenues slumped in 2001, due in part to the bursting of the stock market bubble that had fueled much of its previous growth, and in part to a momentary shift in donations to charities such as the Red Cross following the attacks of September 11. Stock market–related impacts are arguably most apparent for those organizations that derive significant income from investments, including the Sierra Club Foundation, Audubon Society, and World Wildlife Fund. Aggregate revenues then pick up somewhat in 2002, to over $2 billion. Overall, there seems to be a significant resource base for environmental action in the United States.

A more nuanced perspective emerges as we disentangle revenues a little. Table 4.3 shows the average percentage of revenues derived from direct contributions by individuals, corporations, and foundations, as reported on lines 1

Table 4.2. Annual Revenues, FY1991–FY2002

	1991	1994	1995	1996	1997	1998	1999	2000	2001	2002	FY94–FY00	FY00–FY02
Keystone Organizations												
Sierra Club	$40.6	$38.5	$44.2	$46.6	$41.2	$48.4	$48.6	$55.5	$52.2	$60.1	44%	8%
Sierra Club Foundation[†]	n/a	8.6	12.3	9.7	14.6	17.9	26.6	63.8	73.8	23.6	642%	–63%
Natural Resources Defense Council	$16.9	27.0	25.0	25.4	27.5	30.1	34.6	39.1	55.7	46.4	45%	19%
Environmental Defense	$15.8	21.2	22.4	27.0	26.7	29.0	31.2	35.5	42.9	43.8	67%	23%
National Wildlife Federation	$77.3	88.4	87.4	88.1	95.6	98.5	98.0	98.9	112.0	102.1	12%	3%
World Wildlife Fund—U.S.	n/a	74.6	66.6	75.4	79.4	102.3	104.2	110.2	118.4	93.2	48%	–15%
Sectoral Actors												
Greenpeace USA[#]	65.0	n/a	n/a	2.5	3.5	10.2	9.9	n/a	14.5	17.2	n/a	n/a
Greenpeace Fund[†]	n/a	7.2	8.4	7.3	8.4	7.1	10.7	7.9	10.7	8.7	10%	10%
Friends of the Earth	2.5	2.5	2.4	2.6	2.5	2.9	3.8	3.6	3.8	3.8	44%	6%
Wilderness Society	17.0	15.5	13.9	14.5	15.0	14.7	18.4	17.2	24.1	18.8	11%	9%
Defenders of Wildlife	5.2	6.2	6.6	8.6	12.2	14.9	18.9	16.1	24.1	21.8	160%	35%
National Audubon Society	38.0	35.0	47.9	46.9	47.5	64.0	63.5	85.3	98.2	78.6	144%	–8%
National Parks Conservation Association	9.6	17.9	16.2	18.7	18.8	17.7	17.9	20.1	22.8	20.9	12%	4%
Nature Conservancy	254.2	293.9	305.8	307.6	358.7	411.2	569.4	784.3	546.6	972.4	167%	24%
Izaak Walton League	1.8	2.8	1.8	2.5	2.8	3.0	3.5	3.6	5.2	4.3	29%	19%
Ducks Unlimited	63.7	60.8	65.8	70.6	81.6	93.7	108.6	119.6	123.8	125.1	97%	5%

Table 4.2. Annual Revenues, FY1991-FY2002 (*Continued*)

	1991	1994	1995	1996	1997	1998	1999	2000	2001	2002	FY94–FY00	FY00–FY02
Niche Players												
Earth Island Institute	1.6	2.9	2.9	3.3	3.9	4.8	3.2	4.7	4.5	4.9	62%	4%
Clean Water Fund†#	14.6	n/a	n/a	1.7	1.6	2.1	2.0	2.5	3.2	4.4	47%	76%
League of Conservation Voters Fund†	n/a	0.6	1.0	0.6	0.9	1.6	5.3	11.1	6.2	7.0	1750%	–37%
Earthjustice	9.7	11.3	14.5	13.3	17.1	16.2	16.5	27.7	21.5	17.9	145%	–35%
Trust for Public Land	n/a	28.6	29.9	49.6	52.9	89.4	104.9	120.9	154.5	126.5	323%	5%
Ocean Conservancy	5.6	6.3	7.2	7.2	6.5	8.0	9.1	9.4	9.5	8.9	49%	–5%
American Rivers	1.6	2.2	2.6	2.6	3.8	3.6	3.7	5.8	5.6	5.5	164%	–5%
Sea Shepherds#	n/a	n/a	0.9	0.6	0.7	3.5	0.2	1.5	1.0	0.9	67%	–40%
Center for Health, Environment, and Justice	n/a	0.6	0.8	0.8	0.9	1.7	1.8	2.9	1.6	1.0	263%	–66%
National Park Trust	n/a	2.5	7.8	9.0	4.9	5.9	4.9	4.9	3.6	1.2	96%	–76%
Rainforest Action Network	n/a	1.9	1.9	1.9	2.1	2.6	2.8	3.0	2.4	2.2	58%	–27%
Conservation Fund	n/a	34.5	23.2	31.4	23.6	43.4	66.6	67.1	64.2	60.1	94%	–10%
Conservation International	n/a	14.6	13.0	17.0	17.2	25.5	37.7	41.5	68.9	222.7	184%	437%
Earth Share	n/a	7.7	7.1	7.1	7.1	8.9	7.2	7.7	8.5	7.9	0%	3%
Environmental Working Group#	n/a	n/a	n/a	n/a	n/a	n/a	0.8	1.5	2.2	1.8	88%	20%
National Environmental Trust#	n/a	n/a	1.4	3.0	4.2	6.2	7.5	18.0	11.6	10.7	1186%	–41%
Total revenues	640.7	813.8	840.9	903.1	983.4	1,189.0	1,442.0	1,790.9	1,697.8	2,124.4	120%	19%

* In millions of dollars, rounded. Total revenue can also include the value of in-kind services (e.g., legal support).

† Tax-exempt 501(c)(3) fund-raising affiliates of non-tax-exempt 501(c)(4) main organizations. "Grants" from the 501(c)(3) to the 501(c)(4) are not included in revenue for the latter.

Revenue growth was calculated from first available data point. Growth for Greenpeace USA was not calculated.

Sources: IRS Form 990, line 12, as provided by guidestar.org; annual reports.

Table 4.3. Direct Contributions as a Percentage of Total Revenue, FY1994–FY2002*

Organization	Avg. %
National Wildlife Federation	52.5
The Nature Conservancy	68.2
Sierra Club	69.5
National Audubon Society	69.5
Earthjustice	81.6
Izaak Walton League	84.4
Conservation Fund	85.9
Ducks Unlimited	86.5
Sea Shepherds	87.1
Earth Share	87.1
Environmental Working Group	87.1
National Environmental Trust	87.1
Earth Island Institute	87.7
Defenders of Wildlife	88.0
Trust for Public Land	88.8
National Parks Conservation Association	89.5
Ocean Conservancy	89.6
Center for Health, Environment, and Justice	89.8
Sierra Club Foundation	90.7
World Wildlife Fund	90.9
Environmental Defense	91.6
Natural Resources Defense Council	92.4
The Wilderness Society	92.6
Rainforest Action Network	92.8
American Rivers	93.2
Conservation International	93.9
League of Conservation Voters Fund	95.6
Greenpeace (combined)	95.8
Friends of the Earth	96.4
National Park Trust	97.5
Clean Water Fund	98.9

* Figures represent the average proportion of direct contributions to overall revenue for the years covered.

and 3 of IRS Form 990. This average leaves out revenues from investments, government grants, program income (e.g., access or rental fees), and sales (e.g., land, merchandise), so it is a slightly better indicator of contemporaneous levels of public support for any particular organization. As is clear, direct contributions of some kind dictate fiscal health for most organizations. A few—the land conservancies in particular—generate significant revenues from government grants and sales of land or merchandise, but most depend on the success of their fund-raising and development efforts.

Whether that resource base is finite depends more on a particular organization than anything else, even taking macroeconomic and political factors into account. As discussed later, organizations vary in the types of revenue they seek or accept, so for each organization, the potential resource base has a specific shape and even a specific limit. As Robert Lowry concludes about the capacity of environmental organizations to raise revenues, "the options available to them at any given time are often limited by the group's institutional structure and internal constraints that reflect the opportunity set at the time long run choices were made."[34] Although environmental organizations have shown impressive creativity in tapping new revenue sources, the possible boundaries of any organization's resource base must be considered when discussing organizational maintenance and policy strategies. Some fluctuations may reflect strategic decisions by donors about the optimal use of their funds. For example, the dramatic rise in revenue for the League of Conservation Voters Fund, which supports the tax-exempt "voter education" programs of the otherwise non-tax-exempt league, reflected the opportunity to elect environmentally friendly (generally Democratic) candidates to Congress and the White House in 1998 and 2000. The sharp drop-off thereafter could reflect (besides the general slump in support after 2000) a shift in election-related donations to the Democratic Party in anticipation of the ban on "soft money" with the passage of the McCain-Feingold campaign finance law.[35]

More instructive are variations by sector. The strongest overall rates of growth throughout this period were at the land conservancies—Trust for Public Land, Nature Conservancy, Conservation International, Ducks Unlimited, and Conservation Fund. The fluctuations and then the near collapse in revenue at the National Park Trust may reflect its comparatively narrower purpose—purchasing national park "inholdings"—although poor revenue growth at the NPCA and Wilderness Society suggest a broader public lands–specific explanation. In any case, it is instructive that environmentalism's growth sector is dedicated less to changing the national landscape than to buying it.[36] These organizations, as well as state-level counterparts, such as the 40,000-member Trustees of Reservations in Massachusetts, usually purchase land or the development rights to it, so their actions rarely confront core societal values about private property and generally require little government action.[37] Moreover, donations translate directly into acres purchased or otherwise set aside through conservation restrictions, so it is easier for these organizations to show evidence of performance to donors and, equally important, to increasingly influential ratings outfits such as the American Institute of Philanthropy.[38] Land conservancies also have lower fund-raising overhead expenses and are politically neutral, if not entirely apolitical, giving them greater access to corporate and foundation support. The Nature Conservancy alone reaped $445 million in total contributions in fiscal year 2000, putting it in the top ten of *all* nonprofit recipients of private support.[39] Indeed, taking the Conservancy out of the aggregate has a major impact on the overall revenue picture. The Nature Conservancy thrives, joked one Sierra Club leader, because "when corporate America comes to God someone has to take up the collection."[40]

Revenues are more problematic for more ideological and activist organizations such as Greenpeace USA and the Rainforest Action Network, suggesting limits on their respective messages and tactics to attract a middle-class donor base. This phenomenon is nothing new: advocacy organizations seeking profound social change always have a harder time generating funds from a mass base than do organizations dedicated to saving a particular species or landscape. The World Wildlife Fund, for example, can offer material incentives, such as plush stuffed toys, to its massive actual and potential donor base to promote the preservation of pandas and other endangered species. The Rainforest Action Network, by contrast, is less likely to generate comparable funds based on its boycott of Scott Paper or Home Depot as a way of halting the depletion of tropical forests.[41]

Having said this, however, the spectacular growth of Greenpeace during the late 1980s suggests that under the right conditions, even openly ideological direct-action organizations can catch mass public attention and donations, without stuffed toys. Greenpeace's no-compromise image and flamboyant protest tactics seemed to resonate with a mass public concerned about environmental degradation after Chernobyl and, perhaps, put off by the heavy-handedness of the organization's foes. The sinking of its ship *Rainbow Warrior* by French commandos in 1985 to keep it from sailing into an area slated for nuclear weapons testing had an especially galvanic impact, in part because the explosion killed a photographer on board. As a result, Greenpeace USA took in over $60 million in revenue in 1990.[42] Yet Greenpeace soon discovered that image was not enough to sustain its direct-mail-generated revenue base once public attention shifted to other issues (e.g., recession, the 1991 Persian Gulf war) and middle-class donations shifted to organizations that could (and did) claim tangible results. More than a decade later, Greenpeace USA occupies a more modest advocacy niche and claims only around 250,000 supporters.

Variations also occur *within* advocacy sectors, suggesting the influence of organizational factors such as leadership, strategic plans, and fund-raising techniques. For example, the National Wildlife Federation fared somewhat poorly during the 1990s compared with Defenders of Wildlife and the National Audubon Society. The federation's large size and expansive breadth may have been a factor in these differences, although its net assets were smaller than those of Audubon (see table 4.4). Perhaps Defenders benefited from more stable and effective leadership under Schlickeisen, or perhaps it occupied a more popular species niche (e.g., wolves and other predators) within the larger domestic wildlife sector. Whether its success came at the expense of the National Wildlife Federation is hard to say, although its repeated denunciation of actions by congressional Republicans during the 1990s may have given Defenders an edge with elements of the donor population that were dissatisfied with the National Wildlife Federation's more modulated response. What is clearer, however, is that each sector may have its own resource base, the unique shape and depth of which has impacts on the organizations within it.

To offer just one more angle on the aggregate resource picture, table 4.4 displays net assets for each organization over several years, which, by 2002, had gone beyond an astounding $4 billion in the aggregate. Advocacy organizations, like universities or businesses, are keen to build up reserves from which they can derive investment income in good times or draw funds in bad times. Few environmental organizations had much in the way of assets even two decades ago. The Sierra Club, for example, listed only a little over $1 million in net assets in 1980, but today its combined net assets (the club plus the foundation) exceed $120 million. Even now, however, there is wide variation among types of organizations. The land conservancies account for the major share, with a large proportion of their assets in the land they hold (also true for the Audubon Society). In theory, some of these assets are liquid, but in practice, selling conservation property is politically explosive. One-third of the Nature Conservancy's net assets are in the form of investments, mostly securities, so it has a significant fiscal cushion. By contrast, most niche advocacy organizations have net assets that run below annual revenues, suggesting a degree of vulnerability should they hit a sustained rough patch.

The sharp drop in assets for many organizations after 2000 generally reflects the dismal performance of the stock market, which weakened organizations' investment portfolios at the same time that it deflated the wealth of potential donors. At other times, fluctuations in assets reflected more organization-specific problems. Note in particular the decline in net assets for Greenpeace Fund and

Table 4.4. Net Assets, FY1997–FY2002*

Organization	1997	1998	1999	2000	2001	2002	FY97–FY00	FY00–02
Sierra Club	$10.7	$15.4	$23.5	$28.1	$30.5	$31.0	163%	10%
Sierra Club Foundation[†]	$25.4	$29.3	$41.4	$75.9	$117.7	$96.7	199%	27%
National Audubon Society	$92.1	$116.2	$131.8	$167.9	$173.2	$167.7	82%	0%
National Parks Conservation Association	$2.1	$2.7	$4.7	$6.2	$6.8	$8.9	195%	44%
Izaak Walton League	$5.8	$5.8	$5.5	$5.5	$6.5	$6.4	–5%	16%
The Wilderness Society	$9.6	$11.2	$16.0	$15.9	$18.9	$15.9	66%	0%
National Wildlife Federation	$23.5	$27.2	$30.1	$33.8	$25.5	$16.3	44%	–52%
Ducks Unlimited	$25.9	$32.9	$46.1	$48.6	$46.2	$32.3	88%	–34%
Defenders of Wildlife	$8.8	$10.9	$14.5	$15.6	$15.8	$16.1	77%	3%
The Nature Conservancy	$1,484.5	$1,770.7	$2,183.4	$2,571.3	$2,670.1	$2,932.0	73%	14%
World Wildlife Fund—US	$84.5	$114.5	$133.6	$152.6	$148.9	$134.1	81%	–12%
Environmental Defense	$21.7	$28.2	$33.5	$42.3	$43.5	$44.8	95%	6%
Friends of the Earth	$0.9	$1.7	$2.3	$1.6	$2.0	$1.6	78%	0%
League of Conservation Voters Fund[†]	$0.6	$0.8	$2.9	$2.3	$0.9	$1.3	283%	–43%
Natural Resources Defense Council	$35.6	$44.0	$53.5	$61.3	$71.8	$46.4	72%	–24%
Clean Water Action Fund[†]	$0.7	$0.9	$0.7	$0.8	$0.9	$1.9	14%	138%
Greenpeace Fund[†]	$12.7	$12.4	$11.4	$8.7	$8.9	$7.5	–31%	–14%
Earthjustice	$10.5	$15.4	$18.2	$28.7	$27.8	$23.8	173%	–17%
Trust for Public Land	$47.3	$92.9	$102.3	$145.2	$151.2	$160.6	207%	11%
Ocean Conservancy	$16.0	$19.4	$23.5	$33.2	$22.5	$16.9	108%	–49%

Table 4.4. Net Assets, FY1997–FY2002* *(Continued)*

Organization	1997	1998	1999	2000	2001	2002	FY97–FY00	FY00–02
American Rivers	$0.7	$1.2	$1.6	$2.9	$3.4	$3.5	314%	21%
Sea Shepherds	$0.5	$3.2	$3.5	$4.0	$3.7	$3.2	700%	–20%
Center for Health, Environment, and Justice	$0.6	$1.2	$1.4	$2.2	$1.4	$0.6	267%	–73%
Earth Island Institute	$2.8	$3.4	$3.1	$3.6	$2.9	$2.5	29%	–31%
National Park Trust	$3.0	$4.8	$4.7	$4.7	$4.7	$4.1	57%	–13%
Rainforest Action Network	$0.2	$0.5	$0.6	$0.8	$1.0	$1.2	300%	50%
Conservation Fund	$93.6	$107.8	$126.0	$146.1	$180.7	$193.6	56%	33%
Conservation International	$14.6	$24.2	$81.5	$110.2	$126.9	$279.8	655%	154%
Earth Share	$0.9	$1.0	$1.2	$1.0	$0.9	$1.2	11%	20%
Environmental Working Group	n/a	n/a	n/a	$1.0	$1.1	$1.4	n/a	40%
National Environmental Trust	$3.0	$4.5	$4.7	$4.7	$4.7	$4.1	57%	–13%
Total net assets	$2,038.8	$2,504.3	$3,107.2	$3,726.7	$3,921.0	$4,257.4	83%	14%
(Minus The Nature Conservancy)	$554.3	$733.6	$923.8	$1,155.4	$1,250.9	$1,325.4	108%	15%

* In millions of dollars, rounded.

† Tax-exempt affiliate of non-tax-exempt parent organization. Net assets cannot be discerned for LCV, CWA, and Greenpeace.

Source: IRS Form 990, lines 19 and 21.

the Izaak Walton League during the late 1990s, even as other organizations added to their bases. In the former case, the decline can be explained by a significant drawdown on assets to help its non-tax-exempt affiliate, Greenpeace USA, reduce a multimillion-dollar operating deficit that accumulated as it hemorrhaged members and revenue during the 1990s. Greenpeace got its fiscal house in order following its 2000 merger with—or, from another perspective, takeover by—Ozone Action, a direct-action organization whose founder now leads the reconstituted Greenpeace. In the case of the Izaak Walton League, losses in net assets suggested niche-specific problems. The league may have had difficulty differentiating itself from other wildlife and recreation organizations such as the National Wildlife Federation and Ducks Unlimited and, from another angle, organizations such as American Rivers on freshwater pollution issues. Its better performance since 2000 may reflect a strategic effort to position itself as a viable alternative during a period of Republican dominance. Finally, the collapse in revenue at the National Park Trust, some of which it attributed to problems with mail delivery in the Washington, D.C., area following a spate of anthrax scares, spells serious trouble unless the organization can expand its base of support for what might be an unsustainable policy niche. National Park Trust went through its own strategic planning process in 2001, and chief among its recommendations was the need to "commit to the diversification of and increase in NPT's sources of income."[43]

DIVERSIFYING THE RESOURCE BASE

National Park Trust's desire to diversify its revenue sources is warranted, if only because dependence on one or a few sources unduly restricts an organization's flexibility. No money comes without strings, and where an organization gets its money can affect its goals, tactics, and internal modes of operation, even in subtle ways. Therefore, no organization wants to be too dependent on any one type of support. The broader the fiscal base, the better.[44]

Table 4.5 displays the range of revenue sources pursued by the organizations in this study, based on an assessment of their annual reports and tax forms. As one would expect, the largest and most broadly focused organizations (e.g., Sierra Club, NRDC) also have the greatest range of revenue streams—from individual donations and foundation grants to investments, affinity credit cards, and consumer product marketing deals. Others depend more heavily on a few revenue sources, either because they abjure some (especially corporate donations) or because they have positioned themselves with a specific revenue base in mind. For example, Conservation International occupies a policy and tactical niche that, to date, enables it to rely on major donors,

Figure 4.5. Regular Sources of Revenue

Organization	Dues	Other	Fund	Work	Grants	Gov't	Corp
National Audubon Society	X	X		X	X	X	X
National Wildlife Federation	X	X		X	X	X	X
Ducks Unlimited	X	X	X		X	X	X
Sierra Club	X	X	X		X		
National Parks Conservation Association	X	X		X	X	X	X
The Nature Conservancy	X	X		X	X		X
World Wildlife Fund—US	X	X		X	X	X	X
American Rivers	X	X		X	X	X	X
Izaak Walton League	X	X		X	X	X	X
Natural Resources Defense Council	X	X		X	X	X	
Defenders of Wildlife	X	X		X	X	X	
The Wilderness Society	X	X		X	X		
Environmental Defense	X	X		X	X	X	
Trust for Public Land		X		X	X	X	X
National Park Trust	X	X		X	X	X	
Conservation International		X		X	X	X	X
Earth Island Institute	X	X			X	X	
Conservation Fund		X		X	X	X	X
Ocean Conservancy	X	X			X	X	
Earthjustice		X		X	X		
Friends of the Earth	X	X		X	X		
Center for Health, Environment, and Justice	X	X		X	X		
Rainforest Action	X	X		X	X		
Clean Water Action		X	X		X		
Greenpeace	X	X	X				
League of Conservation Voters	X	X	X				
Earth Share		X		X			
Environmental Working Group		X			X		
National Environmental Trust		X			X		
Sea Shepherds		X					

Legend: Dues, annual membership; Other, non-dues donations; Fund, affiliated foundation; Work, workplace giving; Grants, from foundations; Gov't, government grants; Corp, major corporations such as General Motors; Invest, securities, etc.; Mag, available to general readers and/or accepts advertising; Books, self-produced publications, videos, etc.; List, rents mailing list; Royalty, over-time income from publications, property, etc.; Stuff, merchandise; Trips, sponsored outings; Fees, payments for services, litigation costs, etc.; Card, affinity credit card; License, for use of name on merchandise; Land, regular revenue from land sales, exchanges, etc.

Sources: Based on assessment of annual reports, IRS Form 990, and websites for multiple years. Affiliated foundations obtain revenue from multiple sources.

Invest	Mag	Books	List	Royalty	Stuff	Trips	Fees	Card	License	Land
X	X	X	X	X	X	X	X	X	X	X
X	X	X	X	X	X	X	X	X	X	
X	X	X	X	X	X		X	X	X	X
X	X	X	X	X	X	X	X	X	X	
X	X	X	X	X	X	X	X		X	
X	X	X	X		X		X	X	X	X
X			X	X	X	X	X	X	X	
X			X	X	X	X	X		X	
X		X	X	X	X			X	X	
X	X	X	X	X	X		X			
X	X		X	X	X		X	X	X	
X			X	X	X	X	X			X
X			X	X			X	X	X	
X			X		X		X	X		X
X				X		X	X			X
X		X		X					X	X
	X	X		X	X		X			
X				X			X			X
X			X	X			X			
X		X	X		X		X			
				X	X		X			
	X	X					X			
							X			
			X							
X							X			
							X			
X										

foundations, corporations, and other institutions (e.g., the World Bank) for nearly all its revenue. Although Conservation International accepts smaller donations from its 70,000 supporters, it avoids direct-mail solicitation or the types of member development efforts common at the Sierra Club and other member-based organizations. By contrast, Clean Water Action and its affiliated Clean Water Fund rely almost entirely on smaller individual contributions to support public education and grassroots mobilization efforts; thus, they face a very different set of opportunities and constraints.[45]

The Sierra Club offers a useful case study of diversification and how the relative mix of revenue streams can change over time. Table 4.6 shows the distribution of revenue sources for the Sierra Club from 1976 to 2002. In the mid-1970s, the Sierra Club was still a largely regional organization of outdoors enthusiasts, albeit one with a national reputation. As such, it generated nearly 70 percent of its revenue from three sources: annual dues, outings, and sales of books and calendars. By 2002, it was generating more than 80 percent of its revenue in the form of dues, life memberships, bequests, and other contributions directly to it or through the Sierra Club Foundation.

However, even as the Sierra Club became more dependent on contributions, it grew less dependent on annual dues. As table 4.7 suggests, it was not alone. In fact, some organizations (e.g., Wilderness Society, Defenders of Wildlife) no longer publicly distinguish between "membership dues" and "individual contributions" in annual reports or on federal tax forms. In some instances (e.g., Wilderness Society), this strategy may mask stagnant or declining membership totals. However, this mingling of revenue sources also reflects the more basic reality that many advocacy organizations no longer make a conceptual distinction between types of individual contributions, if they ever did. All contributors are "members."[46] Only seven of the organizations in this study continue to make such a distinction in their annual reports or federal tax returns, and four of them are older conservation organizations. For those that do make this distinction, annual dues make up a relatively small percentage of revenues, and for all but one, that share declined over the 1990s as organizations encountered apparent limits to growth in their membership bases. That revenues and budgets continued to increase suggests that organizations have compensated by expanding their reliance on other types of donations.

Even though annual dues play a relatively small role in revenues, for most organizations, developing a base of loyal members (as opposed to more episodic "supporters") continues to be critical to long-term survival. For example, as part of its 2001 strategic plan, the board of the National Park Trust established a membership program after having relied largely on occasional donations since the organization's creation. Two years later, it proudly announced that it had

Table 4.6. Distribution of Revenue, the Sierra Club, FY1976–FY2002

	FY1976	FY1980	FY1982	FY1986	FY1990	FY1994	FY1996	FY2000	FY2002
Membership dues	32.7%	33.0%	40.2%	35.4%	37.2%	31.7%	30.3%	26.8%	27.5%
Life memberships (as of FY89)					2.7%	1.7%	1.2%	1.2%	1.1%
Sales & royalties (FY77–FY87)	14.9%	22.0%	18.8%	20.2%	9.4%	10.7%	9.1%	1.3%	0.9%
Royalties (as of FY87)	5.3%				3.9%	3.5%	3.8%	3.2%	3.3%
Outings and lodge fees	20.2%	12.0%	10.1%	7.1%	6.5%	6.7%	5.2%	5.5%	5.2%
Other contributions & grants	8.1%	14.0%	11.3%	12.3%	11.3%	12.5%	29.7%	32.2%	22.0%
Transfers from Sierra Club Foundation	7.6%	7.0%	6.4%	5.9%	8.3%	10.0%	11.6%	24.6%	35.5%
Transfers from SC Legal Defense Fund	7.9%	7.0%	7.5%	7.3%	11.9%	9.5%			
Investments and other		2.0%	2.0%	7.1%					
Advertising and other*	3.2%	3.0%	3.7%	4.7%	7.2%	8.8%	7.2%	3.0%	1.6%
Capital/major giving campaign					1.5%	1.6%	1.8%	2.2%	2.9%
Deficit						3.3%			
Total	99.9%	100.0%	100.0%	100.0%	99.9%	100.0%	99.9%	100.0%	100.0%
Total revenues	$6,473,418	$9,742,400	$14,898,400	$25,282,900	$40,659,100	$43,007,700	$52,694,50	$73,941,700	$83,833,600
Operating surplus or (deficit)	($75,000)	$215,300	$308,100	$226,000	$953,300	($1,480,500)	$868,700	$4,661,800	$563,900

* Included with "investments and other" until FY1979, then "advertising," then (as of FY1993) "advertising and other."

Source: Annual reports.

Table 4.7. Annual Dues as a Percentage of Total Revenue, 1994–2002*

Organization	1994	1995	1996	1997	1998	1999	2000	2001	2002
Sierra Club	33.3%	30.7%	30.3%	30.5%	30.0%	31.0%	26.9%	30.0%	27.5%
National Audubon Society	28.5%	20.6%	20.1%	21.1%	16.5%	16.0%	11.9%	10.2%	11.3%
National Parks Conservation Association	n/a	n/a	n/a	n/a	7.0%	6.9%	6.6%	5.6%	3.8%
Izaak Walton League	25.9%	13.1%	31.3%	31.7%	40.9%	30.1%	27.0%	n/a	n/a
National Wildlife Federation	23.8%	30.7%	31.0%	20.7%	17.9%	19.3%	19.5%	16.6%	19.0%
Ducks Unlimited	15.7%	5.3%	4.0%	3.3%	3.5%	n/a	n/a	n/a	n/a
Defenders of Wildlife	15.0%	19.6%	24.4%	15.1%	22.4%	n/a	n/a	n/a	n/a
American Rivers	12.2%	16.0%	16.3%	23.4%	15.0%	26.2%	14.9%	17.7%	15.0%
Center for Health, Environment, and Justice	6.3%	3.5%	3.0%	1.9%	3.3%	1.8%	2.6%	1.8%	2.7%
Earth Island Institute	7.6%	8.0%	7.6%	5.6%	6.5%	6.1%	n/a	5.0%	n/a
Rainforest Action Network	16.3%	13.6%	15.9%	13.5%	12.0%	14.5%	12.9%	14.6%	13.7%

* Percentages reflect contributions listed as "membership dues" or "annual dues" in annual reports or on line 3 of IRS Form 990.

surpassed 33,000 members, a conceptual distinction that was clearly made in its public communications.[47]

Major Gifts

Environmental organizations of all types now depend on larger donations by the kinds of longtime members the National Park Trust seeks to cultivate. At best, annual dues of $20 or $30 cover the costs of member recruitment, but they may not do even that. They do, however, get potential supporters in the door. As Lawrence Rothenberg observes about Common Cause, its leaders "have an incentive to keep the monetary cost of membership so low that the ability to pay is irrelevant and that citizens will sample the organization. If contributors are willing to spend more on membership, which should be particularly true over time for those learning that the group is a good match, they can be assured that they will get requests for additional donations."[48] Annual dues are a development loss leader, the cost of building a base of regular contributors who in time may be convinced to go higher on the "pyramid of support"—where the real money is.[49] For example, in fiscal year 2002, American Rivers generated $5 million in total individual contributions. Of that, $3.9 million (78 percent) came in gifts of $5,000 or more. IRS rules enable nonprofits to shield data on specific donors from public scrutiny, so it is hard to know what proportion of that total figure came from individuals versus companies such as Coca-Cola or Office Depot. Either way, in the case of American Rivers, larger donations vastly outweighed membership dues, which accounted for only $832,000.[50]

For organizations like the Sierra Club or Environmental Defense, which take little if any corporate money, the strategy by which they "grew" their membership bases during the 1980s in response to the Reagan presidency had long-term benefits that paid off in the 1990s and beyond. Hundreds of thousands of "cut-rate" members probably had less immediate impact on the action of a president or the voting decisions of particular members of Congress than these organizations proclaimed in their publications, but they certainly provided the base on which organizations were able to enlarge their fiscal capacity. Revenue from individual contributions continued to climb in the 1990s, even as membership levels stagnated or even dropped, suggesting that the members who remained dug deeper in their pockets to support the cause. The Sierra Club, for example, managed to avoid the drop in revenue suffered by other organizations when the stock market slumped, partly by focusing attention on the 40,000 of its 700,000 members with the capacity to give $10,000 or more.[51] Although such donations may seem large, they pale in comparison to individual gifts of hundreds of thousands and more given to its affiliated

Sierra Club Foundation during the market boom. The foundation's reliance on large individual gifts and foundation grants explains its sharp drop in revenue in after 2001.[52]

Foundation Grants

Private foundation grants to national environmental organizations exceeded $70 million in 1999.[53] This is not a small amount, to be sure, but it is a relatively minor part of overall revenue. In addition, more than $40 million of that amount went to the Nature Conservancy, mostly to purchase land. Even so, foundation money often plays a pivotal and sometimes controversial role in the environmental community.

Foundations provided critical seed capital to virtually every organization created during environmentalism's formative years in the 1960s and early 1970s, and several depended heavily on foundation support until they were compelled to diversify. For example, in the late 1970s, the Natural Resources Defense Council relied on government contracts and foundation support—from the Ford Foundation in particular—for more than half its revenue. But the Ford Foundation got out of public-interest law in 1979, and government grants dried up during the Reagan administration and never really came back. In 2002, by contrast, the NRDC got less than 20 percent of its revenue from private foundations and almost nothing from government grants.[54]

Even with its relatively modest role in financing environmental organizations, and even though smaller organizations may not have the staff resources necessary to obtain and manage a major grant, foundation money is still attractive. It makes an organization a bit less dependent on members, usually takes less time than cultivating significant gifts, and, in some instances, supports programs that may hold little allure for individual donors. For example, organizations with significant activity in developing nations—Conservation International and the World Wildlife Fund in particular—rely heavily on foundation and corporate support.

Foundation money is also attractive because it comes with clear strings attached. Grants are usually earmarked for specific projects, rarely for an organization's general fund, and foundation program officers monitor performance to ensure compliance. But foundation money can drive an organization's agenda unless it maintains sufficient internal safeguards against seeking grants just to maintain itself—always a temptation for small organizations in particular. Moreover, as the public-interest law organizations discovered with the Ford Foundation, changes in foundation priorities can leave a dependent organization high and dry. As noted, most American foundations also are loath to fund organizations with "radical" orientations or tactics, so Greenpeace would be unlikely to get much grant money, even if it sought it. Besides being ideologically centrist, most large foundations are impelled by their own tax status to make grants solely for "exempt purposes," which precludes lobbying or other overtly political activities.[55] Organizations such as Friends of the Earth can turn to a few of the more liberal foundations (e.g., the Charles Stewart Mott Foundation) to support research and public education projects, but little goes directly for organizational development.

Perhaps the greatest and most controversial impact of foundation money is its potential to set the agenda for entire sectors of environmental advocacy. Like the Ford Foundation did for public-interest law in the 1970s, the Pew Charitable Trusts have played a major agenda-setting role within the national environmental community in recent years by funding public education efforts on climate change, oceans, and forests. Some $35 million in Pew support went to environmental initiatives in 1999 alone, but the program officers at Pew were not content to simply support programs at existing organizations. Instead, they created new niche organizations around their key initiatives. Some were joint arrangements—for example, the Pew Wilderness Center with Earthjustice, and the Heritage Forests Campaign run through the Audubon Society. Others, the Pew Center on Climate Change and the National Environmental Trust, in particular, were created as stand-alone operations that in time would obtain revenue from other sources.[56] In 1998, foundations (including Pew and the David and Lucile Packard Foundation) provided nearly $10 million to help the Heritage Forests Campaign and other environmental organizations shape the Clinton administration's eventual ban on road building and commercial logging on 58.5 million acres of national forest lands. In the process, the foundations incurred the wrath of the timber industry and congressional Republicans.[57]

This potential to shape agendas, as well as their closely held decision-making processes, makes foundations controversial, even among environmental activists.[58] Major foundations are accused of ignoring "environmental justice" issues that concern the poor and people of color in favor of more mainstream concerns such as endangered species and land acquisition.[59] For example, in October 2001, the new Gordon and Betty Moore Foundation (he founded the Intel Corporation) made a ten-year, $260 million grant to Conservation International to support its biodiversity programs in rainforest regions. Although many applauded the grant as marking a new stage in the battle to preserve endangered species and habitats, the foundation was criticized by grassroots activists and some scientists who disagreed with Conservation International's focus on setting aside biological "hot spots."[60] Some militant wilderness campaign activists in the United States have accused Pew program officers of demanding major changes in the management of their organizations and of withholding funds from any organization they deem too controversial. Others point out that foundations often have board members who hail from major corporations, so they are unlikely to fund any organization that openly criticizes market capitalism or corporate behavior.[61]

Corporate Donations

No other source of revenue is more consistently problematic and controversial for environmental organizations than funding from corporations. Although corporate support fits most comfortably within the ideological orientations and policy interests of more centrist or conservative organizations, such as the National Wildlife Federation and the Izaak Walton League, a wider array of organizations typically maintain some type of "corporate partnerships" or advisory boards. None, however, replicated the National Wildlife Federation's "corporate conservation council," which included companies such as Conoco, Du Pont, Dow Chemical, Duke Power, Miller Brewing, Monsanto, 3M, U.S. Steel, and Weyerhauser.[62] According to historian Thomas Allen, National Wildlife Federation president Jay Hair created the council in the 1980s, with an annual membership fee of $10,000, out of the "belief that the corporate world and the Federation can work out ways to balance the need for economic growth with the need for protecting natural resources."[63] However, the council sparked criticism among environmentalists and proved to be a public-relations headache for the federation, so it was discontinued after Hair's departure in 1995. The federation continues to seek corporate giving, but apparently with greater concern about the perceptions such funding can create.

The studiously apolitical land conservancies are by far the most successful harvesters of direct corporate support, followed by traditional wildlife organizations (e.g., National Wildlife Federation, Ducks Unlimited) and more market-oriented organizations (e.g., Izaak Walton League). For environmental activists on the left, in particular, such corporate money is tantamount to buying a softer image, if not outright blood atonement. The World Wildlife Fund, for example, accepts donations from, among others, Du Pont, Chevron-Texaco, Alcoa, Philip Morris, and Home Depot. Every one of these corporations has been on some other environmental organization's hit list. Home Depot (the nation's largest home-improvement store operator), for example, was the target of a global boycott organized by the Rainforest Action Network until it agreed to stop selling lumber harvested from endangered forests in the United States and abroad.[64] Similar charges of corporate "green-washing" have been aimed at the Nature Conservancy for including on its board executives from American Electric Power, which the NRDC called the nation's worst power company for its record on air pollution, and General Motors, which Environmental Defense called "Global Warmer Number One."[65]

Besides helping land conservancies buy property, what does corporate money purchase? Although evidence of outright corporate "capture" is slim—after all, corporate money goes to those already considered friends—at a minimum, corporate money is public relations, particularly when the company or industry in question might be under public scrutiny.[66] As the Sierra Club's Michael Fischer recounted, "corporations give money from their public affairs budgets. They are giving money in order to get something. They want to get credibility."[67] In this regard, donations to the Nature Conservancy or the World Wildlife Fund by Home Depot or Chevron cannot help but burnish a company's image, although how much is anyone's guess. More worrisome, argues journalist John Judis, is that when corporate money is important to an environmental organization's revenue stream, its "voice is now more likely to be heard, and, in Washington, the power to get your opinion heard wins battles."[68] During the intramural discord over ratification of the North American Free Trade Agreement, for example, environmentalists opposing NAFTA charged that support for it by other environmental organizations had been "purchased" by corporate donations. At the very least, as Representative Marcy Kaptur (D-Ohio) said of pro-NAFTA organizations such as Environmental Defense, "I think they got caught between their funders, some of whom are large corporations who are in favor of NAFTA, and their membership which is very environmentally conscious. I think they caught themselves politically."[69]

To some critics, corporate money is an outright bribe, and they always point to the case of industry giant Waste Management, Inc., as an especially notorious example of the pernicious potential of corporate money. During the late 1980s and early 1990s, the company disbursed a million dollars annually among organizations such as the World Wildlife Fund, National Wildlife Federation, National Audubon Society, Izaak Walton League, and even Natural Resources Defense Council and Sierra Club Foundation (which thereafter revamped its criteria for corporate donations). Critics, including some within recipient organizations, charged Waste Management with seeking to dampen criticism after it had been fined millions of dollars by the federal government for price fixing and illegal dumping and to improve its reputation as it lobbied for regulatory changes that might give it an edge against competitors. Waste Management also allegedly used its position on the National Wildlife Federation's corporate advisory board to arrange a meeting with William Reilly, EPA administrator during the George H. W. Bush administration, who announced shortly thereafter that he would challenge the rights of states to preempt federal rules on the disposal of hazardous wastes. Reilly expressed surprise when the National Wildlife Federation protested his announcement, since it had "hosted the breakfast at which I was lobbied to do the very thing we are doing."[70]

The dilemma posed by corporate money is even more apparent when it is *withdrawn*. Companies naturally stop supporting organizations that criticize them publicly, as when Exxon officials resigned from the National Wildlife Federation's corporate advisory board after it chastised the company following the 1989 *Exxon Valdez* disaster.[71] But this is rare, if only because organizations that accept corporate money rarely rebuke their benefactors in public. Just as important is the vulnerability of corporate funding to countervailing advocacy pressures. In the early 1990s, the Audubon Society generated about $2 million annually in corporate donations, less than 5 percent of total revenue, but still an important part of its overall budget.[72] Most of these funds went for "safe" educational and recreational programs, and one of the most popular and sponsor-dependent was the "World of Audubon" series that aired on PBS and Turner Broadcasting. In December 1991, "World of Audubon" sponsor General Electric announced that it would no longer fund the series, citing economic reasons. Yet its decision came on the heels of a campaign by the National Inholders Association, a lobby for cattlemen, loggers, and others who own property in or near national parks and forests, which was furious about an Audubon special that questioned federally subsidized grazing on public lands. These interests urged a boycott of General Electric products and took credit for the company's subsequent decision.[73] General Electric was only the latest in a line of sponsors to halt funding for the "World of Audubon" following one furor or another; that list included Stroh's Brewing, Ford, Exxon, and Citicorp.[74] Given that many environmental organizations use consumer boycotts as a tool for public persuasion against corporate activity, use by "the other side" is ironic and underscores the vulnerability of environmental organizations' reliance on corporate funding.

Such episodes have made most—but not all—environmental organizations far more careful about the types of corporate donations they accept, if any. This said, even organizations that do not take direct corporate donations accept grants from their technically independent company foundations, in the process, raising the same kinds of problems. For example, in 2000, the Ford Motor Company Fund—not to be confused with the Ford Foundation—gave out $14 million in grants to environmental organizations, including $5 million to Conservation International for a center for environmental leadership in business and another $5 million to Audubon for bird monitoring and public education. Whereas the grant to Conservation International elicited little comment, the award to Audubon provoked an angry protest from western off-road-vehicle enthusiasts, ranchers, and timber industry workers, for whom Audubon's opposition to the development of federal lands embodied "extremist environmentalism." Many announced their intent to swear off Ford products.[75]

Like any other nonprofit that takes corporate philanthropy—universities included—environmental organizations that accept corporate or corporate foundation money argue that it never comes with outright strings attached. For critics, however, dependence on corporate money threatens to mute voices that must be willing to challenge company practices that affect the environment. Moreover, taking such funds only reinforces perceptions that major environmental organizations speak to (and for) a largely affluent constituency on relatively safe issues such as saving pandas or preserving aesthetically pleasing landscapes. Such perceptions explain why organizations that could reap significant income from relationships with major corporations avoid doing so. Their credibility is at stake.[76]

Other Sources

A relatively small but important source of revenue is the sale of a variety of environmental goods and services. Older organizations such as the Sierra Club, Audubon, and the National Wildlife Federation always sold books and generated revenue from advertising in their magazines, but today, many environmental organizations grasp the opportunity to trade on their public images with all the fervor of any free-marketer. In the process, they have generated proportionately greater (if still relatively small) revenues from merchandise. The reasons are simple: selling calendars, books, coffee mugs, eco-tour packages, and magazines generates money without asking members for another direct contribution. In the same vein, selling or licensing goods for sale in retail stores or through upscale catalogs is a profitable way of getting revenue from nonmembers who, in the process of exchange, might sign up.

Other ventures reflect even greater inventiveness. Most major environmental organizations, having learned well from university development offices, encourage longtime members to remember the organization in their wills, and some of the largest organizations offer attractive gift annuity programs. Many accept gifts of land, residences, or other assets (e.g., artwork) in return for tax considerations. The Audubon Society famously derives royalty income from long-established oil and gas wells on some of its property in Louisiana and Texas. Several organizations offer "affinity" credit cards, whereby they get a small but cumulatively lucrative percentage of the service charge every time the card is used. Most rent out their membership lists, which can add a few thousand vital dollars to revenue. The National Wildlife Federation once ran ads in trade publications calling its mailing list "ideal for reaching responsive, upscale individuals with a social conscience," and the Audubon Society trumpeted, "Here's an affluent, upscale audience it will really pay you to reach."[77] And, of course, forty organizations joined to create Earth Share to allow individuals to donate more painlessly through payroll deductions. Workplace giving through Earth Share exceeded $7 million in 2001, providing yet another part of the revenue base.[78]

MASS MEMBERSHIP ENVIRONMENTALISM, REVISITED

The expansion and diversification of the environmental advocacy revenue base are keys to the fiscal resiliency that most of these organizations have shown over time. Even so, for most organizations, survival ultimately depends on their members. In this regard, the critical factor in the adaptation of the national environmental advocacy community since the early 1970s was the development and maintenance of its mass base, first through direct mail and advertising and now, increasingly, through the Internet. This is especially true for organizations that once depended heavily on foundation grants, government contracts, legal fees, or the favor of a few individual patrons. Now survival is tied inextricably to maintaining a base of tens to hundreds of thousands of supporters, even if the organization does not have "members" in the classic sense of the term.

Mass membership environmentalism has its pathologies, as critics are only too happy to point out, but compared with other revenue sources, it may be the least problematic. Corporate money, in particular, is more troublesome for organizations that may need to confront the environmental effects of business behavior or market dynamics. More important, the need to maintain a mass base of support forces even the more narrowly focused environmental organizations to cultivate a national constituency that simply did not exist thirty years ago. The sheer size and breadth of that constituency, even more than the funds it generates, account for national environmental organizations' ability to position themselves at the center of the political landscape and thereby serve as potent counterweights to their political and corporate adversaries.

As mass-based organizations, however, they must show their supporters some kind of return on investment. Even the most modest dues-paying members will surely drift away or shift to a rival if an organization cannot show results. For all except the land conservancies, however, performance is a relatively evanescent criterion. Environmental advocacy organizations are not insurance providers like the American Association of Retired Persons. They are judged by how well they fight the good fight and whether they are making a difference.

5
Adaptation and Change

DRILLING IN ANWR

In early 2001, the new George W. Bush administration resurrected as a centerpiece of its energy policy a long-standing goal of the oil industry to allow drilling in a previously off-limits section of the Arctic National Wildlife Refuge (ANWR). To the administration, starting oil production out of the ANWR was a key element in its announced drive to foster energy independence by promoting maximum use of the nation's coal, oil, and natural gas. To advocates of wilderness preservation and wildlife protection, however, drilling in the preserve seemed unnecessary, given its limited proven reserves and, more important, the potential for irreversible damage to sensitive tundra and resident wildlife.[1]

Despite their concerns, environmentalists played no role in formulating the administration's energy policy. They didn't even get into the room and charged that the administration's National Energy Policy Development Group was little more than a coterie of energy industry insiders working in secret with their former oil industry colleague, Vice President Richard Cheney. The administration refused to release a list of the energy group's participants, prompting the Sierra Club, Natural Resources Defense Council (NRDC), and other advocacy organizations—including a conservative public-interest law organization known for its lawsuits against Bill Clinton—to sue under the federal Freedom of Information Act to gain access to the records. A federal district court eventually ruled in the claimants' favor, and the administration released heavily edited records that, to critics, showed extensive industry insider participation, but it continued to withhold other records under a broad claim of executive privilege.[2] The case wended its way up through the federal judiciary to the U.S. Supreme Court, which in June 2004 remanded it to a federal appeals court for further adjudication of the administration's central claim.[3] Whatever its ultimate outcome, the lengthy legal tussle over the energy task force only reinforced perceptions about the extent to which the administration's energy and environmental policies reflected the desires of industry above all others.

More troubling to administration critics, the general public seemed open to the idea of drilling in the reserve.[4] With repeated White House warnings of an energy "crisis" in the wake of a momentary spike in gasoline prices, respondents to a poll conducted in the late spring of 2001 were inclined to believe that the energy situation was "very serious"—more serious, according to poll trends, than at any time since the late 1970s.[5] By May 2001, although 57 percent in one Gallup poll opposed oil exploration in the ANWR when specifically asked about it, 63 percent also supported a broader policy of "drilling for natural gas on public lands," and 64 percent agreed with "investing in more gas pipelines." More than half (53 percent) were willing to offer tax incentives to oil and gas companies to encourage drilling.[6] Moreover, despite an expressed belief in the value of energy efficiency and conservation, a combined 70 percent agreed that it was either "very important" or "extremely important" that the president and Congress increase energy production.[7]

Such seemingly contradictory public attitudes reflected the administration's strategic argument that drilling in the ANWR was good energy policy *and* safe for the environment. In this respect, the administration took heed from the past, when mobilized public fear about undermining environmental protection had forced Republicans to back off aggressive efforts to restructure regulatory policy. The most recent case had occurred in 1995, when House Republicans under Speaker Newt Gingrich abandoned the most environmentally pertinent portions of their "Contract with America."[8] This time around, by contrast, a disciplined Bush administration worked with congressional Republicans on arguments designed to shift public attitudes toward its preferred position through continuous references to a sagging economy and an emerging "energy crisis." The spikes in gasoline prices and a much-publicized electricity shortage in California offered defensible ground for at least partial exploration in the Arctic refuge. As columnist William Saletan reasoned in May 2001:

> Right now, most Americans oppose drilling in ANWR. But the more we discuss that idea in terms of energy rather than the environment, the more the political equation changes. Economic considerations enumerated by Bush and Cheney—"sharp increases in fuel prices from home heating oil to gasoline," electrical threats to "the high-tech industry," strangled economic growth and layoffs—add weight to the pro-drilling side of the equation. National security concerns—the dependence on foreign oil that, in Cheney's words, makes it "easy for a regime such as Iraq to hold us hostage"—enter the debate, as well.[9]

Critics dismissed the president's rhetoric as an exercise in misdirection—in the words of one commentator, "smoke and mirrors"—to hide its payoff to allies in the energy sector.[10] However, the administration's argument gained greater traction in the wake of the terrorist attacks of September 11, 2001, which renewed the public debate over the nation's continued reliance on politically vulnerable Middle Eastern oil. By early 2002, the president was forcefully linking the need to drill in the ANWR to energy independence and to his administration's economic stimulus efforts. In remarks to labor union leaders, the president argued, "this energy bill that we're working on is a jobs bill. And when we explore for power, U.S. power, U.S. energy in ANWR, we're not only helping us become less dependent on foreign sources of crude oil and foreign sources of energy, we're creating jobs for American workers, jobs so that men and women can put food on the table."[11]

This convergence of factors—in John Kingdon's terms, the opening of a clear "window of opportunity"—strengthened chances for passage of the president's energy program.[12] The Republican-dominated House had passed a version of the energy bill that authorized oil and gas drilling in the ANWR even before September 11. Only the Senate—barely in the hands of Democrats—stood in the way through 2002, and the president's prospects there improved after midterm elections returned the upper chamber to Republican control. The House again authorized drilling in its 2003 version of the energy bill, and to observers, final congressional approval was only a matter of time.

Environmental organizations mobilized early to fight the proposal, their tactics shaped by the political realities of the moment. With no effective access to the top echelons of the Bush administration, environmentalists could only hope to blunt its capacity to define the issue and to mobilize their own supporters to contact their members of Congress. In this regard, they wasted little time on the conservative Republicans who ran the House, focusing instead on the Senate.[13] For one thing, the defection of moderate Republican James Jeffords of Vermont in mid-2001 enabled Democrats to maintain formal control over the chamber's agenda through 2001–2002.[14] Even when Republicans regained control after the 2002 elections, the narrowness of their partisan advantage, combined with the chamber's tradition of minority rights (as embodied in the filibuster), gave a handful of more moderate Republicans and Democrats political leverage.

It was on these swing senators and their constituents that opponents of drilling focused their attention, following a now-standard mix of "inside" and "outside" strategies.[15] Registered lobbyists representing the NRDC, National Audubon Society, and National Wildlife Federation, among others, worked with their largely Democratic allies to shape a legislative blocking strategy even before the administration's proposal went to Capitol Hill. NRDC lawyers led the legal effort to open up the records of the energy task force, in the hope that evidence of industry dominance over the process might provoke a public backlash. Staff at the Wilderness Society and other organizations mined federal records for data and reports to counter the administration's arguments. At the same time, environmental organizations went to the airwaves to try to shape public opinion and, ideally, motivate constituents in key states to contact their senators. That strategy began in March 2001 when the National Audubon Society launched a $150,000 television advertising campaign against drilling to be run in the Washington, D.C., area, where senators and their staff were likely to see or hear about them.[16] Two weeks later, the NRDC began a $450,000 ad campaign—its first ever—to run on cable television stations in twenty-one cities, including Atlanta, Baltimore, Chicago, Indianapolis, Miami, and Portland, Oregon. A concurrent $250,000 television campaign by a coalition of organizations, including Defenders of Wildlife and state affiliates of the Sierra Club and National Wildlife Federation, aired in Baton Rouge, Indianapolis, Lincoln, Little Rock, and Portland.[17] In both campaigns, the choice of cities reflected the presence of moderate Democratic or Republican senators in those states.

The attacks of September 11 abruptly halted these efforts, muted criticism of the president's energy and environmental polices, and forced environmental organizations to assess their strategic options.[18] But the hiatus proved only momentary when it became apparent that proponents of drilling were capitalizing on the crisis to step up their pressure for authorization. "It is appropriate for Americans to examine again our increasing dependence on foreign oil, especially Mideast oil," argued Senator Frank Murkowski (R-Alaska), a leading proponent of drilling. "Each senator is going to have to recognize his obligations to our national security as opposed to environmental extremists."[19] Senator James Inhofe (R-Oklahoma) went so far as to add an ANWR amendment to an October 2001 defense authorization bill, arguing that after September 11, energy independence was a valid part of national security. That tactic failed to generate sufficient support, but it signaled a new level of intensity in the debate.[20]

Faced with this invigorated effort by proponents of drilling, environmental organizations resumed advertising campaigns and redoubled efforts to mobilize their supporters in opposition. The Sierra Club, National Audubon Society, and National Wildlife Federation, operating through their chapters and affiliates in swing-vote states such as Louisiana and Arkansas, urged members to contact their senators and thereby counteract the pressure being brought to bear by pro-drilling forces. Wilderness Society and Sierra Club staff coordinated efforts with coalitions of native tribes and religious groups to broaden the base of opposition to drilling, an effort that included organizing trips to Washington to enable local activists to meet with their representatives and senators.[21]

At the other end of the spectrum, Defenders of Wildlife used phone banks and its e-mail–based Defenders Environment Network to generate more than 1.2 million e-mails and faxes to Congress and the White House.[22] The NRDC reported that its "online activists" sent more than a million messages, including 100,000 the week the Senate voted in March 2002.[23] Defenders also created new websites (www.savearcticrefuge.org and www.savepolarbears.org) to educate the public and, it hoped, stimulate opposition. Similar ANWR-specific websites were launched by the Audubon Society (www.protectthearctic.com) and the NRDC (www.savebiogems.org/arctic/). In a cyber-based twist, with echoes of the Sierra Club's battle over Hetch Hetchy, sixteen environmental organizations, ranging ideologically from Greenpeace to the World Wildlife Fund, collaborated to create a separate "virtual organization," Saveourenvironment.org, to harness "the power of the Internet to increase public awareness and activism on today's most important environmental issues."[24]

Many of the major national environmental organizations were active in the campaign to stave off drilling, but the intensity and visibility of their roles varied widely, depending on policy niche and, to some degree, ideological orientation. Leading the campaign were the wildlife and wilderness organizations—Defenders of Wildlife, National Audubon Society, National Wildlife Federation, Wilderness Society, and World Wildlife Fund—along with the NRDC, which has long focused on energy as one of its policy interests.[25] Key but subsidiary roles were played by the Sierra Club, Environmental Defense, National Parks Conservation Association, and Earthjustice. Niche organizations (e.g., American Rivers, Earth Island) offered support as far as the issue fit with their respective policy areas. Conspicuous in their general silence on the issue were the domestic land conservancies—in particular, the Nature Conservancy and Ducks Unlimited—and the Izaak Walton League's only statement on the matter was that it might be preferable to raise the corporate average fuel economy standards for automobiles and light trucks.[26]

Supporters of the president's energy package were hardly passive bystanders, of course. Indeed, they used pretty much the same range of tactics to shape public opinion and mobilize support. In a widely publicized memo, public-opinion expert Frank Luntz advised Republicans how to "educate constituents" by consistently emphasizing that "energy development and the environment can and must co-exist, and this balance must be part of a truly comprehensive, long-term solution that reduces American dependence on foreign oil."[27] Luntz's "commonsense" talking points formed the core message expressed by the administration and backers of drilling and were widely credited with enabling Republican candidates in key 2002 Senate races to neutralize attacks on their environmental records and, by winning, shift control of the chamber into Republican hands.[28]

Industry associations pursued aggressive newspaper and television advertising campaigns, put together their own coalitions (e.g., the Alliance for Energy and Economic Growth), and created pro-drilling websites; allied labor unions used their members to make phone calls to potential supporters in key states. Money from energy and natural resource sector industries poured into the campaign coffers of friendly candidates in the 2002 election cycle—by one measure, over $40 million to Republicans (versus $15 million to Democrats)—which undoubtedly helped Republicans retake the Senate.[29]

Even so, on March 19, 2003, the Senate voted fifty-two to forty-eight to remove authorization for drilling in the ANWR from its version of the energy bill. The difference was provided by moderate Republicans (e.g., Gordon Smith of Oregon) and Democrats (e. g., Blanch Lincoln of Arkansas), on whom both sides had focused attention. A House-Senate conference committee was convened to work out a compromise and eventually deleted the provision authorizing drilling when it became clear that its continued inclusion would doom Senate passage of the entire bill.[30] But it didn't matter. By two votes, the Senate failed to stop the threat of a filibuster by opponents of a provision restricting lawsuits over the health effects of the gasoline additive MTBE.[31] The energy bill was thus declared dead for the rest of 2003. Everyone involved knew that the administration would again seek authorization to drill in the ANWR in 2004, but for the moment, at least, the environmental community could chalk one up for its side.

TACTICS IN CONTEXT

The battle over the ANWR is a good case study in its own right. Its dramatic twists and turns; the centrality of problem definition to public discourse; the impacts of institutions, procedures, and rules; the vast amounts of money spent on advocacy tactics; and the active role played by organized interests on both sides all make for an instructive lesson about American national politics. For our broader purposes, however, it is especially pertinent for what it reveals about the range of tactics used by national environmental advocacy organizations. As a result of several major survey-based studies, we know that the typical national advocacy organization deploys a mix of "inside" (e.g., lobbying, lawsuits) and "outside" (e.g., advertising, grassroots mobilization) tactics.[32] As Frank Baumgartner and Beth Leech conclude about these findings, "The typical American interest group is involved in such a wide range of policy areas and such a diverse set of issues that they cannot follow a 'one size fits all' policy of choosing their lobbying tactics."[33]

The national environmental organizations, except perhaps for the smallest or most niche specific (e.g., Earth Share), are exemplars of this general rule. Virtually every organization in this study deploys a mix of inside and outside tactics. The scope and intensity of their actions may vary according to organizational resources, mission, or cultural orientation, but at a minimum, all utilize free and paid media, interact with legislative staff, devise public education campaigns, offer comments on proposed federal and state regulations, and urge supporters to contact their elected representatives. Organizations such as Environmental Defense, with a traditional focus on lawsuits and negotiations with regulators, have active public-relations campaigns, and even direct-action outfits such as Greenpeace testify at congressional committee hearings—when given the opportunity.

That term *opportunity* is an important qualifier. We know from the general surveys that the particular tactics used, and in what mix, are conditioned by the nature of the issue, by internal organizational characteristics (e.g., mission, influence of major donors, ideological orientation of members), and by the context (e.g., policy venue) the organization faces.[34] Context—the political opportunity structure—is particularly important in understanding the strategic decisions made by national environmental organizations on issues such as ANWR, as well as their efficacy. The political opportunity structure of the moment not only affects the creation of advocacy organizations (see chapter 2) but also shapes the tactics they are able and likely to use.

By extension, *changes* in the opportunity structure compel advocacy organizations to adapt accordingly, or risk becoming inconsequential. Yet we pay too little attention to how shifts in partisan control of institutions, revisions in formal rules, or alterations in decision-making procedures affect the way advocacy organizations in a particular policy domain seek access to decision-making, much less the tactics they deploy or judge worthwhile.[35] Even seemingly minor procedural changes, such as alterations in congressional committee jurisdictions, have profound impacts. As Bruce Oppenheimer, in studying the politics of oil, observed, "rules and procedures, in affecting the course of public policy and the actions of congressmen, have a simultaneous effect on interest groups concerned with various pieces of legislation. The way the process operates has a good deal to do with the success of an interest group's position and where interest groups will center their attention to influence the results."[36] Contexts matter.

Some components of the political opportunity structure remain comparatively unchanged. Structural elements such as federalism, the separation of institutional powers, and the array of checks and balances embedded in the constitutional system are relatively fixed topographic features that channel political representation and shape policymaking.[37] In the macrolevel sense, the constitutional system has always afforded local economic and political interests preferential access and has always frustrated the easy building of majorities. As Robert Dahl and Charles Lindblom remind us, "the strategic consequences of this arrangement . . . has been that no unified, cohesive, acknowledged, and legitimate representative-leaders of the 'national majority' exist in the United States."[38] Conversely, as with drilling in the ANWR, the system also grants to organized "minorities," or, in the words of James Madison in *Federalist* number 10, "factions," an array of access and leverage points that may not exist in party-dominant parliamentary systems.[39] A system that contains structural biases toward system-level stability and incremental change tends to force coalition building bloc by bloc, parochial interest by parochial interest, a process by which "majorities of the moment" are knitted together out of many diverse interests. The national environmental advocacy community is but one piece in a vast mosaic of issue-based representation whose dimensions are shaped by some rather fixed structural elements.

Beyond these textbook constants, we can observe changes in the political opportunity structure over time that have forced environmental organizations to adapt their tactics, just as they have had to find new sources of revenue or adjust their ways of operating. After all, the environmental era of the late 1960s and early 1970s took place within profoundly different political contexts. That point seems obvious, but it is often overlooked when considering the kinds of tactics advocacy organizations are able and willing to use, or their potential for success.

Adaptation is once again the watchword. However, unlike biological species, advocacy organizations do not adapt merely to survive. They adapt to continue to have an *impact*. To be sure, organizations adopt new goals to stay in business (with polio conquered, rather than close up shop, the March of Dimes shifted to a broader and more open-ended campaign against birth defects), but convincing supporters about the need to continue is another matter. The demise of Environmental Action was not just about weak finances, organizational pathologies, or a crowded advocacy niche; at heart, it was about whether its continued existence mattered. Tactically speaking, the answer was "not really." Other organizations (Friends of the Earth, NRDC, League of Conservation Voters) were doing what Environmental Action did, but apparently, they were doing it better in the eyes of potential supporters, if not the experts. In contrast, the virtual collapse in mass public support for Greenpeace in the 1990s suggests what can happen when an organization is perceived to veer away from the tactics that made it compelling in the first place. For Greenpeace to take on the trappings of conventional advocacy made no sense to its donor base. Identity and tactics can be inseparable.

SHIFTING TERRAIN FOR ENVIRONMENTAL ADVOCACY

Whatever their impact on individual organizations, changes in the political opportunity structure during the last three decades of the twentieth century forced the entire environmental advocacy community to reconfigure the tactics it employed, where it did so, and in what order of priority. It also had to reconfigure its very role in the political system. The potential cost of not adapting was policy failure and irrelevance—even extinction.

The Conservative Surge

For environmental advocates, among others, the big story of the past thirty years was the ascendance of the conservative wing of the Republican Party and the parallel demise of its more liberal wing, which had been pivotal to bipartisan agreement on environmental policy matters through the 1970s.[40] This dominance of conservative Republicans also came at the expense of conservative southern Democrats, producing a more homogeneous Republican majority now rooted in its populous southern and southwestern strongholds. The parallel leftward movement of the Democrats, despite the centrist tendencies of Jimmy Carter and Bill Clinton, produced by the mid-1990s a partisan polarization that may have given the nation more clearly demarcated, even "responsible," parties but afforded environmental activists—among other issue advocates—remarkably little room to maneuver. Despite campaign contributions to moderate Republican candidates and efforts to include Republicans on the boards of directors of environmental organizations, everyone *knows* that mainstream environmentalists must depend on the Democrats if they want to continue to work through the political party system.[41] Partisan polarization has, ironically, narrowed environmentalists' tactical options.

One need only look at the 2000 presidential election to understand this reality and, for environmentalists, the tactical dilemmas it poses. Most major environmental organizations looked beyond any disappointment with the Clinton administration and backed Al Gore as the only credible alternative to Republican nominee George W. Bush. Such pragmatism was rooted in their realization that holding on to the White House was their sole bulwark against an ideologically hostile one-party government. If, in doing so, mainstream environmentalism had to hitch its fortunes to the Democrats, so be it; there was little choice. Such pragmatism was unacceptable for activists on the left, however, because to them, the parties were barely distinguishable defenders of corporate capitalism and unfettered global trade. The "greens" who fought NAFTA, marched in Seattle against the World Trade Organization, and boycotted Shell Oil for its support of the military regime in Nigeria saw Democrats like Gore as only too willing to accept half measures that still favored corporate interests. Such discontent found a repository in Ralph Nader, whose decision to stand as the presidential candidate of the Association of State Green Parties (ASGP) reflected his own belief that only a third party could force a profound change in national discourse. To the Naderites, the Democratic Party itself was the problem.[42]

This was an old debate, to be sure, but its effects in 2000 were significant. For one thing, there was the firestorm over whether the Greens cost Gore the election. Any argument that votes for Nader in Florida or New Hampshire contributed to Gore's loss must consider that Gore also lost his home state of Tennessee. Yet, with polling data showing that many Green voters would have voted for Gore if Nader had not been in the race, 97,000 votes for Nader in Florida had to have some bearing on the outcome. Votes for Green Party candidates also arguably cost Democrats some House seats—no small consequence, given the narrow Republican margin in that chamber. Candidates carrying Green Party labels ran in forty House races in 2000, getting, on average, 2.3 percent of the total vote in contests that included candidates from both major parties. In most cases, the presence of a Green candidate had no effect, but in at least three instances, it may have benefited a Republican candidate with a poorer record on the environment. In Michigan's Eighth District, previously held by Democrats, the Green candidate's 3,400 votes far exceeded the 150-vote margin that gave victory to the Republican. A similar shift in party control occurred in New Jersey's Seventh District, where a Green candidate's 2.8 percent of the vote exceeded the Republican's 2.4 percent margin of victory. In New Mexico's First District, the Republican incumbent enjoyed a 1.4 percent margin over the Democratic challenger, with the Green candidate taking 7.5 percent of the vote, a virtual repeat of the outcome two years earlier.[43] More telling, in New Jersey's Twelfth District, the Democratic incumbent, backed by the Sierra Club and local environmental groups, barely eked out a 600-vote victory in the face of a 5,600-vote showing by the Green Party candidate.[44]

To be sure, environmentalists could claim that their votes and money had helped Democrats in a number of races. The political action committees of Friends of the Earth, the League of Conservation Voters, and the Sierra Club combined made nearly $2.2 million in direct contributions to dozens of candidates, mostly Democrats, and much more in "independent expenditures" to criticize environmentally suspect candidates. Such support probably made a difference in Representative Debbie Stabenow's narrow victory over incumbent Republican Senator Spencer Abraham in Michigan.[45] Yet, given the six-seat majority by which Republicans held on to the House as the Congress convened in 2001, it is no wonder that Democrats and their allies in the environmental community were bitter about the Green Party challenge. Democrats lost more ground in the 2002 midterm election, which was shaped by national security issues in the wake of the attacks of September 11, 2001, so the impacts of 2000 went beyond a single election.

The long-developing partisan dominance by conservative Republicans is not going to be reversed anytime soon, regardless of which party wins the presidency. Republicans are likely to maintain control over the House as a result of continued population movement and beneficial redistricting in southern and southwestern states, while their Senate counterparts are finally reaping the benefits of the long-term shift of southern conservatives to their party. Some observers now consider the possibility of a Republican "lock" on Congress for years to come.[46] That possibility forces environmentalists to think hard about how close they can get to the Democratic Party. For those old-line organizations such as the National Wildlife Federation and the Audubon Society in particular, being seen as overtly partisan is unacceptable to their cultural orientation and donor base. Yet at the national level at least, Democrats may be the only option; most environmentalists want to win, not just make a statement. In short, Republican dominance at the national level has put environmentalists into a bit of an ideological and partisan box, making the dilemma of how to participate in electoral politics even more acute.[47]

Countermobilization

Concurrent with and part of this conservative surge were sustained countermobilizations by industry, on the one hand, and by well-organized and well-funded conservative groups rallied loosely around "property rights" and "Wise Use" banners, on the other hand. The amply documented mobilization of business beginning in the late 1970s was, in many ways, a reaction to the successes of environmental and other public-interest advocates in the previous decade.[48] By the early 1980s, the explosion in the number of business lobbyists based in Washington was just one indicator that corporate America was no longer content to rely on its "privileged position" to defend its interests.[49]

The mobilization of business at the same time that Reagan came to power forced most environmental organizations to establish or expand their formal presence in the nation's capital. Their heightened emphasis on national politics was unpopular with grassroots activists, for whom "Washington politics" meant succumbing to, in the words of critic Kirkpatrick Sale, "the inherently conservatizing pressure to play by the 'rules of the game' in the compromise world of Washington, D.C."[50] As noted in chapter 3, the perceived need to establish a physical presence in the nation's capital led to David Brower's departure from Friends of the Earth and, in part, to Greenpeace's decision to pursue conventional lobbying. Virtually every major environmental organization was faced with a similar dilemma. This balancing act got more difficult when most national environmental organizations were hit with shrinking membership rolls and softening revenues during the recession of the early 1990s, but their need to be in Washington to counteract the greater physical presence of industry interests arrayed along K Street left them little choice.

At the same time, environmentalists increasingly encountered well-organized and well-funded opposition from a variety of property rights and "Wise Use" groups at the state and local levels. The former agitated for the protection of private property against governmental actions that might adversely affect its "fair market" value, such as when wetlands designation precludes commercial development. Some of these operations were little more than thinly disguised fronts for development interests, but others were genuine groups of small property holders anxious about the impact of federal restrictions on land use. The same distinctions held for the dozens of Wise Use groups clustered particularly in the mountain West, which promoted local control over the region's vast stretches of federal lands. Some, like the Blue Ribbon Coalition, seemed to be little more than industry fronts (in this case, the off-road-vehicle industry), but others reflected the region's long-standing grassroots conservative populism.[51]

The more moderate Wise Users saw themselves as real conservationists who hunted and fished; espoused multiple uses of federal lands for grazing, mining, logging, and recreation; and opposed what they regarded as misguided efforts by suburban-oriented environmentalists that threatened to end traditional rural ways of life.[52] The more militant activists expressed values that dovetailed with conservative populism's strident defense of private property and suspicion of the federal government. Many were veterans of the Sagebrush Rebellion of the 1970s, which spawned Republican secretaries of the interior James Watt and, later, Gail Norton; others came out of the Young Americans for Freedom, the National Rifle Association, and other conservative groups that saw little constitutional basis for restricting private property. At the farthest fringes were the John Birch Society and others in the reactionary right who saw environmentalism as the postcommunist radical threat to core American values. Some supported the various anti-federal "militias" that came to public attention during the mid-1990s, while others were behind an effort by some county governments in western states to use novel interpretations of the Tenth Amendment to assert local legal control over federal lands. These initiatives eventually ebbed, but not before states such as South Dakota joined in.[53]

The grassroots dimensions of the private property and Wise Use countermovements, which seemed to peak with the Republican takeover of the House in the mid-1990s, were always hard to gauge. Their proponents claimed tens of thousands of members, but critics countered that there were no more than a few hundred hard-core activists backed by a phalanx of professional organizers and conservative foundations and promoted by allies in extractive industries, libertarian think tanks, and conservative media personalities such as Rush Limbaugh. Whatever the truth, these activists certainly helped elect fellow conservatives to local, state, and federal office; shaped public debates on land use and resource issues; won lawsuits in federal courts populated by Reagan and George H. W. Bush appointees; and exploited their access to the most sympathetic parts of the federal bureaucracy. Even with the apparent ebbing in their fervor by the late 1990s, their ties to the emerging Republican majority, particularly in the House, continue to give them a degree of influence in setting the agenda and crafting legislation—privileges enjoyed by environmentalists when Democrats ruled the Hill.

To complicate matters, by the 1990s, more authority over the implementation and enforcement of environmental regulations had been shifted to the states, in the name of efficiency and flexibility.[54] Greater state responsibility, and wide variance in state government capacity and priorities, now meant that environmentalists, particularly those focused on federal lands and wildlife, had to extend their attention and efforts to many more venues at more levels of government.[55] The influence of business interests, property rights advocates, and Wise Use activists in many localities meant that environmentalists now had to be engaged on a broader array of fronts at several levels. As Sierra Club executive director Michael Fischer put it in 1990, when arguing about the need to shift club resources from Washington to the states, "we'll have to be covering our opponents because the Wise Use movement and other folks are going to the statehouses. But look, we've just won the Clear Air Act. The next step is implementing the Clean Air Act at the state level. We've got Superfund problems. There are problems at the state level."[56]

In short, mobilization by business in Washington forced environmental organizations to strengthen their presence there, just as mobilization by property rights and Wise Use groups compelled environmentalists to pay more attention to the grassroots. At the same time, economic recession in the early 1990s generated severe fiscal strains for many organizations. Those such as the Sierra Club, Audubon Society, and National Wildlife Federation were the first to feel the cross-pressures as their local chapters or affiliates became entangled in legal and political battles over land use and wilderness protection. National Wildlife Federation affiliates serving a traditional base of hunting and fishing constituencies were hit with especially severe cross-pressures, prompting grassroots members to accuse headquarters staff, led by president Jay Hair, with placing undue emphasis on national and international politics.[57] Membership and revenue suffered, Hair resigned under pressure in 1995, and the federation moved to strengthen its local and state presence.[58] The Audubon Society went through a similar crisis after decades of transforming itself from a chapter-based "bird group" to a national environmental organization.[59] As the society's 1995 strategic planning document put it, "the combination of a diminishing resource base, uncertainty over goals, limited accountability among various Audubon constituencies, and poor communication with its major constituent groups have resulted in divisiveness and dissatisfaction within the Audubon family."[60] President Peter Berle "retired," and, as at the National Wildlife Federation, his successor expressed a renewed commitment to working with and serving members in the chapters. Organizations lacking a chapter base, such as the Wilderness Society, responded to these fiscal pressures by closing state and regional offices and targeting their resources toward national advocacy.[61] Similar strategic decisions were made throughout the environmental community.

A Less Congenial Congress

Overlooked in many critical assessments of the efficacy of mainstream environmental organizations is the reality that Democratic control of Congress during the 1960s and 1970s was an essential factor in the passage of major environmental laws under Republican presidents Nixon and Ford. Although conservative southern Democrats often wrangled with their liberal colleagues over the scope of federal action, their shared desire to maintain party control led to compromises that advanced environmental protection.[62] Their retention of control over the House also enabled Democrats to blunt Reagan's efforts to remake environmental policy, and under George H. W. Bush, their renewed dominance in both chambers enabled Democrats to convene committee investigations into the actions of the executive branch and enact major new laws, including the 1990 amendments to the Clean Air Act. Whatever was happening elsewhere, environmentalists knew that they still enjoyed considerable access to and support in the legislative branch.

That access and leverage evaporated starting with the shift of control to Republicans in 1995. By the early 2000s, environmentalists—and Democrats, for that matter—were virtually excluded from the inner circles of House decision-making; their legislative proposals virtually disappeared from the agenda, and House standing committees no longer offered access points for environmental lobbyists. Indeed, in 1995, under Speaker Newt Gingrich, Republicans renamed the Committee on the Interior and Insular Affairs the Committee on Resources, and the Committee on Energy and Commerce became, simply, Commerce. These changes weren't simply matters of semantics; they reflected a profound shift in the chamber's expressed priorities under Republican leadership. The situation in the Senate was marginally better, given the relatively even balance between the two parties and the chamber's strong norms of collegiality, but even a bare shift in control to Republicans affected the chamber's agenda and the access it granted to outside advocates.

A telling marker of this shift is the trend in congressional committee hearings. Figure 5.1 shows the frequency of environmental organization testimony (either in person or in writing) at committee hearings on environmental and conservation matters from 1970 through 2003. The frequency of such hearings peaked in the 1980s, largely because of their widespread use by congressional Democrats as platforms to promote new legislation and to criticize administration activities under Republican presidents. Almost every major national environmental organization testified at least once a year during this period; some testified many times on many different issues before many different committees and subcommittees. What is most striking is the sharp drop-off in testimony following the Republican takeover of the House in 1995 and its virtual disappearance by 2002. Whatever the reasons—including a strategy of avoiding the provision of public forums for critics of the Bush administration—a once-key access point for environmentalists has essentially disappeared.[63]

Environmental organizations have no choice but to maintain their Washington lobbying staffs. In 2003, for instance, eighteen of the national organizations examined here were registered to lobby Congress under the Lobby Disclosure Act of 1995.[64] However, as in the case of ANWR, they seem to spend most of their time fighting attempts by their industry and ideological opponents to revise existing laws or tuck anti-environmental provisions (called "riders") into appropriations and budget bills.[65] It's an essentially rearguard action, but one imposed on them by the realities of the moment.

The Presidency

By January 2005, Republicans will have controlled the presidency for twenty-four of the previous thirty-six years, or two-thirds of the contemporary environmental era, if we mark its start in 1969. Although this fact is often overlooked

Figure 5.1. Appearances at Congressional Committee Hearings, 1970–2003

by critics on both the left and the right, Republican presidents have actually shaped much of federal environmental policy, whether through legislative proposals, budget allocations, clearing regulations through the Office of Management and Budget, or appointments to federal agencies and the judiciary.[66] More important, as George W. Bush underscored in reversing Bill Clinton's support for the Kyoto Protocol and pushing for drilling in the ANWR, presidents set the national agenda.

Presidents and their administrations also decide who gets access. Whatever their disappointments with the Clinton administration, environmentalists knew that their views would be heard at the highest level, that the top layers of the bureaucracy were in friendly hands, and that Clinton would fight off most of the anti-environmental initiatives pursued by House Republicans in particular. None of this was true with Bush, save for an occasional meeting with "hook and bullets" organizations such as Ducks Unlimited and the National Wildlife Federation.[67] As far as the executive branch was concerned, with the George W. Bush administration, environmental organizations were on the outside looking in. They could still file Freedom of Information Act requests, offer comments on proposed regulatory actions, and even get invited to participate in the odd forum run by a marginalized Environmental Protection Agency (EPA), but arguably, they had less meaningful access to or influence in the executive branch than they had under Reagan.

A More Restrictive Federal Judiciary

Republican dominance of the presidency has contributed to the increasingly conservative orientation of the federal judiciary on environmental and related regulatory matters. Federal judges in the early 2000s are more reluctant to extend standing to environmental claimants, more willing to give priority to property rights over environmental welfare, and less willing to grant discretion to federal regulatory agencies and even to Congress with respect to the constitutional powers of the states.[68] If lawsuits based on the National Environmental Policy Act of 1969 once infused environmental considerations into all aspects of federal policymaking, today they seem to be little more than narrow-gauge tools for forcing overburdened regulatory agencies to adhere to the letter of the existing law. So low has the lawsuit fallen in favor that the two major "science and law" organizations, Environmental Defense and the Natural Resources Defense Council, now use it as only a minor tactical tool, less important than lobbying, research, and public communication. "We concentrate more on the promotion of ideas and programs dreamed up by economists and scientists," one Environmental Defense official commented. "Rather than go to court, we lobby, write reports, court the media."[69] Only Earthjustice, a "boutique" shop that in 1993 considered a merger with the Boston-based Conservation Law Foundation, continues to use lawsuits as a core tactic, but augmented by lobbying and public communication.[70]

The upshot is that national environmental organizations now operate on political terrain that is often dominated by their opponents, facing what may be the most challenging political opportunity structure in the history of contemporary environmentalism. They have comparatively little access to the federal decision-making venues, which favor their well-organized business and ideological adversaries. As a result, once-standard inside tactics such as lobbying, meetings with executive branch officials, and lawsuits are of limited utility. For issue advocates, who always claimed to be outsiders, the reality of their current status must be unnerving.

HEARTS AND MINDS

Awkwardly balanced against these challenges in the political opportunity structure is a mass public that continues to express general support for environmental values, even when (as with the ANWR) those attitudes are diffuse and sometimes contradictory. Americans are willing to be convinced, but environmental goals are always going to be measured against other, often more short-term economic, social, and security needs. More than a generation after the first Earth Day, environmentalists are still fighting for the hearts and minds of the American public. As a result, as Robert Duffy notes, "environmental groups are devoting unprecedented resources and energy to framing issues and perceptions of candidates, in the hope that their preferred policies will be adopted and their preferred candidates will be elected."[71] They are doing so precisely because tactics like lobbying and lawsuits no longer suffice at a time when everyone professes to support environmental goals. Defining those goals, and how to balance them with other needs, makes tactics such as agenda setting and issue framing more nakedly imperative than ever. Environmental advocates are again forced to adapt their tactics to the opportunity structure of the moment.

Without stinting mention of other shifts in tactics—Duffy, for example, shows that environmental organizations have de-emphasized direct donations to candidates in favor of "independent expenditures" to shape public discourse during elections—two tactical adaptations are worth particular attention. One is use of the Internet to communicate directly with the public and supporters. The other is the greater attention being paid to members, not simply as financial backers but as part of a real grassroots force. The tactics are intertwined and must be understood in light of a general recognition that, in Robert Putnam's blunt assessment, the national environmental community had become a "defensive light air force, not a massed infantry for change."[72] What is missing, he argues, is a deep, active, and growing environmental grassroots. In fact, he concludes, "the only systematic evidence I have found on trends in conservation and environmental organizations at the state and local level and on environmental activism tends to suggest a *decline* over the last several decades."[73] Activists and scholars might challenge Putnam's empirical evidence,[74] but nobody disputes the need.

Taking It to the (Cyber) Streets

Environmental advocacy had to become a more visibly "outside" game at the right time, for without doubt, the Internet has presented advocacy organizations of all shapes and sizes with the greatest single technological revolution in memory. Perhaps nobody really knows how or how much the Internet will reshape issue advocacy, but few doubt that it already has.[75] E-mail action alerts, list-servs, chat rooms, special-purpose websites, and even "virtual" organizations (e.g., Saveourenvironment.org, in the struggle over drilling in the ANWR) are examples of the rapid and deep technological transformation of issue advocacy. None of these tactics is exactly new—in another age, the ladies of the various state Audubon Societies used letter-writing campaigns to similar effect—but they are now being pursued through a very different technological form. Although television and radio advertising, traditional direct mail, phone banks, and newspaper opinion pieces still occupy a place in the tactical toolbox, their use is increasingly secondary to Internet-based tactics.

How does the Internet affect advocacy tactics? At a minimum, the Internet, in all its guises (including e-mail, websites, discussion groups, videocams, and web logs), gives any advocacy organization an unparalleled capacity to communicate with and disseminate information *directly* to the mass public and current supporters quickly, conveniently, and at a relatively low cost. Even the smallest advocacy organization can manage a decent website. Organizations no longer need to purchase newspaper or television ads—although they still do—nor do they need to worry that their more "political" messages will be filtered or not run at all by mass media outlets. They can bypass commercial mass media and, through websites and e-mail, make their arguments directly to those who might be interested in the message. Again, traditional mass media avenues will continue to be used, but their limitations may no longer matter so much.

For example, television and radio are unidirectional, less easily targeted "broadcast" technologies, but the Internet makes it possible to "narrow-cast," to target information to specific audiences, with individualized adjustments made according to the stored electronic profile of the recipient. An organization can customize its e-mail messages to different subsets of supporters, depending on the issues of concern, and thus target appeals with a direct eye toward mobilization. In many respects, the first real test of this capacity came in 1995, when environmental organizations used e-mail appeals to mobilize supporters in response to House Republicans' "Contract with America." The NRDC, for example, e-mailed its report "Breach of Faith," documenting the expected impact of the contract on environmental laws, to thousands of activists. Such outreach efforts stirred a backlash among voters in districts of more moderate Republicans, compelling Gingrich to back off the contract's environmental provisions, for fear of harming his party's prospects in 1996.[76] Ten years later, every national environmental organization sends e-mail "action alerts" or newsletters to anyone willing to accept them.

Environmental organizations have lavished increasing attention and resources on their websites. This is no surprise: unlike other forms of outreach, a well-designed website can grab attention, publicize an issue, educate, and even mobilize, all at the same time and in a far less invasive way than through direct mail or direct-action protests. A good example of this potential multiplier effect is found with Scorecard (scorecard.org), run by Environmental Defense. Scorecard combines a wide array of data gathered by the federal government with the

Geographic Information System mapping technology to enable a visitor to find out about pollution threats down to the zip code level. For example, Scorecard reorganizes the data from the EPA's Toxic Release Inventory, collected under the Emergency Planning and Community Right-to-Know Act of 1986, to enable a user to identify which industries are releasing what chemicals into the local air. Such a "right to know" is seen as a necessary condition for energizing citizen action.[77] Thus informed, the concerned resident can use Scorecard to send faxes to the responsible companies and e-mails to the EPA or the governor, sign up for e-mail "action alerts," hold online discussions with others in the area, link up with local environmental organizations, and, of course, donate to Environmental Defense. Never before have advocacy organizations been able to offer such "one-stop shopping" to present and potential supporters.

The World Wide Web's multimedia capabilities are being utilized more heavily with each passing year. Unlike other forms of mass communication—television being an arguable exception—communication via the Internet can occur simultaneously in audio, video, graphic, and text formats, the efficacy of which should increase as broadband technologies advance and gain greater coverage. The World Wildlife Fund, for example, offers streaming videos featuring experts on topics such as the impact of global climate change on polar bears, links to various real-time "Panda-cams" throughout the world, tools for educators, interactive games, and an endangered species screensaver. To use a marketing metaphor, for the typical advocacy organization, a website is now a unified multimedia platform capable of delivering a wide array of products directly to discrete elements of its diverse customer base.

This said, most environmental organizations use their websites chiefly to convey information, recruit and mobilize supporters, and raise money.[78] So far, the more "qualitative" advantages of the Internet do not seem to be as well utilized. For example, organizations without local chapters have always found it difficult to foster social and political interaction among members—assuming they cared, of course. With the Internet, they could offer such benefits through chat rooms, discussion forums, interactive calendars, and organizing tools. Relatively little of this has occurred, however, because of the expense and difficulty of maintaining an active online community, even for a large organization.[79] Pulling together the advocacy equivalent of a "flash mob"—an evanescent, e-mail-generated gathering that is there for a moment and then gone—is one thing, nurturing a sustained community of activists is another.

Nevertheless, the trail blazed by web-oriented advocacy organizations such as the Rainforest Action Network (RAN) and, in the more openly political arena, by Moveon.org suggests a new path for advocacy. RAN relies heavily on the Internet to generate faxes and e-mails to corporate executives and government policymakers.[80] Its activist base is not large—a few thousand at most—but the probability that each individual will forward copies of RAN's message to friends and fellow activists magnifies the organization's outreach and impact beyond what the numbers alone imply.[81] Such Internet-based tactics have been used to target the brand images of companies whose actions or products are, in RAN's opinion, environmentally harmful—with apparent success.[82] For example, in 2000, RAN used an e-mail campaign to organize boycotts and protests against Home Depot until it agreed to stop selling lumber harvested from old-growth forests.[83] It has more recently focused on the global financial sector, getting Citigroup and Bank of America to revise their rules on lending to projects with a potentially adverse impact on rainforests. A sign of its apparent success is the anger RAN has provoked among its foes: conservatives call it "socialist," and in 2004, a House subcommittee demanded its financial records as part of an investigation into its tax-exempt status.[84]

What are we to make thus far of the Internet's impact on environmental advocacy? In one respect, as the case of drilling in the ANWR suggests, these tactics are now ubiquitous, and even a small advocacy organization can create a web-based presence that extends its reach to a global audience. To date, Internet-based tactics seem best suited to providing information and connecting with supporters, and they may be particularly effective in organizing less conventional advocacy campaigns, such as RAN's boycotts. When it comes to trying to influence policymakers, however, its impact is less clear. As Jeffrey Berry cautions, although such "high-tech lobbying" is impressive, "it's important to remember that such lobbying is a variation on a theme, not a whole new symphony. In the last analysis, faxes and e-mail are simply letters that constituents send to their members of Congress—they just get there faster."[85] If Berry is correct, the tens of thousands of messages generated electronically only add to the advocacy white noise and probably have only limited effect on policymakers attuned to "Astroturf"—fake grassroots—campaigns. As a result, the need for advocacy organizations to develop and maintain a *real* grassroots, with real people, is greater than ever.

Nourishing the Grassroots

Having spent much of the 1970s establishing a strong conventional Washington presence and most of the 1980s fighting the Reagan administration, by the 1990s, many national environmental organizations turned their attention to organizing and mobilizing local supporters. This renewed—or, for some, new—emphasis on an active base grew out of acknowledgment that local "feet on the ground" were needed to counteract pressure by property rights and Wise Use groups, particularly in policy areas where the federal government had transferred more responsibility to the states. Equally important, deeper local roots and more enduring local connections would complement the mass communications and lobbying strategies employed to influence members of Congress and state legislators.

The focus on the grassroots also reflected growing friction, even alienation, between national leaders and local activists,[86] as well as criticism within the broader environmental community about the purported failures of the national organizations in comparison to the grassroots—that supposedly purer, more local, and less bureaucratic face of environmentalism.[87] These strains showed up earliest and most clearly in older organizations that maintained local chapters or affiliates. By the late 1980s, the National Audubon Society was experiencing fiscal difficulties brought on by the costs of fighting the Reagan administration and, in part, by its expansion into more policy areas over the years. Active members in the now 500-plus local chapters were questioning the efficacy of these priorities and were growing restive over policy statements that they felt did not adequately take into account local political, social, and economic conditions. These frictions grew into outright rebellion in 1987, after president Peter Berle and the board proposed to address the Audubon Society's financial problems by closing regional offices and reducing the chapters' share of member dues. Several state chapters threatened to withdraw and become autonomous, like the historically separate Massachusetts Audubon Society. Chapter activists campaigned to replace the board, eventually forcing the society's leaders to redirect their budget priorities, redraw the bylaws to enable the chapters to nominate a percentage of board members, and ask nine of the thirty-six sitting board members to step down to make room for chapter nominees.[88]

Similar winds buffeted the Sierra Club, which struggled to balance the imperative of maintaining a strong national presence while moving more resources to state-level advocacy *and* dealing with 400 increasingly insistent and occasionally wayward local chapters. The strains led to the resignation of executive director Michael Fischer in 1992 after five years at the helm; he was replaced by his deputy, Carl Pope (who, as of 2004, continued in that position). In his outgoing address, Fischer noted that during his tenure, the Sierra Club had expended significantly more resources to support the chapters and, equally important, to reach out to previously underrepresented constituencies, "building new alliances with the hundreds of grassroots environmental organizations in the African-American, Native-American, Latino and Asian communities. We have only just begun, however; much, much more lies ahead."[89]

Organizations' membership rolls and revenues improved somewhat by the mid-1990s, but the mixed (in activists' view) record of the Clinton administration and, in particular, the Republican takeover of the House in 1995 convinced many more that their organizations were still ineffectual and out of touch. Another round of leadership changes and organizational self-assessments ensued. Jay Hair was forced out at the National Wildlife Federation, purportedly over his management style and allegations of lavish spending on headquarters operations, but more because of a general perception that, under his leadership, the federation had lost touch with its affiliates. His replacement, Mark Van Putten, came from the federation's Great Lakes regional office and had experience as a grassroots organizer. One of Van Putten's first actions was to sell off the federation's relatively opulent Washington headquarters and move into more modest suburban offices, and he stated a clear intent to revive the federation's grassroots reach.[90] At the same time, Peter Berle "retired" as president of the Audubon Society after a board-authorized strategic planning exercise highlighted continued discontent over the organization's direction and management and, more telling, its relationship with its restive chapters.[91] Berle's successor, John Flicker of the Nature Conservancy, put more stress on chapter development and instituted a more equitable sharing of resources between the national office and the chapters. The irony, of course, is that both Hair and Berle had been selected in an earlier era specifically to transform relatively staid conservation organizations into professional national environmental lobbies. Both did so—to some extent, brilliantly—but in the process, they alienated many of their staunchest members exactly when their support and activism were becoming more critical.

Organizations that lacked a traditional chapter base also began to think about creative ways to build an active grassroots presence. Having become direct-mail-fueled mass member organizations in the 1980s, organizations such as the NRDC, Environmental Defense, Wilderness Society, National Parks Conservation Association, and Defenders now had to figure out how to turn *supporters* into *members* who would be active in local and state arenas, not just names to be mobilized in national campaigns. All went through strikingly similar strategic planning exercises in the 1990s, and all came to strikingly similar conclusions: they needed an effective and locally relevant grassroots presence. "We need to work with our members to better serve, engage, and mobilize them toward our mission," declared incoming National Parks Conservation Association president Thomas Kiernan in 1998, adding, "we will win only with greater activism from our members."[92] As noted in chapter 4, many organizations considered any donor a "member," but now they increasingly recognized the need to transform check writers into activists.

The fortuitous emergence of the Internet offered a way to accomplish this goal without requiring the creation of a network of chapters, which itself might provoke conflicts with established chapter-based organizations. Smaller organizations such as RAN already understood the Internet's potential for linking far-flung activists and for organizing demonstrations or boycotts. More mainstream organizations began to realize that the technology could enable them to develop a "grassroots" capacity.[93] For example, for most of its history, Environmental Defense relied on lawsuits, cost-benefit analyses, and collaboration with corporations—not the kinds of grassroots activism promoted by the various state affiliates of Clean Water Action. Through its electronic Action Network, however, Environmental Defense could develop and maintain its own grassroots of sorts.[94] Environmental Defense is not about to become the Sierra Club, but by using the Internet, it can connect to and energize its supporters in a political context, where such mobilization is necessary, albeit not sufficient, to claim any clout with policymakers. As Robert Duffy observes, "environmentalists need people in communities working to put environmental issues on the agenda and to hold public officials accountable."[95] Heeding Robert Putnam, they are struggling to develop their massed infantry for change.

OUTSIDERS—AGAIN?

In May 2004, a federal district judge in Miami dismissed criminal charges against Greenpeace stemming from the 2002 arrest of two of its activists. The Greenpeace activists were arrested and charged with misdemeanor trespass after they climbed aboard and displayed a protest banner on a ship they thought was carrying illegally harvested Brazilian mahogany. Fifteen months later, federal prosecutors levied felony charges against the organization as an entity, relying on an 1872 law intended to deter brothel keepers from boarding ships to lure sailors to their establishments. The federal government's novel application of the law—and the fact that it hadn't been used in more than a century—was widely interpreted among activists as an effort to "chill" the use of civil disobedience.[96] "It's an incredible abuse of power," said one Sierra Club official. "We think this sets a horrible precedent for political intimidation of public interest groups."[97]

This episode underscores the contextual dimensions of advocacy tactics. We like to think that any particular organization is free to select whichever tactics it deems optimal to meet its goals. And to some degree, it is—Greenpeace chooses to engage in civil disobedience, just as the Nature Conservancy surely doesn't—but the evolution of environmental advocacy since the 1970s suggests limits to the range of action enjoyed by any single organization and the advocacy community as a whole. Not all environmental organizations want to use the same tactics, but the tactics that any of them *can* use are affected by the political opportunity structure of the moment, as much as they are shaped by the values of members or the attitudes of leaders.

Consequently, changes in that opportunity structure—such as how one administration interprets the current applicability of an old law—affect what tactics are available and, more important, deemed effective. In the 1970s, as Jeffrey Berry suggests, environmental organizations and other citizens groups of the time "succeeded precisely because they quickly emerged as well-functioning bureaucracies. The watchword of these organizations was not 'power to the people' but 'policy expertise.'"[98] But the inside strategies that were appropriate in the 1970s no longer suffice thirty years later, when every interest is represented by "well-functioning bureaucracies" and, as is so often the case, access to decision-making is shut off or constricted.

Most of the organizations studied here continue to deploy a broad array of advocacy tactics, but, as the ANWR case suggests, tactics directed at setting issue agendas, defining issues, building coalitions with like-minded advocacy organizations, and, most important, mobilizing grassroots supporters have taken more central roles. Such concerns may seem traditional, but the evident alacrity with which environmentalists concentrate on public communications and grassroots mobilization reflects the realities of the moment. In part, it is a consequence of the maturation of a policy domain characterized by an immense body of long-standing laws, regulations, and court precedents at all levels of government. Thirty-five years after passage of the National Environmental Policy Act, environmental policy issues are commonplace, and environmental concerns are interwoven into the fabric of everyday American life. Just getting an issue atop an already crowded—or consciously constricted—agenda for action takes a lot of effort, as Greenpeace knew when it sent its activists to that ship off Miami.

The widespread commitment to strategies designed to set agendas and mobilize supporters also reflects the opportunity structure of the moment. The "environment" may be a presence in everyday life, but *who* defines its meaning is an open political question. Given conservatives' success in reshaping the ideological center of American politics since the environmental era began, it stands to reason that a conservative definition of "commonsense" environmental policy is positioned to dominate debates over issues ranging from drilling in the ANWR to climate change for years to come. Despite their resources and their hard-won legitimacy, environmental advocates know that they must offer a compelling alternative if they are to keep the hearts and minds of average Americans. Their focus on outsider tactics underscores the reality of their circumstances.

6
The Mature Advocacy Community

In the environmental movement, our defeats are always final, our victories always provisional. What you save today can still be destroyed tomorrow, don't you see?
—Jose Lutzenberger

A TYPICAL MONTH

On February 2, 2004, the Bush administration included $2.4 billion in revenue from oil leases in the Arctic National Wildlife Refuge (ANWR) in its projected budget for fiscal year 2006, based on the expectation that Congress would authorize drilling there in fiscal year 2005.[1] On February 5, the Conservation Fund and Nature Conservancy jointly announced the acquisition of 24,000 acres of forestland in California's Mendocino County, a "public-private partnership" of the state, the private landowner, and a collection of local conservation groups designed to balance "sustainable forestry" with nature preservation.[2] That same day, Defenders of Wildlife reported that it had paid more than $17,000 in 2003 to compensate ranchers for losses caused by grizzly bears in the northern Rocky Mountains, part of its Proactive Carnivore Conservation initiative to reduce conflicts with private landowners over the reintroduction of bears in their region.[3]

On February 6, Conservation International and the World Wildlife Fund together urged President Bush to sign into law the Congo Basin Forest Partnership Act, authorizing federal funds for the preservation and sustainable development of endangered forest areas in central Africa. Both organizations work on projects with governments and nongovernmental organizations in the region, and they stressed the bill's urgency and, equally important, its bipartisan support.[4] The president signed the bill into law on February 13, without apparent fanfare.[5] That same day, Environmental Defense president Fred Krupp published an opinion piece in the *Hartford Courant*, warning his fellow Connecticut residents of specific long-term impacts of global warming and promoting a "climate stewardship" bill authored by Senators Joseph Lieberman (D-Connecticut) and John McCain (R-Arizona) that had obtained support from forty-four senators the previous year.[6]

On February 12, Earthjustice, the Wilderness Society, and the Southern Utah Wilderness Alliance (SUWA), a coalition of local conservation organizations, challenged the state of Utah's decision to withhold information about its legal claims to unimproved roads on federal lands approved by Secretary of the Interior Gale Norton in 2003.[7] The Wilderness Society and SUWA had successfully sued in federal court under the Freedom of Information Act to obtain Department of the Interior documents pertaining to the claims, but the state argued that its documents were privileged for legal reasons. On the same front, on February 23, a Utah court ruled in favor of a suit filed by Earthjustice, the Sierra Club, and SUWA that rejected local county claims to similar unimproved roads in the Grand Staircase–Escalante National Monument.[8]

On February 18, a coalition of environmental organizations, including the National Audubon Society, Wilderness Society, Natural Resources Defense Council, and Sierra Club, sued in federal district court to stop the Interior Department from opening an 8 million–acre section of the National Petroleum Reserve in the Alaskan Arctic for oil exploration.[9] On the nineteenth, a group of leading scientists organized by the Union of Concerned Scientists—and represented by Russell Train, administrator of the Environmental Protection Agency (EPA) under Nixon and Ford—accused the administration of distorting the use of scientific data in its policy decisions on issues such as global climate change.[10] At the same time, Clean Water Action, in a letter to the EPA, offered formal comments on proposed rule changes concerning the Toxic Release Inventory, an issue of concern to its coalition of state clean water organizations.[11]

On February 22, Ralph Nader announced that he would run as an independent candidate for president, a decision roundly criticized by Democrats and by many environmentalists as being unnecessarily divisive, and raising fears that his candidacy would only help to reelect President Bush.[12] A day later, the Sierra Club formally requested that Justice Antonin Scalia recuse himself from any Supreme Court action on the legal questions surrounding Vice President Richard Cheney's energy task force, following the justice's holiday duck-hunting trip with the vice president.[13] Justice Scalia, in a rare and lengthy public statement, refused to do so.[14]

On the twenty-third, American Rivers heralded the demolition of Embrey Dam on Virginia's Rappahannock River, which enabled the river to flow unimpeded from its headwaters in the Blue Ridge Mountains to its mouth in Chesapeake Bay for the first time in a century. "This is the culmination of nearly two decades of grassroots advocacy," said John Tippett, executive director of Friends of the Rappahannock, a local organization that worked with American Rivers.

"It's a true testament to the power of persistence and the influence of constructive community partnerships."[15] On the twenty-fifth, the National Wildlife Federation announced its opposition to President Bush's nomination of former Interior Department solicitor William Myers to the Ninth Circuit Court of Appeals, the first time in its history that the federation openly opposed a president's judicial nomination.[16]

All the while, the Sierra Club was embroiled in yet another turbulent and increasingly public board election. This time, controversy swirled around efforts by a slate of outside candidates—supported by board member and Sea Shepherds leader Paul Watson—who opposed national immigration policy as being environmentally unsustainable. Rumors that right-wing activists were encouraging supporters to join the club just to vote for the immigration reform slate led civil rights activists and liberal advocacy organizations such as Moveon.org to urge their supporters to respond in kind. As usual, the inner machinations of the wondrously permeable Sierra Club reflected broader debates within the environmental community.[17] The insurgent faction ultimately failed to win any board seats, but the debate and visibility of the election combined to attract the votes of 22 percent of all club members, the highest turnout in three decades.[18]

Aside from the spectacle at the Sierra Club—but then again, its divisive election battles have come to be rather commonplace—February 2004 was a typical month in American environmental politics. Issues that had concerned environmentalists for years—drilling in the ANWR, control over and access to public lands, the Cheney energy task force, global climate change, land use, judicial nominations, even Ralph Nader—continued to simmer. More to the point, national environmental advocacy organizations were in the thick of each conflict, sometimes individually, and sometimes as part of broader coalitions of local, national, and, in some instances, international advocacy organizations. Some of the issues were debated in local or state venues, others in Washington, and still others beyond the nation's borders.

The fact that all this seems perfectly normal brings us back to the point of this book: after nearly forty years of contemporary environmental history, national environmental advocacy organizations remain key participants in virtually every environmental debate. Individually and as an advocacy community, they have displayed a remarkable, if not necessarily painless, capacity to adapt to the realities of any particular moment. Their long-term survival and their ability to alter their resource bases, their tactics, and even their self-identities underscore the resiliency of advocacy organizations in general, a characteristic that gets too little attention from students of interest group politics.[19]

To critics in the environmental community, however, such adaptation always seems to be a reaction to some external challenge. In their view, adaptation is not the same as being proactive or even effective. That same February, the Bluewater Network, a relatively new San Francisco–based organization that claims 20,000 members and "e-activists" and a budget of about $1 million, ran ads in major newspapers excoriating the poor fuel efficiency of sport utility vehicles (SUVs) produced by the Ford Motor Company. The ad was hard-hitting and portrayed company chairman Bill Ford as a grotesque Pinocchio, the wooden puppet whose nose grew each time he told a lie. Ford's fib, according to Bluewater, was his pledge in 2000 to improve the fuel efficiency of his company's SUV fleet by 25 percent in five years, a goal toward which little progress had been made. Joining Bluewater in the campaign was Greenpeace and a coalition of state and local activist groups. No other national environmental organization participated. The Sierra Club, although it too had criticized Ford on its fuel-efficiency record, declined to take part in what it saw as an overly adversarial message. In response, Bluewater president Russell Long said simply, "Environmental groups have been ineffective. Despite spending millions of dollars in this battle, we've failed."[20]

AMATEURS NO MORE

This book has been guided by three questions: First, how have those organizations that constitute what I call the national environmental advocacy community adapted over time to ensure their own survival and, by extension, their continued relevance to the national discourse on environmental issues and policy options? Second, how have these processes of organizational adaptation shaped the advocacy community as a whole? Finally, in line with the opinions of their critics, have these organizations mattered?

This last question is relevant to the other two. I was intrigued about these organizations in their own right, but also because of the criticisms leveled at them for as long as I have studied environmental politics, in particular, the charge that, in the words of one Sierra Club dissident, the big groups have become "old, fat, and unimaginative."[21] And that was in the early 1990s. Longtime environmental journalist Philip Shabecoff, though not doubting the dedication of environmental leaders, agrees that the organizations have changed, and not always for the better:

> What has changed is that as the organizations themselves have become more mature and professional, in many areas a certain bureaucratization and institutional fatigue have set in. In size and structure, many of the national and international groups have become like business organizations,

> with sizeable budgets, plush offices, and reasonably attractive salaries and benefits. They are in a kind of comfort zone that makes them somewhat risk averse.[22]

Being "old, fat, and unimaginative" is arguably better than being dead, but the question of efficacy is valid and takes us back to the core question: how have these organizations managed to survive, in some instances for more than a century, despite the supposedly tremendous odds against their longevity? Not only have they overcome the collective action problems that are supposed to afflict all interest groups—member-based public-interest advocacy organizations in particular—but they apparently have done so to such a degree that their very size and relative wealth are cause for alarm. Has solving one set of problems created other ones? If so, why did these organizations evolve in this way?

As shown throughout this book, the short answer to this last question is that the organizations were *forced* to transform themselves over time from relatively amateur outfits, often supported by a few elite patrons, into today's mass-based professional advocacy organizations. That is, they responded to internal organizational stresses and external political pressures by growing larger, diversifying their sources of revenue, replacing volunteers with professional staff, and adopting the kinds of management procedures one expects to find in any well-run nonprofit organization—or any corporation, for that matter. In short, they went from being protest "groups" to advocacy "organizations," with all the positive and negative connotations that come with such a transformation.[23]

Despite what the critics aver, I wonder whether these organizations had any real choice. Their systematic and *universal* transformation was driven first by the need to generate the resources sufficient to maintain themselves beyond their birth years. After all, organizations lacking a sufficient resource capacity cannot stay in the advocacy arena in any meaningful way for very long. Even militant groups such as Paul Watson's Sea Shepherds or the Native Forest Council cannot function for long without the expertise offered by managerial staff and even fund-raisers. Earth First!, every Green's favorite "anti-organization," was always more of a loosely knit and highly romanticized claque of activists than anything else. That may have been the intent, but its long-term policy impacts will probably depend on how other activists in *real* organizations take its ideas and apply them to real issues in real places. Sustained issue advocacy requires organization and resources. Ideals matter, but so does money. It buys more robust organizational capacity, greater independence of action, and, as a result, the ability to maintain an active presence in a variety of decision-making venues over a long period.[24] If being "old, fat, and unimaginative" is bad, being weak and irrelevant is a lot worse.

Finding the resources to survive is a constant challenge, and this study shows the high degree of inventiveness—born of necessity, or even desperation—that environmental organizations have exhibited to tap new sources of revenue as others dried up. In this regard, as suggested in chapter 4, the key to their current and future fiscal health and continued political relevance was their almost universal shift to "mass membership environmentalism" in the 1980s. Specialized niche operations such as the Environmental Working Group or land conservancies such as the Conservation Fund aside, it is hard to imagine any national environmental organization surviving for long without a significant base of middle-class supporters able and willing stick with it through thick and thin for years on end. The demise of Environmental Action, not to mention the virtual collapse of Greenpeace, underscores the degree to which any organization depends on a broad base of loyal supporters. Lose them, and you lose everything.

In a fiscal sense, at least, the charges of elitism often leveled against the major national environmental organizations bear little weight. Very few organizations can afford the luxury of excluding anyone who wants to sign up, no matter how small his or her contribution might be. In comparison to the extent of elite patronage in previous generations—not to mention in their foundation- and corporate-dependent critics on the right—the relative democratization of financial support for environmental advocacy is an underappreciated reality. Writing a check to the Wilderness Society may not have the same civic weight as being an active member of the local Elks Club, but with all due respect to Robert Putnam, the cumulative "votes" of millions of environmental organization supporters must count for something.[25] After all, even passive donors pay attention.

In addition, these organizations transformed themselves to respond to external political challenges threatening to undermine their goals and, by extension, their reason for existence. It isn't always about the money, no matter what the critics say. During the 1970s, for example, environmental organizations had to adjust from seeking the passage of new laws to ensuring the successful implementation of those already enacted.[26] With a spate of new federal laws on the books, the youthful activists of the environmental movement—as well as their mature counterparts in the conservation organizations—now faced the prospect of long meetings with federal bureaucrats and corporate lawyers to hash out rules, standards, procedures, and timetables. What had been won in Congress could have been lost at the conference table, in the courtroom, or in the back alleys of Congress, and environmental organizations adapted by hiring more scientists, policy experts, economists, and lawyers. In similar ways, they were forced to respond to the Reagan revolution of the 1980s, to the emerging Republican congressional majority in the 1990s, and to the Bush administration in the

2000s. In each instance, these organizations were engaged in political conflict within a crowded advocacy arena where they were but one set of actors, and compared with the elected officials, political parties, bureaucrats, and judges, they were rarely the dominant ones. After all, they're *only* interest groups, advocacy outsiders that don't even enjoy the privileged position of business in a capitalist economy.

In this regard, environmental organizations are always adjusting to changes in the political opportunity structure, whether shifts in partisan control of key governing institutions; alterations in legislative procedures, administrative rules, and judicial precedent; or the emergence of new technologies for mass communication. They try to shape the opportunity structure, of course, by supporting candidates, proposing reforms, engaging in lawsuits, and agitating, but more often they find themselves reacting to changes generated elsewhere and by others. They are no different from any other organized interest in any other policy domain; even the National Rifle Association owes its success more to the geographic nature of congressional representation than to its purported power as an organization. But that's the point: failure to adapt to new political conditions can spell deep trouble for any particular advocacy organization, and widespread failure to adapt to major perturbations in the political landscape (e.g., Reagan) can destabilize an entire advocacy community.

This dynamic of organizational adaptation and transformation is hardly uniform, of course. Some environmental organizations were unable to adapt, but their demise was due less to leadership myopia or incompetence (although both certainly matter) than to pressures generated by the *other* organizations in the advocacy population within which they all resided. No organization, no matter how large, is free to act as if it were the only game in town. In particular, as described in chapter 3, Environmental Action ran into trouble because it could not compete with other organizations in its sector or carve out a niche of its own, free from direct competition. The patterns of niche seeking and sector partitioning most clearly surfaced in the 1980s, as the many organizations created during the environmental era—not to mention their conservation-oriented predecessors—struggled to find safe havens for themselves as the movement matured into an advocacy community. Even the Sierra Club struggled. Environmental Action found itself in the worst possible situation, forced to compete in its niche with larger organizations on one side and more nimble ones on the other. Like a local grocery store chain caught between the size of Wal-Mart and the boutique attraction of Whole Foods, Environmental Action was unable to compete in its niche and went out of business. The lesson to be learned from this—as well as from the merger of fellow niche occupants Friends of the Earth and the Environmental Policy Institute—is that we cannot understand the success or failure of any one advocacy organization without understanding its particular position in the broader advocacy marketplace.[27]

But why was Environmental Action an exception, not the rule? I suspect the answer lies more at the population level of analysis than with any individual organization. After all, in theory, every advocacy organization has access to the same types of fund-raising talent, the same management manuals and workshops, and the same well of potential leaders, so the explanation for any one organization's success or demise must lie with its relative place in the particular advocacy community. Greenpeace may be unlikely to tap the same donors as Ducks Unlimited, but the Wilderness Society always has to keep one eye on its close neighbor and occasional competitor, the much larger and far wealthier Sierra Club.[28] Fortunately, the national environmental advocacy community is broad and internally variegated. Its ideological breadth and array of policy and tactical niches offer opportunities for many organizations of all sizes and orientations. In short, there are a lot of national environmental organizations because there is room for them.

Even so, the national environmental advocacy community has a definite topography on which its many constituent organizations must position themselves. Competition among otherwise like-minded organizations is assured unless they can find ways to distinguish themselves from one another. If it were a narrower and more internally homogeneous community, the number and types of organizations within it would be very different, as would the scope and intensity of interorganization competition and niche seeking. In contrast to the vastness of the environmental community, the national gun rights or anti-abortion advocacy communities are narrower and far less internally diverse. The National Rifle Association and the National Right to Life Committee dominate their respective advocacy communities to a degree that no environmental organization—not even the Sierra Club or the Natural Resources Defense Council—finds possible. We look at such market-level factors when studying the behavior and performance of corporations, but we rarely apply the same logic to interest groups. We somehow accept their existence as a matter of fact, as normal, but never ask why this is so. Understanding the topography of a particular advocacy domain, and an organization's place in it, is a good start.

The overall point is that internal maintenance requirements and external pressures—generated by both foes and friends—drove this process of adaptation, particularly as the national environmental advocacy community grew denser and more internally diverse following the spasm of organizational creation in the 1960s and 1970s. As noted, this process was not inevitable—

individual leaders chose what they were going to do—but in the main, it was a uniform organizational response to common imperatives. They grew up because they had no choice.

MAINTAINING PRESENCE

On the fact of their survival there is little disagreement, but whether their adaptation as organizations has been good for environmental policy—or the environment—is a matter of debate. For many environmental advocates, especially those on the left, the answer is no. "The best that can be said with any degree of certainty," argues Mark Dowie, "is that if the movement had not existed things would be worse."[29] During 1980s, he states,

> Most of the mainstream organizations lost the momentum they had developed in previous decades. In a desperate drive to win respectability and access in Washington, mainstream leaders politely pursued a course of accommodation and capitulation with elected officials, regulators, and polluters. Compromise . . . became the habitual response . . . even in the face of irreversible degradation. These compromises have pushed a once-effective movement to the brink of irrelevance.[30]

Not so, responds longtime environmental writer Kirkpatrick Sale: "the movement of the last thirty years has altered American consciousness and American behavior, with consequences as profound as any movement since that against slavery in the nineteenth century."[31]

Irrelevant, or shapers of profound change? Both? We thus come back to the basic question: the organizations that make up the national environmental community have adapted and survived, but have they made a difference? The short answer is, of course they did. Even Dowie admits that. But the question is not as silly or dependent on personal ideology as it sounds, given the sharp critiques about the mainstream environmental advocacy community raised by its foes and friends. The "contemporary environmental movement will endure," argues Ronald Shaiko, "not because it is terribly effective as a collective policy advocate, but because of technological and organizational innovations that, for the time being, allow individual organizations to maintain sufficient membership bases and patron support to meet monthly payrolls."[32] He has a point. The national environmental community is not a great "collective policy advocate" in the way that the gay rights or anti-abortion movement is, or the civil rights movement of the 1960s was. For that matter, the fledgling environmental movement of thirty years ago was only a bit more cohesive than its mature offspring.

In fact, old-line conservation organizations such as Audubon and the National Wildlife Federation were hesitant to embrace the original Earth Day, fearing that the new environmental ethos, with its emphasis on human health and lifestyle issues, would draw attention and resources away from traditional wildlife concerns.[33] The breadth and diversity of the contemporary advocacy community impede casual cohesion, and it is not surprising to find one clutch of environmental organizations facing off against another over issues like NAFTA. If one looks closely at history, the only time the movement displayed any real cohesion was when environmentalists were forced into one another's arms by a potent common foe, whether Reagan, the Gingrich-led House of Representatives, or George W. Bush. Those yearning for cohesion should be careful what they wish for.

In the main, I think critics have it wrong. Had these organizations not adapted, it is unlikely that the policy gains made during the heady early days of the environmental era would have been sustained, and environmentalism as a value system probably would not occupy its current position as a legitimate critique of economic and political orthodoxy. In this regard, to echo Jeffrey Berry's point about liberal citizens groups in general, environmentalists endured because they "built strong, well-managed organizations."[34] As noted, there was nothing inevitable about how the national environmental advocacy community evolved. It could have faded away, joining the nuclear freeze and population control movements as compelling historical footnotes, or it could have evolved into a smaller, less robust collection of organizations. But it did neither.

How do these organizations, especially in their mature form, matter? In 1972, Anthony Downs wondered whether environmentalism would survive the "issue-attention" cycle.[35] It did, but no political party, no president, no member of Congress can claim credit for its endurance. Environmentalists and, in particular, the advocacy organizations they created and maintained should get most of the recognition.

How so? American politics is, above all else, about maintaining a visible *presence*—a constant, continuous presence. Every study of policymaking over time, regardless of issue area, observes roughly the same dynamic: policy change requires persistent participation by organized advocates for change.[36] It is about the struggle to determine the scope of conflict; as E. E. Schattschneider observed more than forty years ago, it is about taking part in the never-ending competition between opposing sides of issues.[37] These organized advocates work to define the issues, get them on the agenda of action, mobilize coalitions of support, and, perhaps most important over the long term, ensure that gains won are not rolled back. They certainly do all this within institutional and macropolitical contexts, where they are not necessarily the dominant actors and do not have any particular advantage, but without their constant presence, it is hard to imagine that U.S. environmentalism, whatever its flaws, would be in any better shape.

This notion of maintaining presence extends to the international sphere as well. Loose transnational environmental advocacy networks, including environmental organizations such as Greenpeace, Rainforest Action Network, Friends of the Earth, Environmental Defense, and World Wildlife Fund, "changed the tone of debate" on tropical forest issues in the 1980s, argue Margaret Keck and Kathryn Sikkink. Their constant participation in a global arena traditionally dominated by the World Bank, the International Monetary Fund, national governments, and multinational corporations has forced the inclusion of environmental and social justice considerations in development decisions, where they had previously received little if any attention.[38] As Paul Wapner observes more broadly, "transnational" environmental organizations such as Greenpeace, Friends of the Earth, and the World Wildlife Fund do not just lobby governments; by being part of what Wapner calls "global civil society," they "significantly shape widespread behavior as it relates to environmental issues."[39]

Wapner's point bears repeating. *Only* environmental organizations consistently advocate for environmental values within local, national, and international policy venues. That's why they exist, after all. If they became large and professional—even bureaucratic—those changes came in response to the perceived need to maintain a sizable and sustained advocacy presence in many policy venues at many levels simultaneously. With Big Business, Big Government, and Big Labor comes Big Environment. In this regard, the evolution of the national environmental organizations reflects the evolution of American advocacy politics writ large. Movements for change become institutionalized, or they die.

But if maintaining a presence is a necessary condition for promoting policy change, it isn't a sufficient one. Critics are correct that although the major national environmental organizations may be adept at the hand-to-hand combat of everyday politics, they rarely generate the ideas that ultimately shape political discourse and shift the tides of history. If the past is any guide, those ideas and impulses come from the outside, from thinkers and activists out on the fringes, from the "militants" whose ideas eventually form the next generation's "mainstream" values. But that process of osmosis doesn't just happen. Rather, it occurs because organized advocates make those ideas central to their discursive appeals in real debates over real issues. In doing so, they take the ideas, smooth the rough edges, and make them palatable to the mass citizenry, whose votes (or at least tacit acceptance) matter. That Americans generally embrace the legitimacy of environmental values despite all the contradictions in their belief system is due in no small part to the ceaseless efforts of environmental activists.[40]

LOOKING TO THE FUTURE

The old environmental movement is over, in a sense. That movement arose as a defense against the industrial economy and to save some precious pieces of the landscape from human industrial endeavor. It was appropriate. But we need now to move to a new era where we find synergy and sympathy between the built and natural environments. We need to move from a strategy of defending bits and pieces of nature to recognizing the links between a healthy community and a healthy environment.
—Spencer Beebe, cofounder, Conservation International

In the early 1990s, I argued that the notion of a movement no longer aptly described the immense array of organizations dedicated to protecting, saving, or fixing some part of the environment.[41] That statement is truer than ever. The imagery of movement no longer fits the reality of a mature advocacy community, so it is time to move on. The environmental movement is no more, but its mature offspring are everywhere, embedded in the very fabric of national and international discourse. Environmentalism is better for it.

What does the future hold? Barring some fundamental reordering in the American value system, major organizations such as the Sierra Club and the Natural Resources Defense Council will continue in their roles as the quasi-green parties of American politics, representing the aggregated views of millions of citizens in the many venues of policy discourse and decision. They will continue to adapt their agendas and tactics to new issues and challenges, with their place as permanent fixtures in the political system continuing to elicit little comment. Following close after the major organizations are the many more sector-specific and niche organizations that act to keep watch, to defend, and to act as representatives of their respective constituencies.

The breadth and diversity of that advocacy community guarantee both its overall stability and its internal turmoil. The environmental community itself is not going away, but its internal composition is not fixed in stone. New organizations like the Bluewater Network will be created to push new values, to occupy underutilized policy or ideological niches, or to take maximum advantage of new technologies. Some existing organizations will die out or merge with others, although we are not likely to see a fundamental reshuffling of the organizational deck, barring a collapse of a major organization.

Having said this, mergers among midsize organizations are not inconceivable. For example, the National Parks Conservation Association and the Wilderness Society pursue complementary agendas on federal lands, broadly understood. A merger might be worth consideration. Their respective supporters might protest that such an idea is unacceptable—ridiculous, even—for a whole host of historical, ideological, and mission-relevant reasons. After all, issues concerning the national parks are fundamentally different from those affecting other types of federal lands. Or are they? Moreover, such a move could be seen as a strategic response (for the Wilderness Society, at least) to the dominance of the Sierra Club on the one hand and the increasingly troublesome competition posed by new organizations such as Bluewater on the other. Given relatively flat membership and fiscal performances at both organizations in the recent past (see tables 3.1 and 4.2, respectively), neither should be sanguine about the future.

More likely are mergers among niche organizations, or between them and relevant sectoral players, especially as new organizations continue to enter the advocacy marketplace. Can a National Park Trust continue to survive on its own, or would it be better off merged into a major land conservancy, or even absorbed back into the National Parks Conservation Association? Lingering personal conflicts among erstwhile association colleagues might preclude the last option for a while, but the extremely constricted nature of its niche makes the trust's long-term viability doubtful. For those without a sustainable niche, bigger will continue to be better for those in the environmental "protest business,"[42] particularly if they want to go toe-to-toe with corporations and governments.

Environmental advocacy will continue to thrive beyond the big organizations. To expect otherwise is to deny the realities of group formation and mobilization in the United States. Part of this process will bubble up from the always turbulent grassroots, but a great deal of it will continue the process whereby long-established major organizations beget splinter groups when frustrated activists decide to pursue their own paths. New policy and tactical niches will continue to be created, while existing ones might disappear or get so crowded that their occupants seek partners. Population-level stability will continue to obscure sector- and niche-specific instability.

The environmental community's ideological wings will also become even more pronounced. On the right, free-market devotees in the Competitiveness Enterprise Institute will jostle with the "commonsense" traditionalists of the Izaak Walton League and the social conservatives in the Evangelical Environmental Network, part of that broader struggle within American conservatism to address acknowledged environmental problems within the confines of economic and political orthodoxy. On the left, the "deep greens" of Earth First! and its anarchist spin-off, the Environmental Liberation Front, plus a broad array of environmental justice advocates of many stripes will demand that environmentalism confront fundamental issues of global market capitalism and social inequality.[43] All will share a core belief in the holism inherent in environmental and social values, but they will differ in priorities, strategies, and tactics.

The environmental movement has evolved into a mature and very typical American interest group community, albeit one with an impressive array of policy niches and potential forms of activism. Its breadth and variety will be its lifeblood and its salvation, for within every major group resides tomorrow's rebels, frustrated believers determined to challenge the status quo by starting their own groups. There are no guarantees that some existing organizations will be around in a decade or two—the marketplace for environmental advocacy is a competitive one—but there will be a vibrant community of organizations dedicated to environmental values in all their many forms, both at home and globally. Its broad dimensions are now before us.

Notes

1. A MOVEMENT ASTRAY?

1. White House press release, "President Announces Wetlands Initiative on Earth Day," April 22, 2004, at www.whitehouse.gov/news/releases/2004/04/print/2004 0422-4.html.

2. White House press release, "President Bush Presents Environmental Youth Awards," April 22, 2004, at www.whitehouse.gov/news/releases/2004/04/2004 0422-7.html.

3. Elisabeth Busmiller, "Bush Promotes Wetlands Plan to Counter Kerry's Attack," *New York Times,* April 24, 2004, A13.

4. Felicity Barringer, "U.S. Won't Narrow Wetlands Protection," *New York Times,* December 17, 2003, A24; editorial, "Rescuing Wetlands," *New York Times,* December 18, 2003, A30.

5. National Wildlife Federation press release, "President Bush's Wetlands Initiative Doesn't Hold Water, NWF's Statement on the President's Earth Day Announcement," April 22, 2004, at www.nwf.org/news/.

6. Katherine Q. Seelye and Jennifer 8. Lee, "Court Blocks U.S. Effort to Relax Pollution Rule," *New York Times,* December 25, 2003, A1.

7. See Norman J. Vig, "Presidential Leadership and the Environment: From Reagan to Clinton," in *Environmental Policy,* 4th ed., ed. Norman J. Vig and Michael E. Kraft (Washington, D.C.: CQ Press, 2000), 98–120.

8. See Deborah Lynn Guber, "Voting Preferences and the Environment in the American Electorate," *Society and Natural Resources* 14, no. 6 (2001): 455–69.

9. See, for example, assessments offered in Norman Vig and Michael Kraft, eds., *Environmental Policy: New Directions for the 21st Century,* 5th ed. (Washington, D.C.: CQ Press, 2003).

10. Christopher Drew and Richard A. Oppel Jr., "How Industry Won the Battle of Pollution Control at EPA," *New York Times,* March 6, 2004, A1, A10.

11. Eric Pianin and Guy Gugliotta, "EPA Chief Whitman to Resign: Former N.J. Governor's Tenure Gets Mixed Reviews," *Washington Post,* May 22, 2003, A1.

12. Charles R. Shipan and William R. Lowry, "Environmental Policy and Party Divergence in Congress," *Political Research Quarterly* 54, no. 2 (June 2000): 245–63.

13. Tom Knudson, "Fat of the Land: Movement's Prosperity Comes at a High Price," *Sacramento Bee,* April, 22, 2001, 1, at www.sacbee.com/news/projects/environment/ index02.html.

14. Michael Frome, "In Defense of Wildlife and Open Expression," *Wild Earth* 3, no. 1 (Spring 1993): 60–62.

15. Knudson, "Fat of the Land."

16. Tim Breen, "House Members Rip Green Groups," *Greenwire* 10, no. 9 (May 10, 2001), at www.greenwire.com.

17. Alexander Cockburn, "Greens, Fears, and Dollars," *Nation* 271, no. 21 (December 25, 2000): 10.

18. Alexander Cockburn, "Roush Axed," *Nation* 262, no. 14 (April 8, 1996): 10; and "Wilderness Society: A Saga of Shame Continues," *Nation* 260, no. 9 (March 6, 1995): 300.

19. Katherine Kerlin, "Giving Greenpeace a Chance: After Internal Turmoil, a More Focused Greenpeace Is Back Fighting Polluters," *E: The Environmental Magazine* 7, no. 5 (September–October 2001): 12–16.

20. David B. Ottaway and Joe Stephens, "Nonprofit Land Bank Amasses Billions: Charity Builds Assets on Corporate Partnerships," *Washington Post,* May 4, 2003, A1.

21. Philip Shabecoff, "New Leaders and a New Era for Environmentalists," *New York Times,* November 25, 1985, D28.

22. Keith Schneider, "Selling Out? Pushed and Pulled, Environment Inc. Is on the Defensive," *New York Times,* March 29, 1992, sec. 4, p. 1.

23. Mark Dowie, *Losing Ground: American Environmentalism at the Close of the Twentieth Century* (Cambridge, Mass.: MIT Press, 1995), xii.

24. A point made by Jeffrey Berry in *The New Liberalism: The Rising Power of Citizen Groups* (Washington, D.C.: Brookings Institution, 1999), 153–70.

25. See, for example, Karlyn H. Bowman and Everett Carll Ladd, *Attitudes toward the Environment* (Washington, D.C.: American Enterprise Institute, 1995).

26. Anthony Downs, "Up and Down with Ecology: The Issue-Attention Cycle," *Public Interest* 28 (1972): 38–50.

27. See Robin Toner, "Step by Step, Abortion's Opponents Claim the Middle Ground," *New York Times,* April 25, 2004, sec. 4, p. 1.

28. See, for example, Berry, *The New Liberalism;* Charles C. Euchner, *Extraordinary Politics: How Protest and Dissent Are Changing American Democracy* (Boulder, Colo.: Westview Press, 1996); Sidney Tarrow, *Power in Movement: Social Movements, Collective Action, and Politics* (New York: Cambridge University Press, 1994).

29. See Grant A. Jordan and William Maloney, *The Protest Business? Mobilizing Campaign Groups* (New York: Manchester University Press, 1997).

30. See Kirkpatrick Sale, *The Green Revolution: The American Environmental Movement, 1962–1992* (New York: Hill and Wang, 1993).

31. Ronald G. Shaiko, *Voices and Echoes for the Environment: Public Interest Representation in the 1990s and Beyond* (New York: Columbia University Press, 1999), 8; see also Jeffrey M. Berry, *Lobbying for the People: The Political Behavior of Public Interest Groups* (Princeton, N.J.: Princeton University Press, 1977).

32. See Robert C. Lowry, "The Political Economy of Environmental Citizen Groups" (doctoral dissertation, Harvard University, 1993), 183; David M. Hart, "The Ecology of High-Tech Business Interests in Washington, D.C.: Assembly Rules and Resource Partitioning" (paper presented at the annual meeting of the Midwest Political Science Association, Chicago, 2001).

33. Naftali Bendavid, "Time Held Them Green and Dying: Unwilling to Compromise or Adapt, Environmental Action Calls It Quits after 26 Years," *Recorder,* December 6, 1996, 1, via Lexis/Nexis.

34. See Virginia Gray and David Lowery, *The Population Ecology of Interest Representation: Lobbying Communities in the American States* (Ann Arbor: University of Michigan Press, 1996), 30.

35. William P. Browne, *Private Interests, Public Policy, and American Agriculture* (Lawrence: University Press of Kansas, 1988).

36. But see, for example, Andrew Savage, John Isham, and Christopher McGrory Klyza, "The Greening of Social Capital: An Examination of Land-Based Groups in Two Vermont Counties," *Rural Sociology* (forthcoming).

37. Frank R. Baumgartner and Beth L. Leech, *Basic Interests: The Importance of Groups in Politics and in Political Science* (Princeton, N.J.: Princeton University Press, 1998), 28; Jack L. Walker Jr., *Mobilizing Interest Groups in America: Patrons, Professions, and Social Movements* (Ann Arbor: University of Michigan Press, 1991); Robert H. Salisbury, "Interest Representation: The Dominance of Institutions," *American Political Science Review* 78, no. 1 (March 1984): 64–76.

38. See Baumgartner and Leech, *Basic Interests;* Shaiko, *Voices and Echoes.*

39. See Gray and Lowery, *Population Ecology.*

40. Ibid.

41. Walker, *Mobilizing Interest Groups;* Berry, *Lobbying for the People;* Kay Lehman Schlozman and John T. Tierney, *Organized Interests and American Democracy* (New York: Harper and Row, 1986); John P. Heinz, Edward O. Laumann, Robert L. Nelson, and Robert H. Salisbury, *The Hollow Core: Private Interests in National Policymaking* (Cambridge: Harvard University Press, 1993); Frank R Baumgartner, and Beth L. Leech, "Issue Niches and Policy Bandwagons: Patterns of Interest Group Involvement in National Politics," *Journal of Politics* 63, no. 4 (November 2001): 1191–213.

42. Berry, *New Liberalism.*

43. Lawrence S. Rothenberg, *Linking Citizens to Government: Interest Group Politics at Common Cause* (New York: Cambridge University Press, 1992).

44. Gray and Lowery, *Population Ecology.*

45. Shaiko, *Voices and Echoes.*

46. Gray and Lowery, *Population Ecology,* 39.

47. Ibid., 65.

48. Ibid., 39.

49. E. E. Schattschneider, *The Semi-Sovereign People: A Realist's View of Democracy in America* (New York: Holt, Rinehart, and Winston, 1960).

50. Baumgartner and Leech, *Basic Interests,* xviii.

2. OPPORTUNITIES AND ORIGINS

1. Thomas B. Allen, *Guardian of the Wild: The Story of the National Wildlife Federation, 1936–1986* (Bloomington: Indiana University Press, 1987), 18.

2. Ibid., 27.

3. See Frank R. Baumgartner and Beth L. Leech, *Basic Interests: The Importance*

of Groups in Politics and in Political Science (Princeton, N.J.: Princeton University Press, 1998).

4. See Robert Salisbury, "An Exchange Theory of Interest Groups," *Midwest Journal of Political Science* 13 (1969): 1–32.

5. Jack L. Walker Jr., *Mobilizing Interest Groups in America: Patrons, Professions, and Social Movements* (Ann Arbor: University of Michigan Press, 1991); James Q. Wilson, *Political Organizations* (New York: Basic Books, 1973).

6. David S. Meyer and Douglas R. Imig, "Political Opportunity and the Rise and Decline of Interest Group Sectors," *Social Science Journal* 30 (1993): 253–70.

7. Elizabeth S. Clemens, *The People's Lobby: Organizational Innovation and the Rise of Interest Group Politics in the United States, 1890–1925* (Chicago: University of Chicago Press, 1997).

8. See Steven Skowronek, *Building the New American State: The Expansion of National Administrative Capacities* (New York: Cambridge University Press, 1981).

9. For example, William P. Browne, *Private Interests, Public Policy, and American Agriculture* (Lawrence: University Press of Kansas, 1988).

10. Walker, *Mobilizing Interest Groups;* Jeffrey Berry, *The New Liberalism: The Rising Power of Citizen Groups* (Washington, D.C.: Brookings Institution, 1999).

11. David B. Truman, *The Governmental Process: Political Interests and Public Opinion* (New York: Knopf, 1951).

12. Clemens, *People's Lobby,* 2.

13. Samuel P. Hays, *Conservation and the Gospel of Efficiency: The Progressive Conservation Movement, 1890–1920* (Cambridge: Harvard University Press, 1959).

14. Skowronek, *Building the New American State.*

15. See Robert D. Putnam, *Bowling Alone: The Collapse and Revival of American Community* (New York: Simon and Schuster, 2000).

16. See Michael Cohen, *The History of the Sierra Club, 1892–1970* (San Francisco: Sierra Club Books, 1988); also, Stephen Fox, *John Muir and His Legacy: The American Conservation Movement* (Boston: Little, Brown, 1981).

17. Cohen, *History of the Sierra Club,* 9.

18. Ibid., 14–16; Hays, *Conservation and the Gospel of Efficiency,* passim.

19. Hays, *Conservation and the Gospel of Efficiency,* 192.

20. Fox, *John Muir,* 144; emphasis in original.

21. Cohen, *History of the Sierra Club,* 26.

22. Ibid., 27.

23. Ibid., 32; see also Fox, *John Muir,* 139–46.

24. See Frank Graham Jr., *The Audubon Ark: A History of the National Audubon Society* (New York: Knopf, 1990), 14. George Bird Grinnell, editor of *Forest and Stream,* formed the original Audubon Society in 1886. Within three months, it attracted more than 38,000 members, overwhelming Grinnell's ability to run the organization from his office. He disbanded the group in 1888.

25. Ibid., 41.

26. Ibid., 45–47.

27. Fox, *John Muir,* 154.

28. Hays, *Conservation and the Gospel of Efficiency,* 25–35; see also Char Miller, *Gifford Pinchot and the Making of Modern Environmentalism* (Washington, D.C.: Island Press, 2001).

29. Hays, *Conservation and the Gospel of Efficiency,* 141.

30. Ibid., 179.

31. An argument made by Paul S. Sutter, *Driven Wild: How the Fight against Automobiles Launched the Modern Wilderness Movement* (Seattle: University of Washington Press, 2002), 13; see also, Fox, *John Muir,* 148–82.

32. Clemens, *People's Lobby,* 302.

33. Cohen, *History of the Sierra Club,* 56.

34. Graham, *Audubon Ark,* 70.

35. Ibid., 110.

36. Ibid., 114–17.

37. Fox, *John Muir,* 158.

38. See John C. Miles, *Guardians of the Parks: A History of the National Parks and Conservation Association* (Washington, D.C.: Taylor and Francis, 1995).

39. Sutter, *Driven Wild,* 105.

40. Miles, *Guardians of the Parks,* 20–21.

41. IWLA, 2001 annual report, 34; James A. Tober, "Izaak Walton League," in *Conservation and Environmentalism: An Encyclopedia,* ed. Robert Paehlke (New York: Garland Publishing, 1995), 373.

42. IWLA, articles of incorporation, as amended in 2001, article 2.

43. Allen, *Guardian of the Wild,* 23.

44. Fox, *John Muir,* 162.

45. Ibid., 169.

46. Ibid., 172.

47. See ibid., 181–217.

48. On the founding of the Wilderness Society, see Sutter, *Driven Wild.*

49. Ibid., 6.

50. Ibid., 233.

51. Ibid., 250.

52. Fox, *John Muir,* 212.

53. James M. Glober, "Wilderness Society," in Paehlke, *Conservation and Environmentalism: An Encyclopedia,* 686–87.

54. David R. Brower, *For Earth's Sake: The Life and Times of David Brower* (Salt Lake City: Peregrine Smith Books, 1990), 229.

55. Allen, *Guardian of the Wild,* 32; see also Fox, *John Muir,* 195–96.

56. Allen, *Guardian of the Wild,* 28.

57. Fox, *John Muir,* 196.

58. Kevin McNamee, "Ducks Unlimited," in Paehlke, *Conservation and Environmentalism: An Encyclopedia,* 183.

59. Ducks Unlimited, annual report, 2001, 30.

60. On the New Deal regime, see George Hoberg, *Pluralism by Design: Environmental Policy and the American Regulatory State* (Westport, Conn.: Praeger, 1992).

61. Cohen, *History of the Sierra Club,* 84.

62. Ibid., 85.

63. See A. Grant McConnell, "The Conservation Movement—Past and Present," *Western Political Quarterly* 7 (1954): 467.

64. Cohen, *History of the Sierra Club,* 100.

65. Miles, *Guardians of the Parks,* 177.

66. Graham, *Audubon Ark,* 186; Christopher J. Bosso, *Pesticides and Politics: The Life Cycle of a Public Issue* (Pittsburgh: University of Pittsburgh Press, 1987), 83–85.

67. Allen, *Guardian of the Wild,* 50.

68. Fox, *John Muir,* 282.

69. Cohen, *History of the Sierra Club,* 152.

70. Ibid., 149.

71. Allen, *Guardian of the Wild,* 51.

72. Fox, *John Muir,* 266–72.

73. Robert Holbert, *Tax Laws and Political Access: The Bias of Pluralism Revisited* (Beverly Hills, Calif.: Sage Publications, 1975).

74. Letter to the Massachusetts Forestry and Park Association from the acting deputy commissioner of the IRS, June 2, 1939, carton 6 of the archives of the Massachusetts Forestry Association/Environmental League of Massachusetts, deposited in the Massachusetts Historical Society. For a discussion, see Christopher J. Bosso (with Vanessa Green), "Beyond Conservation: The Evolution of the Environmental League of Massachusetts" (paper presented to the Boston Environmental History Seminar, Massachusetts Historical Society, February 10, 2004).

75. Cohen, *History of the Sierra Club,* 163–85.

76. Jamie Heard, "Washington Pressures: Friends of the Earth Give Environmental Interests an Activist Voice," *National Journal,* August 8, 1971, 1718.

77. *Frothingham v. Mellon,* 262 U.S. 447 (1923); see also Karen Orren, "Standing to Sue: Interest Group Conflict in the Federal Courts," *American Political Science Review* 70, no. 3 (September 1976): 723–41.

78. Bosso, *Pesticides and Politics,* 94–96.

79. Foundation for Public Affairs, *Public Interest Profiles* (Washington, D.C.: Foundation for Public Affairs, 1980), F14.

80. Chris H. Lewis, "Conservation Foundation," in Paehlke, *Conservation and Environmentalism: An Encyclopedia,* 148–49.

81. David B. Ottaway and Joe Stephens, "Nonprofit Land Bank Amasses Billions, Charity Builds Assets on Corporate Partnerships," *Washington Post,* May 4, 2003, A1.

82. James A. Tober, "Defenders of Wildlife," in Paehlke, *Conservation and Environmentalism: An Encyclopedia,* 168.

83. Robert Cameron Mitchell, "From Conservation to Environmental Movement: The Development of the Modern Environmental Lobbies," in *Government and Environmental Politics: Essays on Historical Developments since World War Two,* ed. Michael J. Lacey (Baltimore: Johns Hopkins University Press, 1991), 83–84.

84. See www.panda.org.

85. Robert Paehlke, "World Wildlife Fund," in Paehlke, *Conservation and Environmentalism: An Encyclopedia,* 699.

86. See Samuel P. Huntington, *American Politics: The Promise of Disharmony* (Cambridge: Harvard University Press, 1981).

87. Michael J. Lacey, "The Environmental Revolution and the Growth of the State," in Lacey, *Government and Environmental Politics,* 2.

88. Jeffrey Berry, *Lobbying for the People: The Political Behavior of Public Interest Groups* (Princeton, N.J.: Princeton University Press, 1977), 34.

89. Andrew McFarland, *Public Interest Lobbies: Decision Making on Energy* (Washington, D.C.: American Enterprise Institute, 1978), 4–5.

90. *Scenic Hudson Preservation Conference v. Federal Power Commission,* 354 F.2d 608 (2d Cir. 1965); see also *Association of Data Processing Organization, Inc. v. Camp,* 397 U.S. 150 (1970), and *Barlow v. Collins,* 397 U.S. 159 (1970).

91. *Sierra Club v. Hickel,* 33 F.2d 24, 33 (9th Cir. 1970); *Sierra Club v. Morton,* 405 U.S. 727.

92. R. Shep Melnick, *Regulation and the Courts: The Case of the Clean Air Act* (Washington, D.C.: Brookings Institution, 1983), 10.

93. *Calvert Cliffs Coordinating Committee et al. v. U.S. Atomic Energy Commission et al.,* 449 F.2d 1109 (1971).

94. See Richard A. Liroff, *A National Policy for the Environment: NEPA and Its Aftermath* (Bloomington: Indiana University Press, 1976).

95. Ford Foundation, annual report, 1979, 15.

96. Cohen, *History of the Sierra Club,* 450; Robert Gottlieb, *Forcing the Spring: The Transformation of the American Environmental Movement* (Washington, D.C.: Island Press, 1993), 149; Phillip S. Berry, "Sierra Club President, 1991–1992: The Club, the Legal Defense Fund, and Leadership Issues, 1984–1993" (oral history conducted in 1993 by Ann Lage, Regional Oral History Office, Bancroft Library, University of California, Berkeley, 1997), 12–18.

97. Heard, "Washington Pressures," 1718.

98. *National Journal,* July 24, 1971, 1557.

99. Cohen, *History of the Sierra Club,* 360.

100. Graham, *Audubon Ark,* 228.

101. Allen, *Guardian of the Wild,* 69.

102. Graham, *Audubon Ark,* 227.

103. Miles, *Guardians of the Parks,* 241.

104. Graham, *Audubon Ark,* 227; Gottlieb, *Forcing the Spring,* 136–40; also Marion Lane Rogers, *Acorn Days: The Environmental Defense Fund and How It Grew* (New York: Environmental Defense Fund, 1990).

105. Thomas Dunlap, *DDT: Scientists, Citizens, and Public Policy* (Princeton, N.J.: Princeton University Press, 1981), 103.

106. See Fox, *John Muir,* 316–22.

107. David B. Brooks, "Friends of the Earth," in Paehlke, *Conservation and Environmentalism: An Encyclopedia,* 298.

108. Gottlieb, *Forcing the Spring,* 146.

109. Brower, *For Earth's Sake,* 241.

110. Ronald G. Shaiko, *Voices and Echoes for the Environment: Public Interest Representation in the 1990s and Beyond* (New York: Columbia University Press, 1999), 50–51.

111. Robert Cameron Mitchell, Angela G. Mertig, and Riley E. Dunlap, "Twenty Years of Environmental Mobilization: Trends among National Environmental Organizations," in *American Environmentalism: The U.S. Environmental Movement, 1970–1990,* ed. Riley E. Dunlap and Angela G. Mertig (Philadelphia: Taylor and Francis, 1992), 17.

112. Gottlieb, *Forcing the Spring,* 140–43; Foundation for Public Affairs, *Public Interest Profiles,* F67.

113. Ronald G. Shaiko, "More Bang for the Buck: The New Era of Full-Service Public Interest Organizations," in *Interest Group Politics,* 3d ed., ed. Allan J. Cigler and Burdett A. Loomis (Washington, D.C.: CQ Press, 1991).

114. Walker, *Mobilizing Interest Groups,* 12.

115. See Walker, *Mobilizing Interest Groups.*

116. Virginia Gray and David Lowery, *The Population Ecology of Interest Representation: Lobbying Communities in the American States* (Ann Arbor: University of Michigan Press, 1996), ix.

3. FILLING ADVOCACY NICHES

1. Friends of the Earth International, at www.foei.org.

2. See David M. Hart, "The Ecology of High-Tech Business Interests in Washington, D.C.: Assembly Rules and Resource Partitioning" (paper presented at the annual meeting of the Midwest Political Science Association, Chicago, 2001).

3. On Brower's ouster, see Michael Cohen, *The History of the Sierra Club, 1892–1970* (San Francisco: Sierra Club Books, 1988), 369–435; for his perspective, see David R. Brower, *For Earth's Sake: The Life and Times of David Brower* (Salt Lake City: Peregrine Smith Books, 1990).

4. Cohen, *History of the Sierra Club,* 286.

5. See Frank Graham Jr., *The Audubon Ark: A History of the National Audubon Society* (New York: Knopf, 1990), 222–38; Thomas B. Allen, *Guardian of the Wild: The Story of the National Wildlife Federation, 1936–1986* (Bloomington: Indiana University Press, 1987), 61–88.

6. John C. Miles, *Guardians of the Parks: A History of the National Parks and Conservation Association* (Washington, D.C.: Taylor and Francis, 1995), 241–79.

7. Cohen, *History of the Sierra Club,* 352.

8. Ibid., 262.

9. Brower, *For Earth's Sake,* 241.

10. Cohen, *History of the Sierra Club,* 425.

11. Ronald G. Shaiko, *Voices and Echoes for the Environment: Public Interest Representation in the 1990s and Beyond* (New York: Columbia University Press, 1999), 23.

12. An attitude captured in Lester Milbrath, *Environmentalists: Vanguard for a New Society* (Albany: State University of New York Press, 1984).

13. See Stephen Fox, *John Muir and His Legacy: The American Conservation Movement* (Boston: Little, Brown, 1981), 1.

14. Cohen, *History of the Sierra Club,* 435.

15. See Michael T. Hayes, "The New Group Universe," in *Interest Group Politics,* 2d ed., ed Allan J. Cigler and Burdett A. Loomis (Washington, D.C.: CQ Press, 1986), 133–45.

16. Jamie Heard, "Friends of the Earth Give Environmental Interests an Activist Voice," *National Journal,* August 8, 1971, 1718.

17. Brower, *For Earth's Sake,* 245.

18. Heard, "Friends of the Earth," 1711–18.

19. Robert Gottlieb, *Forcing the Spring: The Transformation of the American Environmental Movement* (Washington, D.C.: Island Press, 1993), 144.

20. Robert Cameron Mitchell, Angela G. Mertig, and Riley E. Dunlap, "Twenty Years of Environmental Mobilization: Trends among National Environmental Organiza-

tions," in *American Environmentalism: The U.S. Environmental Movement, 1970–1990,* ed. Riley E. Dunlap and Angela G. Mertig (Philadelphia: Taylor and Francis, 1992), 14.

21. See ibid., 11–25; Gottlieb, *Forcing the Spring,* 144–48.

22. Brower, *For Earth's Sake,* 245; on FoE–UK, see Grant A. Jordan and William Maloney, *The Protest Business? Mobilizing Campaign Groups* (New York: Manchester University Press, 1997).

23. On the Reagan challenge, see Peter Borrelli, ed., *Crossroads: Environmental Priorities for the Future* (Washington, D.C.: Island Press, 1988).

24. Philip Shabecoff, "Environmental Movement Is Facing Changes," *New York Times,* April 16, 1985, A16; see also Michael McCloskey, "Twenty Years of Change in the Environmental Movement: An Insider's View," in Dunlap and Mertig, *American Environmentalism,* 77–88.

25. Gottlieb, *Forcing the Spring,* 147.

26. Borrelli, *Crossroads,* 12.

27. Brower, *For Earth's Sake,* 248.

28. Michael L. Fischer, "Executive Director of the Sierra Club, 1987–1992" (oral history conducted in 1992 and 1993 by Ann Lage, Regional Oral History Office, Bancroft Library, University of California, Berkeley), 157.

29. Cass Peterson, "An Alliance in the War for the World," *Washington Post,* February 10, 1990, A5.

30. Christopher Manes, *Green Rage: Radical Environmentalism and the Unmaking of Civilization* (Boston: Little, Brown, 1990).

31. See Robert C. Lowry, "The Political Economy of Environmental Citizen Groups" (doctoral dissertation, Harvard University, 1993).

32. Miles, *Guardians of the Parks,* 259.

33. *Encyclopedia of Associations* (Detroit: Gale Research Company, 2001).

34. Stephen G. Greene, "Technology Helps Small Environmental Group Get Big Results," *Chronicle of Philanthropy,* January 11, 2001, at www.philanthropy.com/free/articles/v13/i06/06001001.htm.

35. See Ronald G. Shaiko, "More Bang for the Buck: The New Era of Full-Service Public Interest Organizations," in *Interest Group Politics,* 3d ed., ed. Allan J. Cigler and Burdett A. Loomis (Washington, D.C.: CQ Press, 1991), 109–29.

36. See Sally K. Fairfax and Darla Guenzler, *Conservation Trusts* (Lawrence: University Press of Kansas, 2001).

37. Sara Bennington, "Thirty Years of the Ocean Conservancy," *Blue Planet* (Fall 2002), at www.oceanconservancy.org/dynamic/aboutUs/publications/blueplanet/fall02/feature2.htm.

38. Miles, *Guardians of the Parks,* 241.

39. American Rivers, annual report, 2003, 3; see also Samuel P. Hays, *Beauty, Health, and Permanence: Environmental Politics in the United States, 1955–1985* (New York: Cambridge University Press, 1987), 141.

40. See, among others, Gottlieb, *Forcing the Spring,* 162–204; Adeline Gordon Levine, *Love Canal: Science, Politics, and People* (Lexington, Mass.: Lexington Books/D.C. Heath, 1982).

41. Miles, *Guardians of the Parks,* 296.

42. See, for example, Donald Snow, *Inside the Environmental Movement: Meeting the Leadership Challenge* (Washington, D.C.: Island Press, 1992).

43. Thomas Lovejoy, "Aid Debtor Nations' Ecology," *New York Times,* October 4, 1984, A27.

44. *Conservation International: The First Decade, 1987–1997* (Washington, D.C.: Conservation International, 1997).

45. Elizabeth Becker, "Web Site Helped Change Farm Policy," *New York Times,* February 24, 2002, A24.

46. Douglas Jehl, "Charity Is New Force in Environmental Fight," *New York Times,* June 28, 2001, A1.

47. Hart, "Ecology of High-Tech Business."

48. See Virginia Gray and David Lowery, "The Expression of Density Dependence in State Communities of Organized Interests," *American Politics Research* 29 (2001): 374–91.

49. McCloskey, "Twenty Years of Change," 85.

50. Jeffrey Berry, *The New Liberalism: The Rising Power of Citizen Groups* (Washington, D.C.: Brookings Institution, 1999), 3.

51. McCloskey, "Twenty Years of Changes," 77–80.

52. See Richard Cohen, *Washington at Work: Back Rooms and Clean Air,* 2d ed. (Boston: Allyn and Bacon, 1995), 64–66.

53. See John J. Audley, *Green Politics and Global Trade: NAFTA and the Future of Environmental Politics* (Washington, D.C.: Georgetown University Press, 1997).

54. Keith Schneider, "Environmental Groups Are Split on Support for Free-Trade Pact," *New York Times*, September 16, 1993, A1; Linda Kanamine, "NAFTA Disturbs Peace in 'Green' Movement," *USA Today,* September 17, 1993, 4A.

55. Lowry, "Political Economy," 76–88.

56. Virginia Gray and David Lowery, *The Population Ecology of Interest Representation: Lobbying Communities in the American States* (Ann Arbor: University of Michigan Press, 1996), 49.

57. See Gottlieb, *Forcing the Spring,* 142–43.

58. Graham, *Audubon Ark,* 302–8; Gottlieb, *Forcing the Spring,* 154.

59. Ned Martel and Blan Holden, "Inside the Environmental Groups—1994," *Outside* 19, no. 3 (March 1994): 69.

60. National Audubon Society, strategic plan, June 18, 1995, 9.

61. Tom Horton, "The Green Giant," *Rolling Stone,* September 5, 1991, 44.

62. Carey Goldberg, "Downsizing Activism: Greenpeace Is Cutting Back," *New York Times,* September 17, 1997, A1.

63. Katherine Kerlin, "Giving Greenpeace a Chance: After Internal Turmoil, a More Focused Greenpeace Is Back Fighting Polluters," *E: The Environmental Magazine* 12, no. 5 (September–October 2001): 12–16.

64. See Gottlieb, *Forcing the Spring,* 134–36.

65. See Robert Holbert, *Tax Laws and Political Access: The Bias of Pluralism Revisited* (Beverly Hills, Calif.: Sage Publications, 1975).

66. Don Hopey, "Earth Day Group Near Its Last Days, *Pittsburgh Post-Gazette,* December 16, 1996, A12; Naftali Bendavid, "Time Held Them Green and Dying: Unwilling to Compromise or Adapt, Environmental Action Calls It Quits after 26 Years," *Recorder,* December 6, 1996, 1, via Lexis/Nexis.

67. See William P. Browne, *Private Interests, Public Policy, and Agriculture* (Lawrence: University Press of Kansas, 1988).

68. Elizabeth Shogren, "Hunters, Anglers Gaining Power: President Listens to "Hook-and-Bullet" Enthusiasts on Environmental Issues," *Los Angeles Times,* January 5, 2004, via Lexis/Nexis.

4. MAINTAINING THE ORGANIZATION

1. Robert Gottlieb, *Forcing the Spring: The Transformation of the American Environmental Movement* (Washington, D.C.: Island Press, 1993), 155.

2. Mark Dowie, *Losing Ground: American Environmentalism at the Close of the Twentieth Century* (Cambridge, Mass.: MIT Press, 1995), 25.

3. Gottlieb, *Forcing the Spring,* 155.

4. Ronald G. Shaiko, *Voices and Echoes for the Environment: Public Interest Representation in the 1990s and Beyond* (New York: Columbia University Press, 1999), 67.

5. Gottlieb, *Forcing the Spring,* 155.

6. Jeffrey Berry, *The New Liberalism: The Rising Power of Citizen Groups* (Washington, D.C.: Brookings Institution, 1999), 28.

7. Michael Cohen, *The History of the Sierra Club: 1892–1970* (San Francisco: Sierra Club Books, 1988); Frank Graham Jr., *The Audubon Ark: A History of the National Audubon Society* (New York: Knopf, 1990); John C. Miles, *Guardians of the Parks: A History of the National Parks and Conservation Association* (Washington, D.C.: Taylor and Francis, 1995); Marion Lane Rogers, *Acorn Days: The Environmental Defense Fund and How It Grew* (New York: Environmental Defense Fund, 1990).

8. For a broader discussion, see Mark A. Peterson and Jack L. Walker, "Interest Groups and the Reagan Presidency," in Jack L. Walker Jr., *Mobilizing Interest Groups in America: Patrons, Professions, and Social Movements* (Ann Arbor: University of Michigan Press, 1991), 141–56.

9. On the importance of venues, see Frank R. Baumgartner and Bryan D. Jones, *Agendas and Instability in American Politics* (Chicago: University of Chicago Press, 1993), and, more specific to environmental issues, Christopher J. Bosso, *Pesticides and Politics: The Life Cycle of a Public Issue* (Pittsburgh: University of Pittsburgh Press, 1987).

10. Gottlieb, *Forcing the Spring,* 130.

11. J. Clarence Davies III, "Environmental Institutions and the Reagan Administration," in *Environmental Policy in the 1980s: Reagan's New Agenda,* ed. Norman J. Vig and Michael E. Kraft (Washington, D.C.: CQ Press, 1984), 143–60.

12. See Norman J. Vig, "Presidential Leadership and the Environment: From Reagan and Bush to Clinton, in *Environmental Policy in the 1990s,* 2d ed., ed. Norman J. Vig and Michael E. Kraft (Washington, D.C.: CQ Press, 1994), 71–96.

13. Marc K. Landy, Marc J. Roberts, and Stephen R. Thomas, *The Environmental Protection Agency: Asking the Wrong Questions* (New York: Oxford University Press, 1994), 245–78.

14. Foundation for Public Affairs, *Public Interest Profiles* (Washington, D.C.: Foundation for Public Affairs, 1980).

15. Gottlieb, *Forcing the Spring,* 123.

16. But see Dowie, *Losing Ground,* 175–203.

17. Carl Pope, "Want to Climb a Mountain?" *Sierra* 78, no. 2 (March/April 1993): 23.

18. Graham, *Audubon Ark,* 311.

19. See Gottlieb, *Forcing the Spring;* Dowie, *Losing Ground.*

20. The definitive work on this relationship is Shaiko, *Voices and Echoes.*

21. See also Baumgartner and Jones, *Agendas and Instability,* 37–38, 69, 186–88.

22. See Stephen Fox, *John Muir and His Legacy: The American Conservation Movement* (Boston: Little, Brown, 1981).

23. Michael L. Fischer, "Executive Director of the Sierra Club, 1987–1992" (oral history conducted in 1992 and 1993 by Ann Lage, Regional Oral History Office, Bancroft Library, University of California, Berkeley), 42.

24. Rochelle Stanfield, "Environmental Lobby's Changing of the Guard Is Part of Movement's Transition," *National Journal,* June 8, 1985, 1350–53; Philip Shabecoff, "New Leaders and a New Era for Environmentalists," *New York Times,* November 29, 1985, D28.

25. Gottlieb, *Forcing the Spring,* 156.

26. *Public Interest Profiles, 1992–1993* (Washington, D.C.: CQ Press, 1992), 462.

27. See Robert C. Lowry, "The Political Economy of Environmental Citizen Groups" (doctoral dissertation, Harvard University, 1993), and "The Private Production of Public Goods: Organizational Maintenance, Managers' Objectives, and Collective Goals," *American Political Science Review* 92 (June 1997): 308–23.

28. Gottlieb, *Forcing the Spring,* 120.

29. John Adams et al., *An Environmental Agenda for the Future* (Washington, D.C.: Island Press, 1985).

30. Carl Pope, remarks to the Sierra Club board of directors, May 16–17, 2003, board minutes, 28.

31. For a different perspective, see Gregg Easterbrook, *A Moment on the Earth: The Coming Age of Environmental Optimism* (New York: Viking, 1995).

32. Virginia Gray and David Lowery, *The Population Ecology of Interest Representation: Lobbying Communities in the American States* (Ann Arbor: University of Michigan Press, 1996), 41; an early version of this section is in Christopher J. Bosso, "Rethinking the Concept of Membership in Mature Advocacy Organizations." *Policy Studies Journal* 31, no. 3 (August 2003): 397–412.

33. The classic statement is Mancur Olson, *The Logic of Collective Action* (Cambridge: Havard University Press, 1965).

34. Lowry, "Political Economy," 6.

35. See Robert J. Duffy, *The Green Agenda in American Politics: New Strategies for the Twenty-first Century* (Lawrence: University Press of Kansas, 2003), 130–35.

36. An observation made by Tom Knudson, "Seeds of Change: Solutions Sprouting from Grass-Roots Efforts," *Sacramento Bee,* April 26, 2001, 1, via Lexis/Nexis.

37. See Sally K. Fairfax and Darla Guenzler, *Conservation Trusts* (Lawrence: University Press of Kansas, 2001).

38. The American Institute of Philanthropy runs Charity Watch, at www.charity watch.org/.

39. Tamar Lewin, "Charity Fund for Investors Moves Higher on Philanthropy List," *New York Times,* October 28, 2001, A18.

40. Carl Pope, "Want to Climb a Mountain?" *Sierra* 78, no. 2 (March/April 1993): 23.

41. Michael McCloskey, "Twenty Years of Change in the Environmental Movement: An Insider's View," in *American Environmentalism: The U.S. Environmental Movement, 1970–1990,* ed. Riley E. Dunlap and Angela G. Mertig (Philadelphia: Taylor and Francis, 1992), 77–88.

42. See Clark Norton "Green Giant," *Washington Post Magazine,* September 3, 1989, 25–39; Tom Horton, "The Green Giant," *Rolling Stone,* September 5, 1991, 42–48, 108–12.

43. National Park Trust, strategic plan, 2001–2005, at www.parktrust.org/strategic plan/plan2001.html.

44. For an early look of these questions, see Christopher J. Bosso, "The Color of Money: Environmental Organizations and the Pathologies of Fund-Raising," in *Interest Group Politics,* 4th ed., ed. Allan Cigler and Burdett Loomis (Washington, D.C.: CQ Press, 1994), 101–30; in the same volume, see also Allan J. Cigler and Anthony J. Nownes, "Public Interest Entrepreneurs and Group Patrons," 77–100.

45. Clean Water Action, financial report, FY2002.

46. See Frank R. Baumgartner and Beth L. Leech, *Basic Interests: The Importance of Groups in Politics and in Political Science* (Princeton, N.J.: Princeton University Press, 1998), 30–31; and David C. King and Jack L. Walker Jr., "The Origins and Maintenance of Groups," in Walker, *Mobilizing Interest Groups,* 82–83.

47. National Park Trust, *Legacy News* (Summer 2003): 6.

48. Lawrence S. Rothenberg, *Linking Citizens to Government: Interest Group Politics at Common Cause* (New York: Cambridge University Press, 1992), 81.

49. Peter Edles, *Fundraising: Hands-on Tactics for Nonprofit Groups* (New York: McGraw-Hill, 1993).

50. American Rivers, IRS Form 990, FY2001.

51. Nicole Lewis, "Sierra Club Hopes New Fund-Raising Steps Counter Economy's Slump," *Chronicle of Philanthropy,* February 6, 2003, 21.

52. Sierra Club Foundation, annual report, 2002, 1.

53. Foundation Center, *Foundation Grants Index* (New York: Columbia University Press, 2001).

54. Data obtained from NRDC annual reports.

55. Cigler and Nownes, "Public Interest Entrepreneurs and Group Patrons."

56. April Reese, "Pew Funds, Designs Programs in Three-Pronged Environmental Effort," *Greenwire,* January 8, 2001, via Lexis/Nexis.

57. Associated Press, "Groups Use Foundation Funding to Influence Road-Less Policy," January 2, 2001, via Lexis/Nexis.

58. See Mark Dowie, *American Foundations: An Investigative History* (Cambridge, Mass.: MIT Press, 2001).

59. See Daniel Faber, "Green of Another Color: Building Effective Partnerships between Foundations and the Environmental Justice Movement" (report by the Philanthropy and Environmental Justice Project, Northeastern University, Boston, with funding provided by the Nonprofit Sector Research Fund of the Aspen Institute, April 2001).

60. The Moore Foundation, at www.moore.org/grantees/grant_summaries_content.asp?Grantee=ci, January 21, 2004.

61. Aaron G. Lehmer, "The Foundations Dilemma: Financing Environmentalism," *Earth Island Journal* 14, no. 3 (Fall 1999): 15.

62. John B. Judis, "The Pressure Elite: Inside the Narrow World of Advocacy Group Politics," *American Prospect* (Spring 1992): 22.

63. Thomas B. Allen, *Guardian of the Wild: The Story of the National Wildlife Federation, 1936–1986* (Bloomington: Indiana University Press, 1987), 176.

64. Tom Price, *Cyber-Activism* (Washington, D.C.: Foundation for Public Affairs, 2000), 18.

65. Editorial, "Big Green Blues," *Washington Post,* May 12, 2003, A18.

66. See Lowry, "Political Economy," 127–50.

67. Fischer, "Executive Director of the Sierra Club, 1987–1992," 109.

68. Judis, "Pressure Elite," 23.

69. Michelle Ruess and Tom Diemer, "Environmentalists Split on Tade Policy," *Cleveland Plain Dealer,* July 18, 1993, 4A.

70. Judis, "Pressure Elite," 23.

71. Margaret Kriz, "Shades of Green," *National Journal,* July 28, 1990, 1827.

72. Keith Schneider, "Natural Foes Bankroll Environmental Group," *New York Times,* December 23, 1991, A12.

73. Jane Hall, "Audubon Specials Are Endangered Species," *Los Angeles Times,* December 17, 1991, F1.

74. Schneider, "Natural Foes," A12.

75. Michelle Cole, "Environmental Gifts Bring Ford a Truckload of Trouble," *Oregonian,* June 16, 2001, via Lexis/Nexis.

76. Cigler and Nownes, "Public Interest Entrepreneurs and Group Patrons," 88–92.

77. James R. Rosenfield, "In the Mail," *Direct Marketing* 54 (September 1991): 19–21.

78. Earth Share, IRS Form 990, 2001.

5. ADAPTATION AND CHANGE

1. An argument made in an editorial, "The Iraq Gambit for Drilling in ANWR," *Seattle Times,* April 15, 2002.

2. Ellen Nakashima, "Bush View of Secrecy Is Stirring Frustration; Disclosure Battle Unites Right and Left," *Washington Post,* March 3, 2002, A4.

3. Linda Greenhouse, "Justices' Ruling Postpones Resolution of Cheney Case," *New York Times,* June 24, 2004, A19. See *Judicial Watch, Inc. v. National Energy Policy Development Group,* 233 F.Supp. 2d 16 (D.D.C. 2002), a consolidation of *Judicial Watch, Inc. v. National Energy Policy Development Group*, and *Sierra Club v. Vice President Richard Cheney, et al.*

4. See Christopher J. Bosso and Deborah Lynn Guber, "The Boundaries and Contours of American Environmental Activism," in *Environmental Policy: New Directions for the 21st Century,* 5th ed., ed. Norman Vig and Michael Kraft (Washington, D.C.: CQ Press, 2003), 79–101, and Deborah Lynn Guber, *The Grassroots of a Green Revolution: Polling America on the Environment* (Cambridge, Mass.: MIT Press, 2003).

5. Lydia Saad, "Americans Mostly 'Green' in the Energy vs. Environment Debate," *Gallup Poll Monthly* 126 (March 2001): 35.

6. Riley E. Dunlap and Lydia Saad, "Only One in Four Americans Are Anxious about the Environment," *Gallup Poll Monthly* 127 (April 2001): 13.

7. Gallup Organization, June 8–10, 2001, at www.gallup.com.

8. See Michael E. Kraft, "Environmental Policy in Congress: Revolution, Reform, or Gridlock?" in *Environmental Policy in the 1990s,* 3d ed., ed. Norman Vig and Michael Kraft (Washington, D.C.: CQ Press, 1997), 119–42.

9. William Saletan, "Is There an Energy Crisis? It Depends on Who You Ask," *Milwaukee Journal-Sentinel,* May 13, 2001, J2, via Lexis/Nexis.

10. Paul Krugman, "Reckonings: Smoke and Mirrors," *New York Times,* January 31, 2001, 21.

11. White House press release, "Remarks by the President in Meeting with Labor Leaders, International Brotherhood of Teamsters, Washington, D.C.," January 17, 2002, at www.whitehouse.gov/news/releases/2002/01/20020117-5.html.

12. John Kingdon, *Agendas, Alternatives and Public Policies* (Boston: Little, Brown, 1984).

13. Charles R. Shipan and William R. Lowry, "Environmental Policy and Party Divergence in Congress," *Political Research Quarterly* 54, no. 2 (June 2000): 245–63.

14. Alison Mitchell, "It's Official: Democrats Rule Senate, G.O.P. Rues Day," *New York Times,* June 6, 2001, A27.

15. See, among others, William P. Browne, *Groups, Interests, and Public Policy* (Washington, D.C.: Georgetown University Press, 1998); Kenneth Kollman, *Outside Lobbying: Public Opinion and Interest Group Strategies* (Princeton, N.J.: Princeton University Press, 1998).

16. Natalie M. Henry, "ANWR: Enviros Launch TV Ad Campaign against Drilling," *Greenwire,* March 14, 2001, via Lexis/Nexis.

17. Natalie M. Henry, "ANWR: Enviros Launch Two More TV Ad Campaigns," *Greenwire,* March 28, 2001, via Lexis/Nexis.

18. Thomas B. Edsall, "Attacks Shift Balance of Power, Alliances among Interest Groups," *Washington Post,* September 19, 2001, A6.

19. Miguel Llanos, "Green Issues Sidelined by September 11: How The Tragedy Changed the Environmental Landscape," MSNBC, November 14, 2001, at www.msnbc.com/news/649869.asp.

20. Editorial, "Oil Opportunism," *Boston Globe,* September 27, 2001, A13.

21. Robert Schlesinger, "Two Tribes Split on Alaska Oil Plan," *Boston Globe,* February 25, 2002; Wilderness Society, annual report, 2002, 2.

22. Defenders of Wildlife, annual report, 2002, 7.

23. NRDC, annual report, 2002, 16.

24. Coalition partners included American Rivers, Defenders of Wildlife, Earthjustice, Environmental Defense, Friends of the Earth, Greenpeace, League of Conservation Voters, National Audubon Society, National Environmental Trust, National Parks Conservation Association, National Wildlife Federation, Natural Resources Defense Council, Sierra Club, Ocean Conservancy, Wilderness Society, and World Wildlife Fund. See Save Our Environment at www.saveourenvironment.org/about/. Other partners included Physicians for Social Responsibility, the state Public Interest Research Groups, and the Union of Concerned Scientists.

25. In 2002, the Natural Resource Council of America, a loose coalition of conservation organizations dating back to the 1950s, recognized those organizations and the Alaska Wilderness League for leadership on the issue; see www.naturalresourcescouncil.org/networking/LeadershipAward.cfm.

26. IWLA, annual report, 2002, 9.

27. Luntz Research Companies, *Straight Talk* (2002), 107.

28. Jennifer 8. Lee, "A Call for Softer, Greener Language, G.O.P. Advisor Offers Linguistic Tactics for Environmental Edge," *New York Times,* March 2, 2003, 18.

29. Federal Election Commission data for the 2002 election cycle, as compiled by the Center for Responsive Politics at www.opensecrets.org/industries/indus.asp?Ind=E.

30. Dan Morgan and Peter Behr, "Bush and Hill Republicans Hail Deal on Energy Bill; Arctic Oil Drilling Proposal Dropped; Democrats Are Skeptical," *Washington Post,* November 16, 2003, A20.

31. Dan Morgan, "Senate Energy Bill Is Blocked; GOP Thwarted in Getting Floor Vote," *Washington Post,* November 22, 2003, A1.

32. Kay Lehman Schlozman and John T. Tierney, *Organized Interests and American Democracy* (New York: Harper and Row, 1986); Jack L. Walker Jr., *Mobilizing Interest Groups in America: Patrons, Professions, and Social Movements* (Ann Arbor: University of Michigan Press, 1991); John P. Heinz, Edward O. Laumann, Robert L. Nelson, and Robert H. Salisbury, *The Hollow Core: Private Interests in National Policymaking* (Cambridge: Harvard University Press, 1993).

33. Frank R. Baumgartner and Beth L. Leech, *Basic Interests: The Importance of Groups in Politics and in Political Science* (Princeton, N.J.: Princeton University Press, 1998), 162.

34. See Thomas L. Gais and Jack L. Walker Jr., "Pathways to Influence in American Politics," in Walker, *Mobilizing Interest Groups,* 123–40; Baumgartner and Leech, *Basic Interests,* ch. 8.

35. A theme forcefully expressed by E. E. Schattschneider, *The Semi-Sovereign People: A Realist's View of Democracy in America* (New York: Holt, Rinehart, and Winston, 1960).

36. Bruce Oppenheimer, *Oil and the Congressional Process* (Lexington, Mass.: Lexington Books, 1975), 63.

37. See Christopher J. Bosso, "Environmental Values and American Democratic Institutions," in *Environmental Risk, Environmental Values and Political Choices: Beyond Efficiency Tradeoffs in Public Policy Analysis,* ed. John M. Gillroy (Boulder, Colo.: Westview Press, 1993), 72–93.

38. Robert A. Dahl and Charles E. Lindblom, *Politics, Economics and Welfare* (New York: Harper and Row, 1953), 336.

39. Alexander Hamilton, James Madison, and John Jay, *The Federalist Papers,* ed. Clinton Rossiter (New York: New American Library, 1961); see also David Vogel, *National Styles of Regulation: Environmental Policy in Great Britain and the United States* (Ithaca, N.Y.: Cornell University Press, 1986).

40. Michael E. Kraft, "Environmental Policy in Congress: From Consensus to Gridlock," in Vig and Kraft, *Environmental Policy: New Directions for the 21st Century,* 127–50.

41. Shipan and Lowry, "Environmental Policy and Party Divergence."

42. The ASGP split with the more "radical" Green Party of the United States (GPUSA) in 1991.

43. Suzanne Dougherty, "Wilson Ekes Out Victory in New Mexico's 1st," *CQ Weekly Report,* November 8, 2000, at washingtonpost.com.

44. All data obtained from *CQ Weekly Report,* November 11, 2000, 2694–703.

45. Reports C00141044, C00252940, and C00135368, Federal Election Commission, at www.fec.gov.

46. Robert Kuttner, "America as a One-Party State," *American Prospect* 15, no. 2 (February 2004): 14–23.

47. On this dilemma, see Robert J. Duffy, *The Green Agenda in American Politics: New Strategies for the Twenty-first Century* (Lawrence: University Press of Kansas, 2003).

48. See David Vogel, *Fluctuating Fortunes: The Political Power of Business in America* (New York: Basic Books, 1989); for empirical evidence of the surge in business lobbyists, see, among others, Schlozman and Tierney, *Organized Interests and American Democracy.*

49. The "privileged position" argument is made in Charles E. Lindblom, *Politics and Markets* (New York: Basic Books, 1977).

50. Kirkpatrick Sale, "The U.S. Green Movement Today," *Nation* 257, no. 3 (July 19, 1993): 94.

51. David Helvarg, *The War against the West* (San Francisco: Sierra Club Books, 1994).

52. For an earlier discussion, see Christopher J. Bosso, "Adaptation and Change in the Environmental Movement," in *Interest Group Politics,* 3d ed., ed. Allan Cigler and Burdett Loomis (Washington, D.C.: CQ Press, 1991), 51–176; and, especially, Jacqueline Vaughn Switzer, *Green Backlash: The History and Politics of Environmental Opposition in the United States* (Boulder, Colo.: Lynne Reiner, 1997).

53. See Switzer, *Green Backlash;* Adam Pertman, "Wise Use Foot Soldiers on the March," *Boston Globe,* October 3, 1994, 25–28; Richard Stapleton, "On the Western Front: Dispatches from the War with the Wise Use Movement," *National Parks* 67, nos. 1–2 (January/February 1993): 32–36; David Helvarg, "Grassroots for Sale: The Inside Scoop on (un)Wise Use," *Amicus Journal* 16, no. 3 (Fall 1994): 25.

54. Daniel A. Mazmanian and Michael E. Kraft, "The Three Epochs of the Environmental Movement," in *Toward Sustainable Communities: Transition and Transformations in Environmental Policy,* ed. Daniel A. Mazmanian and Michael E. Kraft (Cambridge, Mass.: MIT Press, 1999), 3–42.

55. Denise Scheberle, *Federalism and Environmental Policy: Trust and the Politics of Implementation* (Washington, D.C.: Georgetown University Press, 1997).

56. Michael L. Fischer, "Executive Director of the Sierra Club, 1987–1992" (oral history conducted in 1992 and 1993 by Ann Lage, Regional Oral History Office, Bancroft Library, University of California, Berkeley), 148.

57. Keith Schneider, "Selling Out? Pushed and Pulled, Environment Inc. Is on the Defensive," *New York Times,* March 29, 1992, sec. 4, p. 1.

58. Carla Koehl and Mark Peyser, "Green Revolt." *Newsweek,* July 10, 1995, 6.

59. Anne Raver, "Old Environmental Group Seeks Tough New Image," *New York Times,* June 9, 1991, A1, 22.

60. National Audubon Society, strategic plan, June 18, 1995, 5.

61. Scott Allen, "Murky Times for Environmentalism: Economy, Crime Overtake What Was to Be Cause of '90s," *Boston Globe,* November 12, 1994, Metro/Region, 1.

62. For example, see Christopher J. Bosso, *Pesticides and Politics: The Life Cycle of a Public Issue* (Pittsburgh: University of Pittsburgh Press, 1987), 143–77.

63. Trends between 1970 and 1990 are discussed in Frank R. Baumgartner and Bryan D. Jones, *Agendas and Instability in American Politics* (Chicago: University of

Chicago Press, 1993), ch. 9; for trends up to 1997, see Frank R. Baumgartner and Christine Mahoney, "Social Movements, the Rise of New Issues, and the Public Agenda," in *Routing the Opposition: Social Movements, Public Policy, and Democracy,* ed. David S. Meyer, Valerie Jenness, and Helen Ingram (Minneapolis: University of Minnesota Press, in press).

64. *Washington Representatives, 2003* (Washington, D.C.: Columbia Books, 2003).

65. See Kraft, "Environmental Policy in Congress," 139–42.

66. See Norman J. Vig, "Presidential Leadership and the Environment," in Vig and Kraft, *Environmental Policy: New Directions for the 21st Century,* 103–26.

67. Elizabeth Shogren, "Hunters, Anglers Gaining Power: President Listens to "Hook-and-Bullet" Enthusiasts on Environmental Issues," *Los Angeles Times,* January 5, 2004, via Lexis/Nexis.

68. See Rosemary O'Leary, "Environmental Policy and the Courts," in Vig and Kraft, *Environmental Policy: New Directions for the 21st Century,* 151–74; Lettie McSpadden, "The Courts and Environmental Policy," in *Environmental Politics and Policy: Theories and Evidence,* 2d ed., ed. James P. Lester (Durham, N.C.: Duke University Press, 1994), 242–74. See also Michael T. Collins, "The Green Internet: Environmental Public Interest Groups on the World Wide Web" (honors thesis, Program in Environmental Science and Public Policy, Harvard University, March 2001).

69. Tom Graff, quoted in Tom Turner, "The Legal Eagles," in *Crossroads: Environmental Priorities for the Future,* ed. Peter Borrelli (Washington, D.C.: Island Press, 1988), 58.

70. Ned Martel and Blan Holden, "Inside the Environmental Groups—1994," *Outside* 19, no. 3 (March 1994): 71.

71. Duffy, *Green Agenda,* 4–5.

72. Robert D. Putnam, *Bowling Alone: The Collapse and Revival of American Community* (New York: Simon and Schuster, 2000), 154.

73. Ibid., 160–61, emphasis in original; see also 471, n. 54.

74. See, for example, Andrew Savage, John Isham, and Christopher McGrory Klyza, "The Greening of Social Capital: An Examination of Land-Based Groups in Two Vermont Counties," *Rural Sociology,* forthcoming.

75. See Christopher Bosso and Michael C. Collins, "Just Another Tool? How Environmental Groups Use the Internet," in *Interest Group Politics,* 6th ed., ed. Allan Cigler and Burdett Loomis (Washington, D.C.: CQ Press, 2002), 95–114.

76. See Michael Kraft and Diana Wuertz, "Environmental Advocacy in the Corridors of Government," in *Environmental Discourse: Perspectives on Communication and Advocacy,* ed. James G. Cantrill and Chris Oravec (Lexington: University Press of Kentucky, 1996), 95–122; John Cushman Jr., "G.O.P. Backing Off from Tough Stand over Environment," *New York Times,* January 26, 1996, A1.

77. See Frank Fischer, *Citizens, Experts, and the Environment: The Politics of Local Knowledge* (Durham, N.C.: Duke University Press, 2000).

78. See Bosso and Collins, "Just Another Tool"; Collins, "Green Internet."

79. Kim Daus and Drew Banks, "Are We There Yet? The Long and Winding Road to On-line Community," *Business 2.0,* June 27, 2000, 317.

80. Tom Price, *Cyber-Activism* (Washington, D.C.: Foundation for Public Affairs, 2000), 18.

81. An observation made by Sabine Schutte-Morris in an internship paper, "On the Use of Technology in Environmental Nonprofit Organizations" (Northeastern University, October 2000).

82. Price, *Cyber-Activism,* 19.

83. Emily Schwartz, "Activists Now Have Corporate Attention," *Chicago Sun-Times,* February 13, 2000, Money/Life, 40.

84. Marc Gunther, "The Mosquito in the Tent: A Pesky Environmental Group Called the Rainforest Action Network Is Getting under the Skin of Corporate America," *Fortune,* May 31, 2004, 156–60.

85. Jeffrey Berry, *The Interest Group Society,* 3d ed. (New York: Longmann, 1997), 136–37.

86. See Ronald G. Shaiko, *Voices and Echoes for the Environment: Public Interest Representation in the 1990s and Beyond* (New York: Columbia University Press, 1999).

87. See Robert Gottlieb, *Forcing the Spring: The Transformation of the American Environmental Movement* (Washington, D.C.: Island Press, 1993); Nicholas Freudenberg and Carol Steinsapir, "Not in Our Backyards: The Grassroots Environmental Movement," in *American Environmentalism: The U.S. Environmental Movement, 1970–1990,* ed. Riley E. Dunlap and Angela G. Mertig (Philadelphia: Taylor and Francis, 1992), 27–38.

88. Frank Graham Jr., *The Audubon Ark: A History of the National Audubon Society* (New York: Knopf, 1990), 303–8.

89. Fischer oral history, 179.

90. Margaret Kriz, "Mark Van Putten: Wildlife Lobby Returns to Its Roots," *National Journal,* January 25, 1997, 184; see also Shaiko, *Voices and Echoes,* 80–81.

91. "Enviro Groups: Money, Management Woes Paralyze Greens," *Greenwire,* American Political Network Inc., July 18, 1995, via Lexis/Nexis; Carla Koehl and Mark Peyser, "Green Revolt," *Newsweek,* July 10, 1995, 6.

92. Interview, *National Parks* 72, nos. 9–10 (September/October 1998): 42.

93. Thomas Gais and Jack L. Walker, "Pathways to Influence in American Politics," in Walker, *Mobilizing Interest Groups,* 103.

94. Environmental Defense, annual report, 1999.

95. Duffy, *Green Agenda,* 17.

96. Manuel Roig-Franzia, "Judge Dismisses Greenpeace Charges," *Washington Post,* May 20, 2004, A14.

97. Catherine Wilson, "U.S. Uses 1872 Law against Activists," *Boston Globe,* January 26, 2004, 12.

98. Jeffrey Berry, *The New Liberalism: The Rising Power of Citizen Groups* (Washington, D.C.: Brookings Institution, 1999), 155.

6. THE MATURE ADVOCACY COMMUNITY

1. Sam Bishop, "ANWR Sales in 2006 Bush Budget," *Fairbanks News-Miner,* February 3, 2004, via Lexis/Nexis.

2. Conservation Fund press release, "Public Private Partnership Creates Model to Balance Nature Preserves and Sustainable Forestry: Groups Work to Create California's

First Large-Scale Nonprofit-Owned Working Forest," February 5, 2004, at www.conservationfund.org.

3. Defenders of Wildlife press release, "Defenders Pays $17,219 in Grizzly Bear Compensation during 2003," February 5, 2004, at www.defenders.org/releases/pr2004b/pr20040205.

4. Conservation International press release, "Conservation International, Wildlife Conservation Society, and World Wildlife Fund Applaud Passage of Congo Basin Forest Partnership Act," February 6, 2004, at www.conservation.org/xp/news/press_releases/2004/020604.xml.

5. White House press release, "Statement on H.R. 2264," February 13, 2004.

6. Fred Krupp, "Global Warming: Connecticut's Already Feeling Heat," *Hartford Courant,* February 6, 2004, A11, via Lexis/Nexis.

7. Earthjustice press release, "State's Refusal to Share Public Documents Draws Challenge from Conservation Groups," February 12, 2004, at www.earthjustice.org/news/.

8. Earthjustice press release, "Utah Court Rejects Claims to Roads through Utah Monument, Wildlands," February 23, 2004, at www.earthjustice.org/news/.

9. Tom Doggett, "Alaskan Reserve Drilling Plan Draws Lawsuit," *Washington Post,* February 18, 2004, A1.

10. James Glanz, "Scientists Say Administration Distorts Facts," *New York Times,* February 19, 2004, A18.

11. Clean Water Action, "Comments on EPA's 'Burden Reduction Options,'" Toxic Release Inventory Program, February 2004, at www.cleanwateraction.org/tri.html.

12. Adam Nagourney and Jim Rutenberg, "Nader, Gadfly to the Democrats, Will Again Run for President," *New York Times,* February 23, 2004, A1, 16.

13. Charles Lane, "Sierra Club Wants Scalia to Sit out Task Force Case," *Washington Post,* February 24, 2004, A19; Michael Janofsky, "Scalia's Trip with Cheney Raises Questions of Impartiality," *New York Times,* February 6, 2004, A14.

14. Michael Janofsky, "Scalia Refusing to Take Himself off Cheney Case," *New York Times,* March 19, 2004, A1.

15. Press release, "Embrey Dam Demolition Frees Rappahannock River," February 23, 2004, at www.americanrivers.org.

16. National Wildlife Federation press release, "National Wildlife Federation Opposes Myers Circuit Court Nomination," February 25, 2004, at www.nwf.org/news/.

17. Glen Martin, "Board Election Divides Sierra Club: Environmentalists Renew Bitter Fight over Controlling U.S. Immigration," *San Francisco Chronicle,* February 11, 2004; Terrence Chea, "Rival Factions Vie for Sierra Club Control," *Seattle Post-Intelligencer,* February 17, 2004, via Lexis/Nexis.

18. Felicity Barringer, "Establishment Candidates Defeat Challengers in Sierra Club Voting," *New York Times,* April 22, 2004, A18.

19. But see Theda Skocpol, *Diminished Democracy: From Membership to Management in American Civic Life* (Norman: University of Oklahoma Press, 2003).

20. Fara Warner, "Environmental Group Depicts Ford's Chief as Pinocchio," *New York Times,* February 26, 2004, C8. The ad ran in the *Times* on February 11, A11.

21. Kirkpatrick Sale, *The Green Revolution: The American Environmental Movement, 1962–1992* (New York: Hill and Wang, 1993), 99.

22. Philip Shabecoff, *Earth Rising: American Environmentalism in the 21st Century* (Washington, D.C.: Island Press, 2000), 46.

23. On the transformation of FoE United Kingdom, see Grant A. Jordan and William Maloney, *The Protest Business? Mobilizing Campaign Groups* (New York: Manchester University Press, 1997).

24. On venues, see Frank R. Baumgartner and Bryan D. Jones, *Agendas and Instability in American Politics* (Chicago: University of Chicago Press, 1993).

25. See Robert D. Putnam, *Bowling Alone: The Collapse and Revival of American Community* (New York: Simon and Schuster, 2000).

26. See, for example, Christopher Bosso, *Pesticides and Politics: The Life Cycle of a Public Issue* (Pittsburgh: University of Pittsburgh Press, 1987), especially ch. 8.

27. See William P. Browne, *Private Interests, Public Policy, and American Agriculture* (Lawrence: University Press of Kansas, 1988).

28. See Robert C. Lowry, "The Political Economy of Environmental Citizen Groups" (doctoral dissertation, Harvard University, 1993).

29. Mark Dowie, *Losing Ground: American Environmentalism at the Close of the Twentieth Century* (Cambridge, Mass.: MIT Press, 1995), 7.

30. Ibid., 6.

31. Sale, *Green Revolution,* 8.

32. Ronald G. Shaiko, *Voices and Echoes for the Environment: Public Interest Representation in the 1990s and Beyond* (New York: Columbia University Press, 1999), 114.

33. Dowie, *Losing Ground,* 25.

34. Jeffrey Berry, *The New Liberalism: The Rising Power of Citizen Groups* (Washington, D.C.: Brookings Institution, 1999), 142.

35. See Anthony Downs, "Up and Down with Ecology: The Issue-Attention Cycle," *Public Interest* 28 (Summer 1972): 38–50.

36. Bosso, *Pesticides and Politics;* Baumgartner and Jones, *Agendas and Instability;* Robert J. Duffy, *Nuclear Politics in America: A History and Theory of Government Regulation* (Lawrence: University Press of Kansas, 1997); Charles O. Jones, *Clear Air: The Policies and Politics of Pollution Control* (Pittsburgh: University of Pittsburgh Press, 1975); Gary Mucciaroni, *The Political Failure of Employment Policy, 1945–1982* (Pittsburgh: University of Pittsburgh Press, 1990).

37. E. E. Schattschneider, *The Semi-Sovereign People: A Realist's View of Democracy in America* (New York: Holt, Rinehart, and Winston, 1960).

38. Margaret E. Keck and Kathryn Sikkink, *Activists beyond Borders: Advocacy Networks in International Politics* (Ithaca, N.Y.: Cornell University Press, 1998), 160–62.

39. Paul Wapner, *Environmental Activism and World Civic Politics* (Albany: State University of New York Press, 1996), 152.

40. See Deborah Lynn Guber, *The Grassroots of a Green Revolution: Polling America on the Environment* (Cambridge, Mass.: MIT Press, 2003).

41. See Christopher J. Bosso, "Adaptation and Change in the Environmental Movement," in *Interest Group Politics,* 3d ed., ed. Allan J. Cigler and Burdett A. Loomis (Washington, D.C.: CQ Press, 1991), 174.

42. A term coined by Jordan and Maloney in *The Protest Business?*

43. See Robert Paehlke, *Environmentalism and the Future of Progressive Politics* (New Haven, Conn.: Yale University Press, 1990).

Selected Bibliography

Adams, John, et al. *An Environmental Agenda for the Future*. Washington, D.C.: Island Press, 1985.

Allen, Thomas B. *Guardian of the Wild: The Story of the National Wildlife Federation, 1936–1986*. Bloomington: Indiana University Press. 1987.

Audley, John J. *Green Politics and Global Trade: NAFTA and the Future of Environmental Politics*. Washington, D.C.: Georgetown University Press, 1997.

Baumgartner, Frank R., and Bryan D. Jones. *Agendas and Instability in American Politics*. Chicago: University of Chicago Press, 1993.

Baumgartner, Frank R., and Beth L. Leech. *Basic Interests: The Importance of Groups in Politics and in Political Science*. Princeton, N.J.: Princeton University Press, 1998.

———. "Issue Niches and Policy Bandwagons: Patterns of Interest Group Involvement in National Politics." *Journal of Politics* 63, no. 4 (November 2001): 1191–213.

Baumgartner, Frank R., and Christine Mahoney. "Social Movements, the Rise of New Issues, and the Public Agenda." In *Routing the Opposition: Social Movements, Public Policy, and Democracy*. Edited by David S. Meyer, Valerie Jenness, and Helen Ingram. Minneapolis: University of Minnesota Press, 2004.

Berry, Jeffrey M. *Lobbying for the People: The Political Behavior of Public Interest Groups*. Princeton, N.J.: Princeton University Press, 1977.

———. *The New Liberalism: The Rising Power of Citizen Groups*. Washington, D.C.: Brookings Institution, 1999.

Borrelli, Peter, ed. *Crossroads: Environmental Priorities for the Future*. Washington, D.C.: Island Press, 1988.

Bosso, Christopher J. "Adaptation and Change in the Environmental Movement." In *Interest Group Politics,* 3d ed. Edited by Allan Cigler and Burdett Loomis. Washington, D.C.: CQ Press, 1991.

———. "After the Movement: Environmental Activism in the 1990s." In *Environmental Policy in the 1990s,* 2d ed. Edited by Norman Vig and Michael Kraft. Washington, D.C.: CQ Press, 1993.

———. "The Color of Money: Environmental Groups and the Pathologies of Fund-Raising." In *Interest Group Politics,* 4th ed. Edited by Allan Cigler and Burdett Loomis. Washington, D.C.: CQ Press, 1994.

———. "Environmental Groups and the New Political Landscape." In *Environmental Policy in the 1990s,* 4th ed. Edited by Norman Vig and Michael Kraft. Washington, D.C.: CQ Press, 1999.

———. "Environmental Values and American Democratic Institutions." In *Environmental Risk, Environmental Values and Political Choices: Beyond Efficiency Trade-offs in Public Policy Analysis*. Edited by John M. Gillroy. Boulder, Colo.: Westview Press, 1993.

———. *Pesticides and Politics: The Life Cycle of a Public Issue*. Pittsburgh: University of Pittsburgh Press, 1987.

———. "Rethinking the Concept of Membership in Mature Advocacy Organizations." *Policy Studies Journal* 31, no. 3 (August 2003): 397–412.

———. "Seizing Back the Day: The Challenge to Environmental Activism in the 1990s." In *Environmental Policy in the 1990s,* 3d ed. Edited by Norman Vig and Michael Kraft. Washington, D.C.: CQ Press, 1997.

Bosso, Christopher J., and Michael Collins. "Just Another Tool? How Environmental Groups Use the Internet." In *Interest Group Politics,* 6th ed. Edited by Allan Cigler and Burdett Loomis. Washington, D.C.: CQ Press, 2002.

Bosso, Christopher J., and Deborah Lynn Guber. "The Boundaries and Contours of American Environmental Activism." In *Environmental Policy: New Directions for the 21st Century,* 5th ed. Edited by Norman Vig and Michael Kraft. Washington, D.C.: CQ Press, 2003.

Bowman, Karlyn H., and Everett Carll Ladd. *Attitudes toward the Environment*. Washington, D.C.: American Enterprise Institute, 1995.

Brower, David R. *For Earth's Sake: The Life and Times of David Brower.* Salt Lake City: Peregrine Smith Books, 1990.

Browne, William P. *Groups, Interests, and Public Policy.* Washington, D.C.: Georgetown University Press, 1998.

———. *Private Interests, Public Policy, and American Agriculture*. Lawrence: University Press of Kansas, 1988.

Cigler, Allan J., and Anthony J. Nownes. "Public Interest Entrepreneurs and Group Patrons." In *Interest Organization Politics,* 4th ed. Edited by Allan Cigler and Burdett Loomis. Washington, D.C.: CQ Press, 1994.

Clemens, Elizabeth S. *The People's Lobby: Organizational Innovation and the Rise of Interest Group Politics in the United States, 1890–1925*. Chicago: University of Chicago Press, 1997.

Cohen, Michael. *The History of the Sierra Club, 1892–1970*. San Francisco: Sierra Club Books, 1988.

Cohen, Richard. *Washington at Work: Back Rooms and Clean Air,* 2d ed. Boston: Allyn and Bacon, 1995.

Davies, J. Clarence III. "Environmental Institutions and the Reagan Administration." In *Environmental Policy in the 1980s: Reagan's New Agenda*. Edited by Norman J. Vig and Michael E. Kraft. Washington, D.C.: CQ Press, 1984.

Dowie, Mark. *American Foundations: An Investigative History.* Cambridge, Mass.: MIT Press, 2001.

———. *Losing Ground: American Environmentalism at the Close of the Twentieth Century.* Cambridge, Mass.: MIT Press, 1995.

Downs, Anthony. "Up and Down with Ecology: The Issue-Attention Cycle." *Public Interest* 28 (1972): 38–50.

Duffy, Robert J. *The Green Agenda in American Politics: New Strategies for the Twenty-first Century.* Lawrence: University Press of Kansas, 2003.

———. *Nuclear Politics in America: A History and Theory of Government Regulation.* Lawrence: University Press of Kansas, 1997.

Dunlap, Riley E., and Angela G. Mertig, eds. *American Environmentalism: The U.S. Environmental Movement, 1970–1990.* Philadelphia, Taylor and Francis, 1992.

Dunlap, Thomas. *DDT: Scientists, Citizens, and Public Policy.* Princeton, N.J.: Princeton University Press, 1981.

Easterbrook, Gregg. *A Moment on the Earth: The Coming Age of Environmental Optimism.* New York: Viking, 1995.

Edles, Peter. *Fundraising: Hands-on Tactics for Nonprofit Groups.* New York: McGraw-Hill, 1993.

Euchner, Charles C. *Extraordinary Politics: How Protest and Dissent Are Changing American Democracy.* Boulder, Colo.: Westview Press, 1996.

Faber, Daniel. "Green of Another Color: Building Effective Partnerships between Foundations and the Environmental Justice Movement." Report by the Philanthropy and Environmental Justice Project, Northeastern University, Boston, with funding provided by the Nonprofit Sector Research Fund of the Aspen Institute, 2001.

Fairfax, Sally K., and Darla Guenzler. *Conservation Trusts.* Lawrence: University Press of Kansas, 2001.

Fischer, Frank. *Citizens, Experts, and the Environment: The Politics of Local Knowledge.* Durham, N.C.: Duke University Press, 2000.

Fox, Stephen. *John Muir and His Legacy: The American Conservation Movement.* Boston: Little, Brown, 1981.

Freudenberg , Nicholas, and Carol Steinsapir. "Not in Our Backyards: The Grassroots Environmental Movement." In *American Environmentalism: The U.S. Environmental Movement, 1970–1990.* Edited by Riley E. Dunlap and Angela G. Mertig. Philadelphia: Taylor and Francis, 1992.

Gottlieb, Robert. *Forcing the Spring: The Transformation of the American Environmental Movement.* Washington, D.C.: Island Press, 1993.

Graham, Frank Jr. *The Audubon Ark: A History of the National Audubon Society.* New York: Knopf, 1990.

Gray, Virginia, and David Lowery. "The Expression of Density Dependence in State Communities of Organized Interests." *American Politics Research* 29 (2001): 374–91.

———. *The Population Ecology of Interest Representation: Lobbying Communities in the American States.* Ann Arbor: University of Michigan Press, 1996.

Guber, Deborah Lynn. *The Grassroots of a Green Revolution: Polling America on the Environment.* Cambridge, Mass.: MIT Press, 2003.

Hart, David M. "The Ecology of High-Tech Business Interests in Washington, D.C.: Assembly Rules and Resource Partitioning." Paper presented at the annual meeting of the Midwest Political Science Association, Chicago, 2001.

Hayes, Michael T. "The New Group Universe." In *Interest Group Politics,* 2d ed. Edited by Allan J. Cigler and Burdett A. Loomis. Washington, D.C.: CQ Press, 1986.

Hays, Samuel P. *Beauty, Health, and Permanence: Environmental Politics in the United States, 1955–1985.* New York: Cambridge University Press, 1987.

———. *Conservation and the Gospel of Efficiency: The Progressive Conservation Movement, 1890–1920.* Cambridge: Harvard University Press, 1959.

Heinz, John P., Edward O. Laumann, Robert L. Nelson, and Robert H. Salisbury. *The*

Hollow Core: Private Interests in National Policymaking. Cambridge: Harvard University Press, 1993.

Helvarg, David. *The War against the West*. San Francisco: Sierra Club Books, 1994.

Holbert, Robert. *Tax Laws and Political Access: The Bias of Pluralism Revisited*. Beverly Hills, Calif.: Sage Publications, 1975.

Hoberg, George. *Pluralism by Design: Environmental Policy and the American Regulatory State*. Westport, Conn.: Praeger, 1992.

Hula, Kevin. *Lobbying Together: Interest Group Coalitions in Legislative Politics*. Washington, D.C.: Georgetown University Press, 1999.

Huntington, Samuel P. *American Politics: The Promise of Disharmony*. Cambridge: Harvard University Press, 1981.

Johnson, Paul E. "How Environmental Groups Recruit Members: Does the Logic Still Hold Up?" Paper presented at the annual meeting of the American Political Science Association, Chicago, 1995.

Jones, Charles O. *Clear Air: The Policies and Politics of Pollution Control*. Pittsburgh: University of Pittsburgh Press, 1975.

Jordan, Grant A., and William Maloney. *The Protest Business? Mobilizing Campaign Groups*. New York: Manchester University Press, 1997.

Keck, Margaret E., and Kathryn Sikkink. *Activists beyond Borders: Advocacy Networks in International Politics*. Ithaca, N.Y.: Cornell University Press, 1998.

Kingdon, John. *Agendas, Alternatives and Public Policies*. Boston: Little, Brown, 1984.

Kollman, Kenneth. *Outside Lobbying: Public Opinion and Interest Group Strategies*. Princeton, N.J.: Princeton University Press, 1998.

Kraft, Michael E. "Environmental Policy in Congress: From Consensus to Gridlock." In *Environmental Policy: New Directions for the 21st Century*, 5th ed. Edited by Norman Vig and Michael Kraft. Washington, D.C.: CQ Press, 2003.

———. "Environmental Policy in Congress: Revolution, Reform, or Gridlock?" In *Environmental Policy in the 1990s*, 3d ed. Edited by Norman Vig and Michael Kraft. Washington, D.C.: CQ Press, 1997.

Kraft, Michael E., and Diana Wuertz. "Environmental Advocacy in the Corridors of Government." In *Environmental Discourse: Perspectives on Communication and Advocacy*. Edited by James G. Cantrill and Chris Oravec. Lexington: University Press of Kentucky, 1996.

Lacey, Michael J., ed. *Government and Environmental Politics: Essays on Historical Developments since World War Two*. Baltimore: Johns Hopkins University Press, 1991.

Landy, Marc K., Marc J. Roberts, and Stephen R. Thomas. *The Environmental Protection Agency: Asking the Wrong Questions*. New York: Oxford University Press, 1994.

Levine, Adeline Gordon. *Love Canal: Science, Politics, and People*. Lexington, Mass.: Lexington Books/D. C. Heath, 1982.

Lindblom, Charles E. *Politics and Markets*. New York: Basic Books, 1977.

Liroff, Richard A. *A National Policy for the Environment: NEPA and Its Aftermath*. Bloomington: Indiana University Press, 1976.

Lowry Robert C. "The Political Economy of Environmental Citizen Groups." Doctoral dissertation, Harvard University, 1993.

———. "The Private Production of Public Goods: Organizational Maintenance, Managers' Objectives, and Collective Goals." *American Political Science Review* 92 (June 1997): 308–23.

Manes, Christopher. *Green Rage: Radical Environmentalism and the Unmaking of Civilization.* Boston: Little, Brown, 1990.

Mazmanian, Daniel A., and Michael E. Kraft. "The Three Epochs of the Environmental Movement." In *Toward Sustainable Communities: Transition and Transformations in Environmental Policy.* Edited by Daniel A. Mazmanian and Michael E. Kraft. Cambridge, Mass.: MIT Press, 1999.

McCloskey, Michael. "Twenty Years of Change in the Environmental Movement: An Insider's View." In *American Environmentalism: The U.S. Environmental Movement, 1970–1990.* Edited by Riley E. Dunlap and Angela G. Mertig. Philadelphia: Taylor and Francis, 1992.

McConnell, A. Grant. "The Conservation Movement—Past and Present." *Western Political Quarterly* 7 (1954): 467.

McFarland, Andrew. *Public Interest Lobbies: Decision Making on Energy.* Washington, D.C.: American Enterprise Institute, 1978.

McSpadden, Lettie. "The Courts and Environmental Policy." In *Environmental Politics and Policy: Theories and Evidence,* 2d ed. Edited by James P. Lester. Durham, N.C.: Duke University Press, 1994.

Melnick, R. Shep. *Regulation and the Courts: The Case of the Clean Air Act.* Washington, D.C.: Brookings Institution, 1983.

Meyer, David S., and Douglas R. Imig. "Political Opportunity and the Rise and Decline of Interest Group Sectors." *Social Science Journal* 30 (1993): 253–70.

Milbrath, Lester. *Environmentalists: Vanguard for a New Society.* Albany: State University of New York Press, 1984.

Miles, John C. *Guardians of the Parks: A History of the National Parks and Conservation Association.* Washington, D.C.: Taylor and Francis, 1995.

Miller, Char. *Gifford Pinchot and the Making of Modern Environmentalism.* Washington, D.C.: Island Press, 2001.

Mitchell, Robert Cameron, Angela G. Mertig, and Riley E. Dunlap. "Twenty Years of Environmental Mobilization: Trends among National Environmental Organizations." In *American Environmentalism: The U.S. Environmental Movement, 1970–1990.* Edited by Riley E. Dunlap and Angela G. Mertig. Philadelphia, Taylor and Francis, 1992.

Mucciaroni, Gary. *The Political Failure of Employment Policy, 1945–1982.* Pittsburgh: University of Pittsburgh Press, 1990.

O'Leary, Rosemary. "Environmental Policy and the Courts." In *Environmental Policy: New Directions for the 21st Century,* 5th ed. Edited by Norman Vig and Michael Kraft. Washington, D.C.: CQ Press, 2003.

Olson, Mancur. *The Logic of Collective Action.* Cambridge: Harvard University Press, 1965.

Oppenheimer, Bruce. *Oil and the Congressional Process.* Lexington, Mass.: Lexington Books, 1975.

Orren, Karen. "Standing to Sue: Interest Group Conflict in the Federal Courts." *American Political Science Review* 70, no. 3 (September 1976): 723–41.

Paehlke, Robert. *Environmentalism and the Future of Progressive Politics.* New Haven, Conn.: Yale University Press, 1990.

———, ed. *Conservation and Environmentalism: An Encyclopedia.* New York: Garland Publishing, 1995.

Price, Tom. *Cyber-Activism.* Washington, D.C.: Foundation for Public Affairs, 2000.
Putnam, Robert D. *Bowling Alone: The Collapse and Revival of American Community.* New York: Simon and Schuster, 2000.
Rogers, Marion Lane. *Acorn Days: The Environmental Defense Fund and How It Grew.* New York: Environmental Defense Fund, 1990.
Rothenberg, Lawrence S. *Linking Citizens to Government: Interest Group Politics at Common Cause.* New York: Cambridge University Press, 1992.
Sale, Kirkpatrick. *The Green Revolution: The American Environmental Movement, 1962–1992.* New York: Hill and Wang, 1993.
Salisbury, Robert H. "An Exchange Theory of Interest Groups." *Midwest Journal of Political Science* 13 (1969): 1–32.
———. "Interest Representation: The Dominance of Institutions." *American Political Science Review* 78, no. 1 (March 1984): 64–76.
Savage, Andrew, John Isham, and Christopher McGrory Klyza. "The Greening of Social Capital: An Examination of Land-Based Groups in Two Vermont Counties." *Rural Sociology,* forthcoming.
Schattschneider, E. E. *The Semi-Sovereign People: A Realist's View of Democracy in America.* New York: Holt, Rinehart, and Winston, 1960.
Scheberle , Denise. *Federalism and Environmental Policy: Trust and the Politics of Implementation.* Washington, D.C.: Georgetown University Press, 1997.
Schlozman, Kay Lehman, and John T. Tierney. *Organized Interests and American Democracy.* New York: Harper and Row, 1986.
Shabecoff, Philip. *Earth Rising: American Environmentalism in the 21st Century.* Washington, D.C.: Island Press, 2000.
Shaiko, Ronald G. "More Bang for the Buck: The New Era of Full-Service Public Interest Organizations." In *Interest Group Politics,* 3d ed. Edited by Allan J. Cigler and Burdett A. Loomis. Washington, D.C.: CQ Press, 1991.
———. *Voices and Echoes for the Environment: Public Interest Representation in the 1990s and Beyond.* New York: Columbia University Press, 1999.
Shipan, Charles R., and William R. Lowry. "Environmental Policy and Party Divergence in Congress." *Political Research Quarterly* 54, no. 2 (June 2000): 245–63.
Skocpol, Theda. *Diminished Democracy: From Membership to Management in American Civic Life.* Norman: University of Oklahoma Press, 2003.
———. "Voice and Inequality: The Transformation of American Civic Democracy." *Perspectives on Politics* 2, no. 1 (March 2004): 20.
Skowronek, Steven. *Building the New American State: The Expansion of National Administrative Capacities.* New York: Cambridge University Press, 1981.
Snow, Donald. *Inside the Environmental Movement: Meeting the Leadership Challenge.* Washington, D.C.: Island Press, 1992.
Sutter, Paul S. *Driven Wild: How the Fight against Automobiles Launched the Modern Wilderness Movement.* Seattle: University of Washington Press, 2002.
Switzer, Jacqueline Vaughn. *Green Backlash: The History and Politics of Environmental Opposition in the United States.* Boulder, Colo.: Lynne Reiner, 1997.
Tarrow, Sidney. *Power in Movement: Social Movements, Collective Action, and Politics.* New York: Cambridge University Press, 1994.
Truman, David B. *The Governmental Process: Political Interests and Public Opinion.* New York: Knopf, 1951.

Vig, Norman J. "Presidential Leadership and the Environment." In *Environmental Policy: New Directions for the 21st Century,* 5th ed. Edited by Norman Vig and Michael Kraft. Washington, D.C.: CQ Press, 2003.

———. "Presidential Leadership and the Environment: From Reagan and Bush to Clinton." In *Environmental Policy in the 1990s,* 2d ed. Edited by Norman J. Vig and Michael E. Kraft. Washington, D.C.: CQ Press, 1994.

Vogel, David. *Fluctuating Fortunes: The Political Power of Business in America.* New York: Basic Books, 1989.

———. *National Styles of Regulation: Environmental Policy in Great Britain and the United States.* Ithaca, N.Y.: Cornell University Press, 1986.

Walker, Jack L. Jr. *Mobilizing Interest Groups in America: Patrons, Professions, and Social Movements.* Ann Arbor: University of Michigan Press, 1991.

Wapner, Paul. *Environmental Activism and World Civic Politics.* Albany: State University of New York Press, 1996.

Wilson, James Q. *Political Organizations.* New York: Basic Books, 1973.

Index